Beautiful
accommodation

New South Wales & Queensland

**Your guide to
the very best**

Beach houses
Country cottages
Eco lodges
Boutique hotels
Bed and breakfasts
Holiday apartments
Day spa retreats

Beautiful
Accommodation
Contents

New South Wales

Queensland

Welcome to
Beautiful Accommodation
New South Wales & Queensland

If you love staying in amazing places as much as we do, this is the book for you. We have handpicked more than 200 incredible properties and day spas across New South Wales and Queensland – each one visited, reviewed and photographed by our team. All you have to do is choose your next special getaway.

Welcome to *Beautiful Accommodation New South Wales and Queensland* – where we uncover incredible holiday experiences.

Whatever your taste, this book is filled with escapes for all occasions. Choose between everything from traditional B&Bs, rustic cottages and jaw-dropping beach houses to slick apartments, rainforest eco lodges and boutique hotels. The choice is yours, whether you are a couple seeking some time away, a family needing some room to move or a large group of friends looking for somewhere to celebrate together.

To ensure each property featured in this book meets our criteria, we invite the owners to get involved after an extensive research process. Our philosophy is to include as many different styles of quality accommodation as possible, but they must have a few critical elements in common.

Each property must be among the best in their region, with distinctive style and high service standards. They must also represent value for money in a fantastic location. And for those choices that have on-site hosts, they must be welcoming and love to share their inside tips about the area with guests.

Once invited by us, the property owners are asked to contribute a fee to defray production costs, which includes a personal visit and photo shoot by our team (see page 6).

This guide is divided into key regions across New South Wales and Queensland. Each section opens with images and details about the region's geography, appeal and attractions.

A comprehensive index features at the back of the guide, starting on page 294. Properties are listed by name and location, as well as by category to identify whether they offer a notable garden, good food, day spa facilities

or eco-oriented features. It also includes separate listings for properties that are great for groups – sorted by the number of guests that can be accommodated – as well as the properties that are suitable for children.

To further assist your travels, a set of maps can be found at the back of the guide, covering the featured accommodation. Each property's own page includes a reference to its corresponding map in the book. Similarly, all purple map plots refer to the respective properties' page numbers. The maps start on page 279.

All prices are correct as at publication but always check rates on enquiry as they are subject to change. Any updates should also be available on our website, www.beautifulaccommodation.com

The quoted rates vary in format, with some listings relating to whole property costs while others are dependent on the number of guests. We have also indicated whether meals are included in the rate, but many properties offer special packages on request and can tailor their services accordingly.

Any stars in this guide refer to the AAA STAR Rating system. Not all properties choose to participate in the system and the search for *Beautiful Accommodation* properties is not restricted to a particular rating. Eco-Friendly STAR Accreditation is an additional endorsement that indicates the property is committed to reducing the environmental impact of their business.

Some property groups represented in this guide include:

- Ecotourism certified

- Bed and Breakfast and Farmstay Association Australia (BBFAA)

- Select Hotels and Resorts International

- Accommodation Association of Australia (AAA, formerly the HMAA)

- Tourism Accreditation Australia Ltd

The accepted forms of payment referenced in this guide are:

Visa	=	Visa card
AMEX	=	American Express
MC	=	MasterCard
DC	=	Diners Club
JCB	=	Japan Credit Bureau
DD	=	Direct deposit
Chq	=	Cheque
Eftpos	=	Debit card processing
PayPal	=	Online transfers

Meet the team

Reviewer
Simon St John

Having spent many long months researching properties for five titles in the *Beautiful Accommodation* series, Simon says all the hard work pays off when he finds those elusive perfect getaways. The freelance travel writer never tires of uncovering incredible accommodation, meeting the owners who are so passionate about what they do and sharing these experiences with readers.

Visit us online

If you want to know more about a property or region featured in this guide, visit **www.beautifulaccommodation.com**. Each property is showcased on our website, and here you can view additional images, enquire direct to the property and book your stay without any added commission or booking fees.

The online property pages feature up-to-date information including tariff changes and details of any new rooms, cottages or other features, as well as information on special events, discounts and package deals.

You can keep up-to-date by joining our Beautiful Accommodation Club. Membership is free and you will receive email newsletters that include special member offers, news, updates and exclusive giveaways. Go to **www.beautifulaccommodation.com/club** to register.

If you book through a property's own website, be sure to let the owners know you found them in *Beautiful Accommodation*.

Photographer
Ross Doonan

It's all about the challenge of capturing the essence of a property for photojournalist Ross. As a specialist in interior and architectural tourism photography, Ross knows an undiscovered gem when he finds one. Having the privilege of visiting so many beautiful places and photographing them is a dream job come true for Ross.

www.beautifulaccommodation.com

SYDNEY

Sydney

Is there any city with a broader appeal than Sydney? Whatever your demographic – with kids, no kids, single, a couple, a bunch of friends – there's a sweet spot for you in sunny Sydney. The world's most beautiful harbour is split into dozens of points, islands, beaches and headlands. Each has its own distinctive history and vibe, ranging from the elegant terraces of Glebe to iconic beaches such as Bondi, Coogee and Manly, and historic Cockatoo Island. Get out and explore.

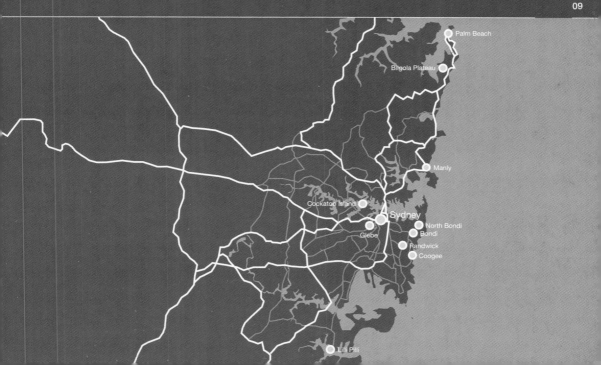

Palm Beach

Bilgola Plateau

Manly

Cockatoo Island

Sydney

North Bondi
Bondi
Glebe
Randwick
Coogee

Lilli Pilli

Sydney's beaches offer a potent mixture of surf, sand, salt, suntan lotion, hot chips and a soundscape of cries from happy gulls and children.

Sydney has its internationally recognised landmarks that include the majestic Opera House and the Harbour Bridge. When these icons appear in your holiday snaps, your friends and family instantly know where you've been. However, Sydney has a far deeper appeal than these monuments of steel and stone.

Of course, Sydneysiders love their city's glamorous looks. But their real passion is for the sensual experiences it offers: the taste of fresh sushi at the Sydney Fish Market, the fragrant smell of cafes and restaurants in Glebe or the rolling swell as the Manly Ferry crosses the harbour heads. Nowhere quickens their senses more than Sydney's grand beaches – Bondi,

Coogee, Manly and a dozen others. They offer a potent mixture of surf, sand, salt, suntan lotion, hot chips and a soundscape of cries from happy gulls and children. Childhood memories are made on these sands.

Bondi is a huge natural amphitheatre focused on its world-famous half-mile strip of sand. Behind the beachfront are streets filled with groovy places to eat, drink, party and stay. Local and foreign celebs love parading its streets, and so do backpackers from around the world.

Coogee is Bondi's beguiling and more relaxed cousin. As you drive into Coogee, it feels as though you are leaving the jostle of Sydney far behind. Coogee has a 19th century

ambience with its magnificent sea baths such as Wylie's (1907) and the women-only McIver's Baths (1886). The surf at Coogee is softened by Wedding Cake Island, making it ideal for kids. There are endless eateries where you can buy everything from souvlaki and baklava to fish and chips, best eaten with vinegar or tomato sauce – or both.

Circular Quay is the doorstep to Sydney's CBD. Turn right when you leave the wharf and follow the waterline around to Sydney's oldest urban precinct, The Rocks. The Museum of Contemporary Art has an astonishing collection and its outdoor cafe is a fine spot for a coffee and people watching. Many of Sydney's

Accredited Visitor Information Centres

oldest pubs are in the area, including the Fortune of War (1828). Be sure to climb the stairs of the Glenmore Hotel and take in the view with a drink in-hand. The Rocks is a marvellous place to let serendipity be your guide.

Turn left as you depart the Manly Ferry and you can't miss one of the world's most recognised buildings, the Sydney Opera House. Ideally, you will book in for a performance in the stunning interior. But the building's steps and foreshore cafes are splendid places to sit in the sun and take in the glorious view.

Sydney has dozens of special corners. At the tip of upmarket Mosman is the stunningly situated terrace of Taronga Zoo. If you wander up ritzy Woollahra's Ocean Street, you will end up in Oxford Street and Sydney's gay centre. Slip over to Sydney's biggest harbour island, Cockatoo, for music, history and a different perspective.

The northern and southern outskirts of Sydney are also full of sensational beaches and waterways. Palm Beach is a playground for Sydney's millionaires and Pittwater is a brilliant setting for sailing and fishing. To the south is Port Hacking, which is the 'other' Sydney Harbour. The area has quiet tongues of land like Lilli Pilli or beautiful bays like Bundeena, which make for ideal escapes.

Mascot
Sydney International Airport
1300 402 060
www.gnconcierge.com

The Rocks
Cnr Argyle & Playfair Street
02 9240 8788
www.sydneyvisitorcentre.com

Darling Harbour
Palm Grove, between Cockle Bay
Wharf & Harbourside
02 9240 8788
www.sydneyvisitorcentre.com

Manly
Manly Wharf Forecourt,
East Esplanade
02 9976 1430
www.manlyaustralia.com

The Pittwater

Bilgola Plateau (near Palm Beach)

15 Farview Road, Bilgola Plateau ▪ 02 9918 6932
www.beautifulaccommodation.com/thepittwater

Rates
Per couple $175-$200
Full breakfast included,
dinner by prior arrangement
Visa, MC, AMEX

Location
50 minutes or 35km north
of Sydney. Map 4.

Minimum stay
Two nights

Facilities
Two suites: one one-bedroom
(queen, ensuite), one two-bedroom
(one queen, one king/twin, spa
bathroom). Guest lounge, office,
WiFi, RC AC. Solar-heated
swimming pool.

Member
BBFAA

Host details
Colette and James Campbell
▪ colette@thepittwater.com.au
▪ www.thepittwater.com.au

Plateau of elegance

The Pittwater achieves perfect pitch with every element that goes into making a superb bed and breakfast: stunning location, gourmet food, delightful bedrooms and attentive but very discreet hosts. It is one of our perennial favourites and is tucked away in the exclusive Palm Beach area making it ideal for a luxurious break from the stresses of city life.

Let's start with the astonishing food. We highly recommend booking ahead for one of Colette Campbell's sumptuous celebrations of fresh Sydney produce. She is a Le Cordon Bleu-trained chef and her table features creative, delectable dishes. Guests are welcome to invite friends for a hosted dinner at this very elegant house. And, needless to say, the breakfasts are real feasts (with early morning tea or coffee delivered to your room as requested).

The rooms at The Pittwater are restful retreats with windows that welcome in the sea breezes. The main lounge has a stunning new picture window that takes in the whole valley view below so you can just sit and gaze. A pool and terrace complete this wonderful property.

The central Bilgola Plateau location means you can easily slip away for some boutique cruising at Palm Beach, Whale Beach or Avalon.

Bondi Salt
Bondi

3/2 Castlefield Street, Bondi ▪ 0400 324 096
www.beautifulaccommodation.com/bondisalt

Brilliant Bondi holiday pad

It's easy to love Bondi Salt when it so perfectly captures the relaxed vibe of Sydney's celebrity beach. The style is freshly contemporary with an appealing marine theme (we love the surfboard coffee table and the Eco-Marine bathroom product).

Even better, this Bondi residence has those very rare inner-city commodities: off-street parking for two cars, a private courtyard and a quiet location tucked behind this boutique apartment block.

Bondi Salt has a king-size main bedroom with an ensuite and a second bedroom with twin singles, making it ideal for a family with kids.

The thoughtful owners have even included a mini table to seat your littlies and just ask if you need high chairs or a portacot.

This is a real holiday retreat, combining a brilliant position with every interior comfort. There is a barbecue in the courtyard, an LCD TV for movies (there are kids' DVDs too) and stylish yet practical furnishings. The polished floorboards welcome sandy feet from the beach.

Everything you love about Bondi is nearby: restaurants, pubs, beaches, cafes and wonderful cliff walks to neighbouring beaches. The vibrant local cultural calendar includes Flickerfest in January and the City to Surf in August.

Rates
Whole apartment per night from $280-$500 (up to 4 people, $25 per extra person per night; additional $80 cleaning fee) Accommodation only
Visa, MC, DD

Location
12 minutes or 8km from Sydney CBD. Map 4.

Minimum stay
Three nights

Facilities
One apartment with two bedrooms (king with ensuite, twin singles), lounge (LCD TV, DVD, CD), dining, kitchen, bathroom, RC AC, internet. Deck (BBQ), courtyard, off-street secure parking.

Other
Suitable for children

Manager details
Barbara
▪ info@bondisalt.com.au
▪ www.bondisalt.com

Bondi Aqua

North Bondi

116 Clyde Street, North Bondi ▪ 0413 482 588
www.beautifulaccommodation.com/bondiaqua

Rates
Penthouse per night from
$400-$700 (up to 6; $150
cleaning fee per stay)
Accommodation only
Direct deposit, no credit cards

Location
12 minutes or 8km from Sydney
CBD. Map 4.

Minimum stay
Five to seven nights (seasonal)

Facilities
Penthouse: three bedrooms (two
queens, one ensuite; twin
singles), lounge (Foxtel TV, DVD,
CD), dining, kitchen, second
bathroom, laundry. Duplex: two
bedrooms (queen; bunk, single),
lounge (Foxtel TV, DVD, CD),
dining, kitchen, bathroom. Pool,
BBQ, WiFi, off-street parking.

Other
Suitable for children

Owner details
Sharifa and Ian Wallace
▪ sharifaw@bigpond.net.au
▪ www.beautifulaccommodation.
com/bondiaqua

Bondi penthouse style

Bondi is the iconic Sydney beach
suburb for good reason. It has the
city's finest arc of golden sand,
perfect waves for board or body
surfing, wonderful architecture
and endless places to eat, drink
and be merry.

They are all good reasons to perch
yourself in the Penthouse at Bondi
Aqua and lap up the good life as a
short-term resident.

Bondi Aqua is a classic design for
Sydney beach holiday relaxation.
The rooms are bright and airy,
drawing in healthy draughts of sea
air and offering vistas in all directions,
from the Sydney Harbour Bridge
to the sea.

The polished floorboards are perfect
for beachside living and there are two
balconies for relaxing with a morning
coffee or a sunset G&T. Your kids will
love the huge aqua pool and
landscaped back garden. The owners
can even arrange babysitting,
allowing you some time off together.

The North Bondi location is ideal:
close to the city and far enough from
the hustle of the main beach strip but
only 800 metres stroll to the beach
and shops. For larger groups, talk to
the owner about combining the
Penthouse with the duplex below –
this will sleep up to 10 guests.

Cockatoo Island

Cockatoo Island (Sydney Harbour)

Cockatoo Island ▪ 02 8898 9774
www.beautifulaccommodation.com/cockatooisland

Harbour views with history

The *MasterChef* TV program chose Cockatoo Island as the glamorous Sydney Harbour location to film the first weeks of the 2011 series. Lucky contestants – this is one of the most sensational island stays anywhere in Australia, facing the grand arch of the Harbour Bridge and surrounded by Sydney's twinkling lights at night.

The island has been part of the harbour city's history since the 1830s, first as a prison for convicts who were doing hard labour and later as a shipyard.

The accommodation options are wonderfully diverse, ranging from a studio in the old Cockatoo Island fire station to a four-bedroom house once used by the chief medical officer. You can even go "glamping" in comfy permanent tents overlooking the harbour. We love the one- and two-bedroom luxury holiday houses where smart interior design perfectly melds the historic architecture with every modern comfort. Plus there are views, views, views everywhere over glorious Sydney Harbour.

These island stays make a perfect getaway for everyone from out-of-towners wanting a unique Sydney experience to Sydneysiders after something special.

The island is host to a variety of large events and cultural programs, including the Biennale Of Sydney and offers fascinating self-guided tours as well. Cocktails at the funky Island Bar are a must and you can eat at The Canteen.

Rates
Whole house/studio per night from $220-$520 (for 2-10 people)
Glamping per night $125-$148
Accommodation only
Visa, MC, AMEX, DD, Eftpos

Location
Ten minutes by ferry from Circular Quay. Map 4.

Minimum stay
Two nights (single nights for Glamping welcome)

Facilities
A range of studio, one-, two- and four-bedroom apartments and houses, all with lounge (TV, DVD), dining, kitchen, courtyard garden or balcony. Pre-erected luxury tents with camping beds and mattresses, chairs and lantern; shared bathroom facilities.

Other
Suitable for children
Cafe open seven days

Manager details
Victoria Uriarte
▪ reservations@harbourtrust.gov.au
▪ www.harbourtrust.gov.au/accommodation

Dive Hotel
Coogee

234 Arden Street, Coogee ▪ 02 9665 5538
www.beautifulaccommodation.com/dive

16

Rates
Per couple from $165-$310
Continental breakfast included
Annexe house from $310-$395
(up to 6 people)
Visa, MC, AMEX, DC, DD, Eftpos

Location
15 minutes or 9km southeast
of Sydney CBD. Map 4.

Minimum stay
Two nights at weekends
Five nights (Annexe only)

Facilities
16 ensuite rooms (kitchenette, TV,
AC). Breakfast room, laundry
facilities. Three-bedroom Annexe
with lounge, dining, kitchen, two
bathrooms, courtyard (BBQ).

Other
Suitable for children (Annexe)

Host details
Terry Bunton and
Mercedes Mariano
▪ thedive@bigpond.net.au
▪ www.divehotel.com.au

A plunge into Coogee

Three of Sydney's great city beaches
are Manly, Coogee and Bondi – and
many people rate Coogee as the
finest of them all. Why? Because
it has fabulous sea baths like the
theatrical Wylie's and the women-only
McGiver's Ladies Baths. The main
beach is sensational and there are
streets full of little bars, takeaways
and upmarket eateries.

The must-stay place in Coogee is
the funky boutique hotel Dive, which
combines a straight-to-the-sea
location with stylish design and a
relaxed family-run vibe.

The guest rooms are alluring. They
feature king or queen beds that are
crisply set with fine linen sheets,
windows that open to draw in the air
and sunlight, kitchenettes, and
totally hip bathrooms with little blue
tiles, white grouting and stainless
steel fittings.

The primo rooms are numbers 1, 2
and 19, which look out to sea and
offer their happy guests stunning
sunrises and the soothing sounds
of the waves. A complimentary
continental breakfast is served in the
communal dining area, which is a
great place to swap tourist tips with
your fellow travellers.

For families or a group of up to six,
Dive also has the three-bedroom
Annexe townhouse around the
corner. It has its own courtyard,
full kitchen and lounge.

Tricketts Luxury Bed & Breakfast
Glebe

270 Glebe Point Road, Glebe ▪ 02 9552 1141
www.beautifulaccommodation.com/tricketts

Glad to be in Glebe

To be honest, we think Liz Trickett is undercharging for rooms in her stunningly restored Victorian B&B in Glebe. It is the result of a 25-year labour of love, which saved this historic inner-city mansion from the wrecker's ball and restored it to its original grandeur.

Here you can sweep past the rich, red cedar staircase and relax in the gilded ballroom (now a guest lounge) amid antiques and curios. The carpets are exquisite, the kauri floors beautiful, and the whole ambience invites rest and relaxation after a busy day in the city.

Liz has made the bedrooms impressive havens of heritage style and contemporary comfort. The two guest rooms – both with ensuites – are appointed with carefully chosen antiques, more Persian carpets and beds fit for a Victorian prince. Our favourite place is the front verandah. Here you can sit, read, snooze or watch the passing parade from a distance while watching birds play in the gardens.

The location in Glebe is ideal. You can take quiet walks to Wattle Bay, visit the fish market or explore an endless assortment of world cuisines all along Glebe Point Road (try the renowned Glebe Point Diner). The CBD is a short bus ride away.

Rates
Per couple from $198-$220
Continental breakfast included
Visa, MC, AMEX, DC

Location
10 minutes or 3km west
of Sydney CBD. Map 4.

Facilities
Two guest rooms (one queen, one ensuite), guest lounge, conservatory breakfast room. Off-street parking.

Host details
Liz Trickett
▪ trickettsbandb@hotmail.com
▪ www.tricketts.com.au

Alcheringa
Lilli Pilli

8 Apollo Place, Lilli Pilli ▪ 02 9524 5396, 0405 471 334
www.beautifulaccommodation.com/alcheringa

Rates
Apartment per night
from $180-$195
Studio per night from $160-$175
Accommodation only
Direct deposit, no credit cards

Location
60 minutes or 27km south of
Sydney CBD; 40 minutes from
Sydney airport. Map 4.

Minimum stay
Two nights

Facilities
One apartment and one studio:
apartment with separate queen
bedroom, ensuite, lounge (TV,
DVD, CD), dining, kitchen and
laundry. Studio with queen bed,
ensuite, kitchenette, TV, DVD.
Fans, electric or gas heating.

Host details
Nona and Richard Putral
▪ info@alcheringa.net.au
▪ www.accommodation
southsydney.com.au

Dreamy waterfront bliss

What makes a perfect Sydney escape? We suggest one version has to include absolute waterfrontage, a private pontoon for fishing or boating, breathtaking water views, exotic birdlife, sea breezes, and places to eat and shop within easy reach. If that fits your picture, Alcheringa will too. Its apt name means "dreamtime" in Aboriginal dialect.

There are two options here. The Retreat is a fully self-contained, ground-floor apartment with everything you need for a longer holiday, including laundry facilities, a queen-size bed, ensuite and walk-in robe, and space to lounge and breathe in the view.

Then there is the Studio, which has one of the finest bedroom views of Port Hacking you are likely to see. You can cook a meal in the kitchenette, throw some steaks on the barbecue in the garden or pop off to nearby Cronulla to sample the many local cafes, bars and restaurants. What a pleasure it is to slip back to this private retreat after a day of adventure.

A real treat at Alcheringa is the astonishing birdlife, which includes kookaburras, rosellas, sulphur-crested cockatoos and pelicans. There are three golf courses nearby and you can reach the airport without trawling across the city.

Rimrock Retreat
Palm Beach

330 Whale Beach Road, Palm Beach ▪ 02 9954 9343, 0412 202 814
www.beautifulaccommodation.com/rimrockretreat

Breathtaking Palm Beach beauty

The jewel of Sydney's northern beaches is undoubtedly the very upmarket, absolutely gorgeous Palm Beach. This is where the emerald city's rich and beautiful choose to hang out, so why shouldn't you join them for a while?

Getting a spot in the sun is easily done at Rimrock Retreat, which commands a headland above the sparkling blue waters of the Pacific. As you settle into a day bed and don the sunglasses, you could be aboard a liner cruising the most beautiful coastline in the world.

Rimrock is superbly designed to cater for mixed parties of friends or family members. The architect has done a brilliant job at maximising liveability and comfort with a three-bedroom, two-bathroom upper level and a self-contained studio apartment downstairs. You can take them separately or together, enabling up to 10 people to relax into holiday mode in comfort. There's no doubt you'll spend most of your time on the grand louvered decks that provide sunny shelter and add a vast extra room on each level.

Rimrock is placed between Palm Beach and Whale Beach, which presents plenty of options for dining out, walking the coastline and picnicking on the beach. If you need it, the owners have a second Pittwater apartment at nearby Snapperman Beach.

Rates
Whole house per night from
$500-$1000 (up to 10 people)
Studio only per night from
$170-$360 (up to 4 people)
Accommodation only
Direct deposit, no credit cards

Location
50 minutes or 35km north of
Sydney. Map 4.

Minimum stay
Three to seven nights (seasonal)

Facilities
One house: upper level with three bedrooms (two queens, one with ensuite, twin singles), lounge (TV, DVD, CD), dining, kitchen, large deck and second bathroom (laundry), BBQ. Lower studio with queen, lounge, kitchen, bathroom and large deck, BBQ.

Other
Suitable for children

Owner details
Shane Tiernan
▪ bookings@rimrockretreat.com
▪ www.rimrockretreat.com

Avonmore on the Park Boutique Hotel

Randwick

34 The Avenue, Randwick ▪ 02 9399 9388
www.beautifulaccommodation.com/avonmore

Rates
Room per couple $155-$230
Accommodation only
Visa, MC, AMEX, DC, DD, Eftpos

Location
10 Minutes or 8km from
Sydney CBD. Map 4.

Facilities
Hotel with a range of Garden,
Family and Heritage rooms, each
with double and/or twin singles,
TV, kitchenette and ensuite. WiFi.
Limited off-street parking.

AAA Star Rating
★★★★

Other
Suitable for children
Disabled facilities

Manager details
George Calopedos
▪ info@avonmoreonthepark.com.au
▪ www.avonmoreonthepark.com.au

An elegant terrace

Avonmore is like a wonderfully layered confectionary, with twirls of creamy stone and delightfully sculpted highlights in chocolatey timber and cool white marble.

This authentic piece of Sydney's history was built in 1888 by the Irish-born railroad contractor John Walsh. Now it is one of the city's charming boutique hotels, with 23 elegant rooms, a shaded courtyard and mosaic floors.

The attention to period detail here is marvellous. In the bedrooms there are carved wooden bedheads, bentwood chairs and parlour tables draped in rich fabrics. Naturally, every room has its own ensuite bathroom.

Modern distractions, such as the LCD HD TVs, are discreetly placed in a way that doesn't detract from the late-Victorian style. And there is also a bonus you don't normally see in most hotels: each room has a small kitchenette for preparing snacks, light meals or breakfast.

There are plenty of places to eat in nearby Alison Road and Avoca Street. You can stroll over to watch the footy or cricket at the SCG, catch a race at Randwick, wander through Centennial Park or hop on a bus for the beaches at Bondi or Tamarama. The Ritz Theatre and the University of New South Wales are both easily reached.

The Russell Hotel
The Rocks, Sydney

143A George Street, Sydney ▪ 02 9241 3543
www.beautifulaccommodation.com/therussell

Heritage on The Rocks

The Russell is one of our favourite Sydney CBD places to park the bags and explore the harbour city. It's a gorgeous heritage hotel – there are only 30 rooms – that has just undergone a complete makeover, including the installation of a new lift for modern convenience. We loved it before and we love it more now with the pearl stripe feature walls, muted fabrics and high-ceilinged rooms. The Russell Wine Bar downstairs has also been refurbed with a luscious peacocky theme.

A very cosy small-hotel vibe fills the whole place, infusing it with the charming atmosphere of a big B&B that has plenty of attentive hosts at your beck and call.

The rooms range from those that have ensuites to very affordable standard rooms that have a shared (but private) bathroom.

Upstairs there is a roof garden with 270-degree views of the whole Rocks-Circular Quay-Opera House panorama. It's a great place to lap up the sun and retreat from the hustle of central Sydney.

The Rocks needs no introduction to those who love Sydney. It's all there, from early 18th century pubs (the 1828 Fortune of War is next door) to museums, restaurants and wonderful walks around the foreshore.

Rates
Room per couple from $135-$290
Continental breakfast included
Visa, MC, AMEX, DC, DD, Eftpos

Location
In the heart of Sydney's historic Rocks area. Map 4.

Facilities
30 rooms: 20 with ensuites and TV, 10 with share bathrooms. Roof garden, sitting room (TV), lift. Car parking available (fee).

Other
Suitable for children
Wine Bar open from 12pm, seven days

Managers details
Judy Beardsell and Louise Marshall
▪ manager@therussell.com.au
▪ www.therussell.com.au

GRAND CANYON
WALKING TRACK →

O SYDNEY
Sydney Surrounds

Sydney Surrounds

Sydney Harbour always draws crowds of snap-happy tourists. But those who keep to the glittering city will miss many astonishing experiences within an hour or so of town. To the north is the inspiring Hawkesbury River, which flows to the sea past historic settlements such as Windsor and Ebenezer and idyllic spots that include Bar Point. To the west is the mysterious maze of the Blue Mountains, which is filled with dramatic lookouts, spas, walking trails and fantastic high-country accommodation.

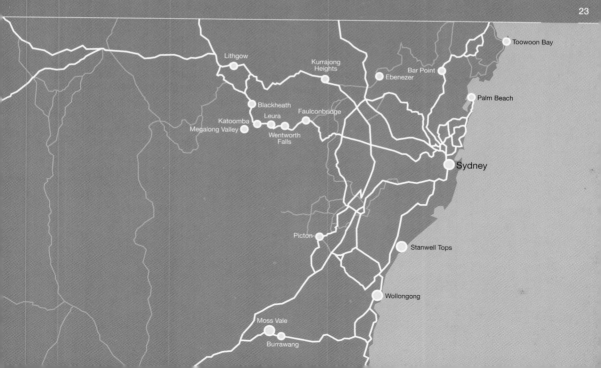

Toowoon Bay

Lithgow

Kurrajong
Heights

Bar Point
Ebenezer

Palm Beach

Blackheath
Leura   Faulconbridge
Katoomba
Megalong Valley
Wentworth
Falls

Sydney

Picton

Stanwell Tops

Wollongong

Moss Vale

Burrawang

Follow the winding route of the Great Western Highway, which cuts across the mountains, passing natural wonders and groovy little alternative lifestyle towns.

The Blue Mountains form a deceptively low ridge on the western horizon of Sydney. But, up close, it is clear why it took European explorers 25 years after landing in 1788 to find their way through this jigsaw of sandstone escarpments. Only 15 years ago, a stand of about 100 Wollemi Pines – last seen in 200-million-year-old fossils – was discovered here in a forgotten valley.

The Mountains have a distinctive highland micro-climate that is very different from sub-tropical Sydney. The geography has spawned a string of charming little towns and villages along the winding route of the Great Western Highway. Faulconbridge is a great first stop. Here, Norman Lindsay (subject of the film *Sirens*) set up his studio, which is now a gallery with the charming Lindsay's Cafe. The district also captured the heart of Australia's father of Federation, Sir Henry Parkes, who bought 600 acres here in 1877. He is buried in the town's cemetery.

Wentworth Falls is named after the eccentric William Charles Wentworth, one of the explorers who first found a route through the mountains in 1813 (you can visit his mansion in the Sydney suburb of Vaucluse). Wentworth Falls is a vibrant village with great places to eat, shop and stay. Make sure you walk the tracks to see Wentworth's waterfalls and the magnificent Jamison Valley. The evolutionary theorist Charles Darwin toured the area in 1836 and you can still follow his route today.

Leura and Katoomba have been drawing visitors to the mountains for 130 years. Leura is a gorgeous village with a real shopping mall – not a faux shopping centre – that has antique shops, booksellers and places to eat. Also worth checking out are the Everglades gardens, built by Paul Sorensen in the 1930s.

Katoomba has been at the heart of Blue Mountains tourism for more than a century. Nearby is the iconic Three Sisters rock formation, which could be the most photographed natural feature in NSW. Stop in at the sensational Hydro Majestic Hotel, which is scheduled to re-open in 2012.

Blackheath has some of the most awe-inspiring vistas in the Blue Mountains, including the panorama from Govetts Leap in the wild Grose Valley. Blackheath is also an entry point to the Megalong Valley, which is a marvellous place for horse riding. The newly restored Six Foot Track was designed for riders heading to the subterranean world of the Jenolan Caves.

The Hawkesbury River rises in the Blue Mountains and flows through some of Australia's oldest agricultural districts, including Windsor. The town has a historic building register that dates back to the earliest years after settlement. This includes the Macquarie Arms Hotel (1815)

and the stunning St Matthew's Anglican Church (1817), designed by convict architect Francis Greenway. Nearby Ebenezer is the oldest surviving free settlement in Australia.

The Hawkesbury meets the Pacific Ocean via a dramatic sunken river valley. This fertile waterway is filled with birdlife, beds of Sydney rock oysters and fish. Bar Point offers a wonderful perspective on this beautiful estuarine landscape.

On the southern edge of Sydney are some of Australia's most spectacular coastal landscapes. Stanwell Tops, where aviation pioneer Lawrence Hargrave perfected the first workable box-kite wings in the 1880s, is among the best spots to savour the views.

Blackheath
End of Govetts Leap Road
02 4787 8877
www.nationalparks.nsw.gov.au

Katoomba
Echo Point Road
1300 653 408
www.visitbluemountains.com.au

Windsor
8 Baker Street
02 4560 4655
www.hawkesbury.nsw.gov.au

Wollongong
Princes Highway, Bulli Tops
02 4227 5545
www.visitwollongong.com.au

Wagon Wheels Country Retreat
Stanwell Tops

20 Lawrence Hargrave Drive, Stanwell Tops ▪ 02 4294 2449, 0419 429 458
www.beautifulaccommodation.com/wagonwheels

The wheel of good fortune

You can sleep, entertain or even get married at the very adaptable Wagon Wheels Country Retreat. This classic 1895 country house on Stanwell Tops has a small ballroom, Ye Old Barn for larger functions and plenty of marquee space in the immaculately kept garden. The location – mid-way between Wollongong and Sydney – makes it accessible for travellers from either direction.

Geoffrey Pybus has done an extraordinary job at creating the right mood in each of the homestead's four bedrooms. Pure romantics will love the honeymoon suite with its blazing log fire – ideal for newlyweds post-reception.

There is also the funky Panoramic Loft with dormer picture windows and fireplace, the Fountain Room, which looks over a splashing cascade outside and the Farm Room, with twin single beds for the kids. Wagon Wheels is perfect for kids to explore, with cute alpacas, ponies, horses, donkeys and cows to admire. Guests will enjoy indulging themselves in the grand spa bathroom that looks out over the green surrounds.

The property is surrounded by forest and features marvellous walks to spots like Kelly's Falls, which you can reach via the back gate. Ask Geoffrey to take you on a tour.

Rates
Rates per couple from $120-$185 (extra guests $55)
Continental breakfast included
Visa, MC, DD

Location
60 minutes or 52km south of Sydney. Map 2 and 4.

Minimum stay
Two nights preferred

Facilities
One suite (queen, log fire, ensuite); two rooms (one queen, one twin singles) and one loft (two queens and one single), shared spa bathroom. Guest kitchen, lounge/dining (wood fire, TV, DVD). Ballroom and 'Ye Old Barn'. Pool.

Other
Suitable for children

Host details
Geoffrey Pybus
▪ info@wagonwheels
retreat.com.au
▪ www.wagonwheels
retreat.com.au

Tumbling Waters Retreat

Stanwell Tops

End of Stonehaven Road, Stanwell Tops ▪ 02 4294 1888
www.beautifulaccommodation.com/tumblingwaters

Rates
Rates per couple from $495-$575
Full breakfast provisions included
Visa, MC

Location
60 minutes or 52km south
of Sydney. Map 2 and 4.

Minimum stay
Two nights at weekends

Facilities
Four suites, one Bath House
(queen, ensuite, cable TV, DVD,
CD, kitchenette, RC AC), BBQ,
WiFi; suites with soaking tub
and eco fireplace; Bath House
with spa, steam room).
Restaurant, function centre, day
spa suite. Pool and spa.

Other
Restaurant
Wedding and functions (various
packages available)

Contact details
▪ info@twr.com.au
▪ www.twr.com.au

Falling into paradise

There is a distinct echo at Tumbling Waters Retreat of the renowned US architect Frank Lloyd Wright's most famous house, Fallingwater in Pennsylvania. Tumbling Waters similarly integrates a contemporary design with a majestic location, achieving a wonderful synthesis of place and building. But unlike the forest-enclosed Fallingwater, Tumbling Waters looks from the Illawarra escarpment over the grand spectacle of the Pacific Ocean with a constantly changing interplay of light and water.

This is unapologetically an adult's retreat. It's for those couples who appreciate all the extras, such as a boutique day spa, which shares the breathtaking view (read our review on page 271), candlelit dinners in the restaurant and well-appointed guest rooms. The luxurious guest suites have ocean vistas and are generously supplied with complimentary aromatherapy oils and sparkling wine to start your chill-out. There is also the Bath House, which has a private steam room and its own place in the garden next to the pond.

Tumbling Waters has a divine function centre that can cater for dreamy weddings and other celebrations. Naturally, guests are free to roam the magnificent gardens, which include Shona sculptures from Zimbabwe, and to relish the spectacular views.

If you want stunning wedding photos, framing yourselves against this backdrop will cap off a memorable day.

Amaroo Cottage
Bar Point (the Hawkesbury)

Location on enquiry, Bar Point ▪ 02 9922 2934, 0414 959 564
www.beautifulaccommodation.com/amaroocottage

Hawkesbury River paradise

Pardon us if we rave on about Amaroo Cottage and its truly romantic, blessedly blissful location. This place is the stuff of lovers' dreams: castaway together on a distant shore, far from the cares of the world and surrounded by idyllic natural beauty.

The setting is utterly beguiling. You arrive by boat (there are no roads) to find a charming boathouse and cottage nestled in verdantly terraced gardens on the Hawkesbury River. As the outboard engine lapses into silence, bird calls echo across the water and mullet happily plop in and out of the water. Fishing anyone?

The living is easy in the relaxed rooms of the cottage, which has beds for six (so couples could bring friends, if they wish), a country kitchen and a sun deck that will have you basking in the warmth. The boathouse has been converted into a groovy waterfront lounge with a petite studio overlooking the jetty.

What to do here? In a word: relax. Throw a line into the waters for a fresh fish barbecue, put your feet up on the deck with a book or sit on the private beach. The local restaurant at Peats Bite will pick you up for a long lazy lunch.

Rates
Whole cottage per night from $345-$495 (up to 2 people, $100 per extra person per night) Accommodation only
Visa, MC

Location
60 minutes from Sydney CBD. Map 4.

Minimum stay
Two nights

Facilities
One cottage: two bedrooms (queen and twin singles), lounge, kitchen, bathroom, deck. Boathouse: studio bedroom (double), jetty, deck.

Owner details
Jonathan and Mary Threlfall
▪ Jthrelfall@tpg.com.au
▪ www.amaroocottage.com.au

Tizzana Winery Bed and Breakfast

Ebenezer (near Windsor)

518 Tizzana Road, Ebenezer ▪ 02 4579 1150
www.beautifulaccommodation.com/tizzana

Rates
Rates per couple from $220-$275
Full breakfast included,
five-course dinner by prior
arrangement
Visa, MC, AMEX, DC, JCB,
DD, Eftpos

Location
90 minutes or 70km northwest
of Sydney. Map 4.

Facilities
Two suites: king bed, ensuite,
AC, heating. Guest lounge (wood
fire). Cellar door.

AAA Star Rating
★★★★★

Member
BBFAA

Other
Cellar door open seven days

Host details
Peter and Carolyn Auld
▪ enquiries@tizzana.com.au
▪ www.tizzana.com.au

Winelovers' slow-food escape

At Tizzana Winery your feet are on the ground of Australian winemaking history. It was established in 1887 by one of the most remarkable pioneers of the Australian wine industry: Dr Thomas Fiaschi. After studying medicine in Pisa and Florence, Fiaschi migrated to Australia in the 1870s and worked as a GP, military surgeon, medical pioneer and winemaker. The provincial Italian ambience of this wonderful estate is not a faux design – it's the real thing.

The winery's setting, glorious views and superb food make it one of our favourite regional hideaways and we highly recommend it for wedding nights, anniversaries and special double-couple getaways.

The Provincial Room is a glorious exposition of timber, woodwork and crisp white linen, while the Rose Room has big French doors that open onto a courtyard rose garden. Both are generously appointed with fluffy towels, toiletries and plump pillows, and guests have their own sun-filled lounge.

For the ultimate indulgence, opt for the five-course dinner with the estates' own wines – this is slow food and artisan wines at its most heartfelt.

Tizzana is a beguiling slice of Tuscany in Australia, just a stone's throw from historic Windsor and only a short drive from Sydney.

Kims Beach Hideaway
Toowoon Bay

16 Charlton Street, Toowoon Bay ▪ 02 4332 1566
www.beautifulaccommodation.com/kims

Barefoot luxury with panache

Life doesn't get any sweeter than this luxurious, personalised beachfront retreat. Kims consists of a cluster of architect designed deluxe timber bungalows and spa villas immersed in a subtropical rainforest and shaded by grand Norfolk pines. Inside you'll find the perfect beach house, with high ceilings, timber floors, cane furnishings and louvered glass windows to let in the sea breeze. Some have extra luxuries – an open fireplace, private pool, even a personal sauna – but each comes with a wealth of stylish details.

Served in the pavilion-style restaurant overlooking an infinity of blue sea, the buffet style meals at Kims are legendary, a celebration of Australia's finest, freshest produce.

Three times a day, you'll find a buffet table overflowing with outstanding seafood, meats, fruits, preserves, vegetables and cheeses, all included in the tariff.

The beachfront location is perfect. Throw open your door, walk across the shady lawn and you're on the golden sands of Toowoon Bay. This idyllic location easily explains why Kims is Australia's oldest resort, transformed from its humble early days to one of Australia's most luxurious today.

In a perfect world everyone would have a beach house like this.

Rates
Bungalow or spa villa per couple, $510-$1860
Dinner, breakfast and lunch included
Visa, MC, AMEX, DC, DD, Eftpos

Location
90 minutes or 90km north of Sydney. Map 4.

Minimum stay
Two nights at weekends

Facilities
34 bungalows and villas with ensuites, all with spa bath or Jacuzzi. Some with private pool and sauna. RC AC, ceiling fans. DVD/CD. Bar, dining room. Massage available.

Member
SLH, Select

Owner details
Diana and Peter Kershaw
▪ kims@kims.com.au
▪ www.kims.com.au

Bluecliffe

Blackheath

16 Grose Street, Blackheath ▪ 02 9546 5309, 0412 894 786
www.beautifulaccommodation.com/bluecliffe

Rates
Whole house per night $600
(up to 6, extra persons $50)
Whole cottage per night $200
(up to 4, extra persons $50)
Accommodation only
Direct deposit, no credit cards

Location
2 hours or 110km west
of Sydney. Map 3.

Facilities
One house: three bedrooms (two
queen, one king/twin singles),
lounge (gas log fire, TV, DVD),
dining, reading room, kitchen,
RC AC, laundry. One cottage:
two bedrooms (queen, king/twin
singles), lounge (two singles, two
doubles, TV, DVD, CD), kitchen,
laundry. Undercover parking.

Owner details
Tanya Hough
▪ papide@bigpond.com
▪ www.bluecliffe.com.au

Garden for all seasons

If you like the idea of ensconcing
yourself for a few days in an
impressive Blue Mountains house,
surrounded by one of the most
beautiful cool-climate gardens we
have seen, then Bluecliffe is for you.

This elegant three-bedroom home is
complemented by a two-bedroom
cottage, allowing a party of up to 16
to be cosseted in total comfort. The
drawcard here is the wonderful sense
of space, with generous interiors to
gather in with friends and a stunning
garden to escape for quiet moments.

The interior of Bluecliffe's main house
is a dreamy blend of white and gold,
with delicate porcelains and
statuettes placed at selected focal
points. Your family or friends will
naturally gravitate to the grand sitting

room, which features a magnificent
bay window that brings views of the
garden into the house.

The bedrooms are light-filled havens
of serenity with comfy beds and
views to the garden. Depending on
the season, the garden provides a
stunning backdrop with cherry trees,
camellias, Japanese maple,
rhododendrons and a rare Japanese
birch tree.

Larger groups will love the option
of combining the house with the
cottage, adding another spacious
lounge (complete with bar and piano),
kitchen and two further bedrooms to
the grand home.

Brantwood Cottage
Blackheath

Location on enquiry, Blackheath ▪ 0405 187 297, 0404 479 411
www.beautifulaccommodation.com/brantwood

Elegant Federation gem

Some of the best accommodation experiences begin with a sensitive renovation, where period charm melds with modern convenience to offer a stay of serenity and comfort.

Brantwood Cottage is like having the weekender of your dreams waiting ready in the hills but without any maintenance worries. Just leave work, arrive, pass the keyless entry and find the beds dressed, the log fire ready to light and every modern comfort provided for your enjoyment.

The style is French provincial, with delicate colour schemes that ensure serenity. The three bedrooms feature carved wooden bed heads, elegant lamps on the side tables and the bathroom has a deep soaking tub, fluffy towels and indulgent toiletries.

For those who love to cook, the country-style kitchen will impress, as will the thoughtful touch of a generous breakfast hamper for your first morning. A bottle of wine, cheese crackers and chocolates together with the collection of magazines, games and DVDs and toys are a further hint at the owners' generosity of spirit.

The idea is to relax as if this were your own home. Entertain, relax, explore and if golf is your thing, the spectacularly beautiful Blackheath Golf Course – adorned with vivid rhododendrons, azaleas and conifers – is nearby, along with a range of dining options.

Rates
Whole cottage per night $275-$595 (up to 6 people)
Weekly rates available
Continental breakfast provisions included (first morning)
Visa, MC, DD

Location
2 hours or 110km west of Sydney. Map 3.

Minimum stay
Two nights

Facilities
One cottage: three bedrooms (queen, double, twin singles), lounge (fire, LCD TV, Austar, Bluray DVD, iPod dock, CD), kitchen/dining, bathroom. BBQ, laundry, ducted central heating, RC AC, garage.

AAA Star Rating
★★★★☆

Other
Suitable for children

Owner details
John & Tanya Georges
▪ brantwoodcottage@unwired.com.au
▪ www.brantwoodcottage.com.au

Falls Mountain Retreat Luxury Apartments

Wentworth Falls

The Avenue (off Falls Road), Wentworth Falls ▪ 02 4757 8836
www.beautifulaccommodation.com/thefalls

34

Rates
Apartment per night from
$180-$690 (up to 6 people)
Accommodation only
Visa, MC, AMEX, DC, DD, Eftpos

Location
1½ hours or 95km west
of Sydney. Map 3.

Minimum stay
Two nights at weekends (three
at long weekends)

Facilities
Studio, loft studio and one- and
two-bedroom suites, with king or
queen bed, lounge (TV, DVD, CD,
RC AC), real-flame gas fireplace,
double spa ensuite, kitchen or
kitchenette, some with laundry.

AAA Star Rating
★★★★☆

Member
Accommodation Association
of Australia

Other
Suitable for children
Disabled facilities

Manager details
Aaron Crockett
▪ stay@fallsmountainretreat.com.au
▪ www.fallsmountainretreat.com.au

Modern mountains high

The Falls Mountain Retreat ticks
all our boxes for a contemporary
self-contained stay in the Blue
Mountains. Waking up on a misty
morning in one of the spacious
apartments is a dreamy experience.
Soon the mist will lift, revealing
towering pines and walkways to
dramatic landscapes of sandstone
canyons and waterfalls.

You can bring your partner, family or
whole company here and be assured
of a sublime stay. We love the lofts,
with their flickering flame gas fires,
peaked roofs and fine views.

The designers have brought a real
contemporary verve to these large,
gracious spaces: the furnishings and
fittings are quietly sophisticated with
nods to the past such as port-hole
mirrors and restrained mantels
around the fireplaces.

There are also one- and two-
bedroom apartments, and some very
groovy (and very affordable) studios
for those who prefer cosy comfort.
Whichever you choose, all have one
or two bathrooms, each with a
two-person hydrotherapy spa bath
with 18 adjustable jets.

There are connections to 16 different
walking trails within 200 metres of
The Retreat, including a 20-minute
stroll to lookouts over the crashing
power of Wentworth Falls.

Galleries, restaurants, golf courses
and gorgeous public gardens are
within easy reach.

Hills Havens
Leura

Various locations, Leura ▪ 02 4782 7777, 0409 811 182
www.beautifulaccommodation.com/hillshavens

Lovely Leura hideaways

The Blue Mountains is a mystical landscape of misty mountains, waterfalls and awe-inspiring canyons that have drawn lovers, artists and jaded urbanites for decades.

Nestled within the gorgeous town of Leura are the three delightful Hills Havens, each lovingly restored to resonate with the history of their surrounds. Antiques, spas, artistic touches and cosy fires are the hallmarks of these impeccably presented hideaways.

Come as you like to the three Hills Havens – as singles, couples or as group members who want to be near one another without falling over each other.

Little Pomander is the largest Hills Haven cottage, with three bedrooms, beautiful English gardens (the owner is a horticulturalist), a sunny entertainment deck and a cosy lounge. It is also close to Leura's very elegant shopping and dining precinct.

Little Haven (one bedroom) and Iorana (two bedrooms) are tucked away in a secluded semi-rural part of Leura and each has its own quiet garden – a point noteworthy for friends who can meet under the trees for social times yet still have their own privacy.

Leura is a great location for idle walks to discover second-hand bookshops, antiqueries and sensational eating spots such as Silks restaurant. Naturally, walks to admire the views are close at hand.

Rates
Whole cottage per night from $165-$345 (2 people; $30 per extra person per night) Continental breakfast provisions included (first night) Accommodation only Visa, MC, DD

Location
90 minutes or 100km west of Sydney. Map 3.

Minimum stay
Two nights preferred

Facilities
Three cottages (one-, two- and three-bedrooms), each with lounge (wood or gas fire, TV, DVD, CD), dining, kitchen, spa bathroom, BBQ, RC AC.

Other
Suitable for children (Little Pomander)

Owner details
Sandra and Clem Hill
▪ hilhaven@bigpond.net.au
▪ www.hillshavensleura.com.au

Lavender Blue Mountains and Lavender Majestic

Blackheath and Katoomba

Locations on enquiry, Blackheath and Katoomba ▪ 02 4782 2385, 0412 884 061
www.beautifulaccommodation.com/lavendermajestic

Rates
Whole Cottage/Manor $245-$625
(2-6 people, $90/$110 per extra
guest) Full breakfast provisions
included (first morning)
Lavender Majestic per person
per weekend from $450-$750
Full breakfast, plus massage
or facial included
Visa, MC, DD

Location
1¾ hours or 112km west
of Sydney. Map 3.

Minimum stay
Two nights

Facilities
Lavender Majestic: three
bedrooms, lounge (fire, TV, Austar,
DVD, CD), conservatory, dining,
kitchen, two bathrooms (spa),
outdoor spa, BBQ. Manor: four
bedrooms, lounge (fire, TV, DVD,
CD), dining, kitchen, three
bathrooms, BBQ. Cottage: two
bedrooms, lounge/dining, sunroom,
second lounge (fire, TV, DVD,
libraries) kitchen, BBQ. Day spa.

Other
Suitable for children

Owner details
Nicky Vaux
▪ info@lavenderbluemountains.com
▪ www.lavenderbluemountains.com

Magical mountain fun

Sydneysiders have loved the mountain spa pleasures of the Blue Mountains for well over 100 years. Thoughts turn to warm fires, great company and indulgent pastimes, and this is exactly what Nicky Vaux offers with her stunning range of accommodation options and activity packages.

There is something for everyone, from honeymooners and girls on a jaunt to singles wanting to learn French cooking or simply mix with a like-minded group. Nicky offers three choices: The Lavender Manor and Cottage are self-contained, and the aptly named Lavender Majestic offers butler service for groups.

Lavender Manor is a graceful four-bedroom property that is ideal for self-catering groups.

The gorgeous Lavender Cottage has a storybook-like enchantment for one or two couples. Lavender Majestic, which was owned and built for the same family who built the famous Hydro Majestic Hotel, is a very special experience, with a butler to make the beds, serve up hearty breakfasts and keep your fires stoked.

For those seeking an organised escape, Nicky's residential Bliss Retreats are a real treat, including mums and babes sojourns, exclusive shopping and much more.

There are day spa services at each property with the sensuous Lavenderluscious Day Spa (see page 270) exclusive to guests.

The Studio Cottages

Faulconbridge (near Wentworth Falls and Katoomba)

169 Chapman Parade, Faulconbridge ▪ 02 4757 2816, 0414 514 766
www.beautifulaccommodation.com/thestudiocottages

Birdsong in the hills

There is something about these hand-built wooden cottages that creates an immediate sense of peace and security. Think sweet-smelling timbers, fresh mountain breezes, a crackling fire, bushland views and a delightfully soothing garden to roam at your leisure. Now add the indulgence of chocolates, red roses, sparkling wine and other goodies into your Romance arrival package and the feeling of being generously welcomed to your country retreat is complete.

The owner, Andy MacDonald, built these three cottages (Cottage, Treetops and the Hideaway), bringing all his aesthetic taste and craftsmanship to the task. Each has slate floors, an open fireplace to roar away on cold nights, a full kitchen for preparing your daily breakfast supplies and a private deck for basking in the peace and solitude.

The views are painterly shades of green, which are animated by birdsong and meandering wildlife. There is no need to haul in your own supplies here: seafood platters, barbecue packs and other treats are available on request.

Nearby is Norman Lindsay's historic home and now gallery, Springwood, and the Lindsay Cafe, which has won a swag of foodie awards. Laid out before you is all the majesty of the Blue Mountains to explore, but forgive yourself if you just put your feet up and relax.

Rates
Whole cottage per couple from $228-$298 (extra persons $35-$50) Full breakfast provisions included, gourmet platters available
Visa, MC, DD, Eftpos

Location
1 hour or 75km west of Sydney. Map 3.

Minimum stay
Two nights at weekends preferred

Facilities
Three cottages, each with queen, lounge (wood fire), dining, kitchen, spa bathroom, RC AC. Pool, BBQ, mountain bikes, laundry.

Other
Suitable for children
Accredited Tourism Business Australia

Owner details
Andy MacDonald
▪ studio5@bigpond.net.au
▪ www.studiocottages.com.au

Villa Athena Boutique Accommodation
Wentworth Falls

165-169 Falls Road, Wentworth Falls ▪ 02 4757 1998
www.beautifulaccommodation.com/villaathena

38

Rates
Whole suite or villa per couple
from $255-$750
Full breakfast included, dinner by
prior arrangement
Visa, MC, AMEX, DC, JCB, DD,
PayPal, Eftpos

Location
1½ hours or 95km west
of Sydney. Map 3.

Minimum stay
Two nights

Facilities
Two suites (king) and one
two-bedroom Stable Farmhouse
(king and queen, lounge/dining),
all with wood fire, mini bar, TV,
Austar, DVD, RC AC. Indoor
heated pool, spa, sauna, croquet
lawn. Butler and room service.

General Manager details
Craig McCallum
▪ reservations@villa-athena.com.au
▪ www.villa-athena.com.au

Vive les Montagnes Bleues

We often discover properties with
a delightful folly. At some it is the
idiosyncratic art or sumptuous suites,
at others it is the gastronomic
creations or romantic gardens.
Rarely, however, are all these
elements as beautifully orchestrated
as they are at Villa Athena.

It helps to start with a grand estate
like The Falls, a private garden
surrounding an imposing home.
It dates back to the late 1840s, when
it was Tolls Hotel – one of the first in
the Blue Mountains. Today majestic
trees cast a dappled light across its
manicured gardens and the three
exquisite accommodations – Villa
Athena's Studio Suite, Stable King
Suite and Stable Farmhouse.

The renowned interior designer
Jean-Christophe Burckhardt,
of Christophe Living in Woollahra,
has achieved an extraordinary
transformation here, recreating an
18th century French provincial style.

Villa Athena will transport you away
from mundane cares. The bed linens
are fragrant and the furnishings are
superbly matched by the cuisine,
which is a *fusion magnifique* of
French and Australian influences.
It starts with exceptional breakfasts
and there is the option to continue
with picnic baskets, lunches,
afternoon teas and dinner served in
your suite or in the gardens.

For the ultimate gourmet adventure,
join the monthly Chef's Table
Gastronomique where you dine with
the hosts in gothic splendour in the
original wine cellar.

Woodbridge Country Estate
Megalong Valley

Location on enquiry, Megalong Valley • 02 9949 6441
www.beautifulaccommodation.com/woodbridge

Valley of content

If we were going to advise a high-profile celebrity about where to hold their birthday or special anniversary celebration, one place would immediately spring to mind: Woodbridge Country Estate in the Megalong Valley. This wonderfully secluded manor is a private little kingdom of luxury that can sleep up to 16 guests.

It has beautifully manicured gardens that include a pool, a six-hole bush golf course, croquet lawn and tennis court – all great spaces for team bonding, individual retreats or group relaxation.

The comfort level is exemplary with a gracious dining room, expansive guest lounges, five bedrooms and three heated bathrooms in the main house.

The garden wing has three bedrooms, each with ensuites. Every room delights in gorgeous garden vistas and there is a magnificent outdoor terrace for casual dining or afternoon tea. There are also two kitchens that are well-stocked with every tool a master chef could want.

The Megalong Valley is a hidden gem on the floor of the Blue Mountains, with forests, waterfalls and horse riding tracks (horse riding is available next door to Woodbridge).

But it is all too easy to sit back with a book from the library or play spot the native wildlife.

Rates
Whole estate per night from $1250-$1950 (up to 16 people)
Accommodation only
Visa, MC, AMEX, DD

Location
2 hours or 120km west of Sydney; 18km from Katoomba. Map 3.

Minimum stay
Two nights

Facilities
Homestead and attached Garden Wing: total of 8 bedrooms, 6 bathrooms, extra toilet, two lounges (piano, open fires), dining (seats 16), breakfast room, living/dining room (fire, piano), laundry; TV, DVD, central heating, two kitchens. Pool, bush golf course, tennis, BBQ, horse riding nearby.

Other
Suitable for children

Host/Manager/Owner details
Bruce and Tilli Polain
▪ brucepolain@ozemail.com.au
▪ www.bluemts.com.au/
woodbridge

Hunter Valley
SYDNEY

The Hunter Valley

Sydneysiders are blessed to have the Hunter Valley within easy reach of their city. Just a few hours away is this stunning wine-growing region, with the internationally acclaimed districts of Pokolbin, Lovedale and Rothbury. However, this surprising area also includes the spectacular high plateau of the Barrington Tops and historic country towns such as Dungog. You can do everything here from mustering cattle to cruising cellar doors or hiking mountain trails. And the region offers sensational places to stay.

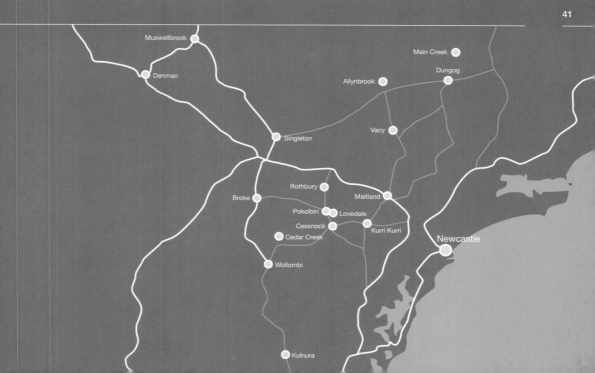

Muswellbrook
Main Creek
Dungog
Denman
Allynbrook
Vacy
Singleton
Rothbury
Maitland
Broke
Pokolbin
Lovedale
Cessnock
Kurri Kurri
Cedar Creek
Newcastle
Wollombi
Kulnura

The Hunter offers much more than fabulous reds and dry whites. It also has the Barrington Tops, one of Australia's most distinctive high country plateaus.

The ambrosial delights of wine are the focus of many visitors' trips to the Hunter Valley and with good reason. Its soil and climate produce some of the world's finest dry white wines, notably including wonderful semillons that only improve with age. This variety was introduced into the region in the 1820s and has thrived here like nowhere else. Other notable Hunter varieties include chardonnays, verdelhos and delicious shiraz.

With more than 120 wineries to explore, your cellar-door hopping and tasting will only scratch the surface in a few days. In the Pokolbin area, Tyrrell's produces its premium shiraz and semillons, which are regular trophy winners at Australian wine shows. But as you cruise the back-country roads from Pokolbin through Rothbury towards Branxton, expect to stumble across boutique wineries. Be sure to stop in and collect a case or two. Look in on Rothbury Estate; it was founded in 1968 by the late wine aficionado Len Evans, triggering the modern Australian wine renaissance.

Over the past 15 years, Lovedale has become famous on the global foodie trail for its annual Long Lunch in late May. This involves a weekend of progressive wine and food tastings at seven local wineries including Wandin Valley Estate and Allandale Winery. Music and other artistic pursuits add to the local flavour. Indeed, the Hunter has made a real signature style of combining gourmet events with the arts. Jazz in the Vines and the Hunter Valley Harvest Festival regularly draw thousands of repeat visitors for fun, fine food and good wine. Can it get more enticing than that?

The Hunter offers much more than fabulous reds and dry whites. It also has the Barrington Tops, one of Australia's most distinctive and unusual high country plateaus. This 1200 square kilometre landscape of extinct volcano cones, subtropical rainforests and ancient stands of Antarctic beech is a unique microclimate.

Two of the best vantage points in this eerie, evocative area are Devil's Hole

Hunter Valley
455 Wine Country Drive
02 4990 0900
www.winecountry.com.au

Maitland
Cnr New England Highway
& High Street
02 4931 2800
www.maitlandhuntervalley.com.au

Morpeth
173 Swan Street
02 4933 2612
www.morpethwinecellar.com.au

Dungog
Corner Dowling and Brown Street
02 4992 2212
www.barringtontopstourism.com.au

and Thunderbolt's Lookout, which recall the lawless bushranging of the mid-1800s. Many visitors to the Hunter who are after a real retreat from urban life book themselves into the cottages and cosy B&Bs in the uplands. They make ideal bases to venture down to the wineries and historic country towns below. The innovative Farm Gate Trail wanders through the region leading to places such as Johnson's Farmgate with its jams, relishes and Over The Moon milk from jersey cows.

Almost any road you take in the area will lead to some historic or enthralling spot in an unexpected or out-of-the-way place. The Anglican cemetery at Allynbrook has been in continuous use by locals since 1852 and is well worth a contemplative stroll to pay your respects to the region's pioneers. At Vacy, you get to cross one of the famous NSW timber truss bridges, which dates from 1898.

Dungog is one of the Hunter's brilliant historic towns and dates back to 1834, when a military post was set up to hunt down the bushrangers who hid out in the wilderness. The town is noted for its well-preserved buildings from the colonial era onwards. Tocal Homestead, which dates from 1822, has many of its original buildings intact. The annual Dungog Film Festival is a celebration of Australian cinema and it is held in the town's beautiful Spanish Mission-style James Theatre.

Cedar Creek Cottages at Stonehurst Vineyard

Cedar Creek (near Wollombi)

1840 Wollombi Road, Cedar Creek ▪ 02 4998 1576
www.beautifulaccommodation.com/cedarcreek

44

Rates
Cottage per couple from $159-$199
Full breakfast provisions included
Visa, MC, AMEX, Eftpos

Location
2¼ hours or 140km north
of Sydney. Map 5.

Minimum stay
Two nights at weekends

Facilities
Six cottages with one or two
bedrooms (queen), each with
lounge (wood fire, TV, DVD, CD),
dining, kitchen, spa bathroom,
RC AC. BBQ. Cellar door.

Other
Suitable for children
Cellar door open seven days
20% guest discount at cellar door
Disabled facilities

Owner details
Phillipa and Daryl Heslop
▪ relax@cedarcreekcottages.com.au
▪ www.cedarcreekcottages.com.au

Authentic, organic goodness

If we had to use one picture to illustrate the glories of the Hunter Valley, it would be a snap of the Stonehurst Vineyards' cellar door. It's the dream scenario: curling green grape vines on one side, a stunning stone chapel and the fruits of those vines on the other.

What's more, you can stay on this glorious Hunter Valley estate, poke your nose into all aspects of the vigneron's day and buy their prize-winning wines with an exclusive guest's discount to boot. Importantly, Stonehurst is committed to producing organic wines and does not use any modern preservatives. Wine aficionados, start your cars.

Cedar Creek Cottages on the Stonehurst estate radiate an ambience that recalls the early European settlers of this land.

They are timber-lined on the inside, with cosy wood fires, deep comfy beds, decanters of port and chocolates to keep your mood indulgent. Each has a verandah, some framed by dripping bursts of wisteria, that gazes over the rolling vineyards. The bounty extends to the packed breakfast hampers in the kitchen and spas in the bathrooms.

Nearby there are a string of other Hunter wineries to discover, dining including Bistro Molines at Tallavera Grove, historic Wollombi and you can even indulge in a massage in your cottage.

Noonaweena
Kulnura

1442 George Downes Drive, Kulnura ▪ 02 4376 1290
www.beautifulaccommodation.com/noonaweena

Indulgence among the treetops

Noonaweena is one of those special places spoken in whispers, the kind that is hidden in a location you might not expect. Overlooking the awesome Yengo National Park at the gateway to the Hunter Valley, Noonaweena is a purpose-built retreat for couples who need time out and groups seeking a secluded get-together in a place of stunning beauty.

The interior design of the various retreats is sumptuous yet unpretentious, the recreation facilities are fabulous and the restful atmosphere calls on you to commune with nature.

Couples will gravitate to the one- and two-bedroom retreats such as Boronia or Treetops, which are fully self-contained pleasure havens.

A group could opt for the grand gesture and choose the very contemporary Gymea house. All are blessed with decks overlooking escarpment and garden views.

In Treetops, the kitchen is a rainbow of vibrant hues and the king bedroom a spacious nest, complete with a restful bay window lounge. Each retreat is blessed with engaging art and interior tones that are in harmony with the natural surrounds.

All the facilities one could hope for are here, including a tennis court and a parkland garden to explore. You are also right on the food and winery trail with roads branching out towards dozens of cellar doors.

Rates
Room per couple from $200-$220
Full breakfast provisions included, catering available
Visa, MC, AMEX, DC, DD, Eftpos, Chq

Location
1¼ hours or 90km northwest of Sydney. Map 4.

Minimum stay
Two nights

Facilities
Treetops Suite: king bedroom, spa ensuite, lounge (TV, Foxtel, DVD), dining, kitchen, outdoor entertaining. Boronia Cottage: two bedrooms, lounge (TV, DVD), dining, kitchen, bathroom. Biram and Gymea houses: eight and five bedrooms, ensuite or private bathrooms, lounge (entertainment systems, fire), dining, kitchen, alfresco entertaining (BBQ), RC AC, fans. Function and conference facilities. Pool, spa, tennis court.

Other
Disabled facilities

Manager details
Rodney, Maureen and Adam Forsythe
▪ manager@noonaweena.com.au
▪ www.noonaweena.com.au

Adina Vineyard

Lovedale

492 Lovedale Road, Lovedale ▪ 02 4930 7473
www.beautifulaccommodation.com/adina

Rates
Lodge per night from $170-$800
(up to 6 people)
Full breakfast on weekends,
continental breakfast mid-week
Visa, MC, AMEX, DC, JCB,
DD, Eftpos

Location
2½ hours or 200km north
of Sydney. Map 5.

Minimum stay
Two nights at weekends

Facilities
Four three-bedroom lodges (one
king, two queen) all with ensuite,
lounge (gas log fire, TV, DVD, CD),
dining, kitchen, RC AC, fans. Pool,
BBQ, laundry. Cafe, cellar door,
olive mill, tastings.

Other
Suitable for children
Disabled facilities
Cafe: breakfast (Sat-Sun),
lunch (Wed-Sun)
Cellar door open daily

Owner details
Peter O'Meara
▪ info@adinavineyard.com.au
▪ www.adinavineyard.com.au

In the pleasure grove

Australians love authentic travel experiences and top of the list would be those that combine wine, food and gourmet produce, which goes some way to explaining why Adina Vineyard is so popular.

Here you can stay in superb accommodation on a working vineyard and olive oil producer. The ambience is very Italian, right down to the cuisine offered in the innovative menus. The pleasure of being a guest is that you can immerse yourself in this wondrous experience and truly become a part of the estate, whether you come as a couple with a group of friends or choose Adina as your wedding venue.

The accommodation options at Adina range from totally contemporary (three stunning lodges, each with three bedrooms) to the original estate manager's house, which has been completely renovated and sleeps up to six people.

The Lodges are avant-garde in design and each bedroom has its own ensuite. Floor-to-ceiling picture windows and decks give breathtaking vistas across the vines and olive trees. Adina House could be a provincial Italian farmhouse, complete with its refectory dining table and gourmet kitchen.

You can peer into every facet of winemaking and olive growing here, with experts providing information and sips of freshly milled olive oil and the estate's award-winning wines.

The Albion Hotel
Newcastle (Wickham)

72 Hannell Street, Wickham ▪ 02 4962 2411
www.beautifulaccommodation.com/thealbion

Eat, drink, play, sleep

Australia's historic pubs are the vastly underrated grande dames of the boutique accommodation industry. With their high ceilings and lovely facades, they make for a uniquely interesting stay.

These features have been carefully restored at Newcastle's The Albion, and better still, it has turned itself into a funky gastronome's pub with an excellent bill of comedians, celebrity speakers and degustation lunches by local wine makers. All you have to do afterwards is roll upstairs and snuggle into your crisp, white linen sheets.

The Albion has been a mainstay of Newcastle since it was built in 1922. Its revival beyond its original glory is truly brilliant.

You get a choice of twin single or queen rooms plus there is a self-contained apartment. We love the sparely refined treatment of the rooms, with plain walls, gorgeous lamps, tall windows, beds with comfy doonas and L'Occitane soaps. The shared bathroom facilities are well presented and do the trick or choose the apartment for your own bathroom. There is a private residents' lounge upstairs with sea views.

Across the road is the Newcastle Marina and foreshore for walks and cycling. The hotel can arrange boating and fishing trips. Newcastle's CBD is a two-minute drive away.

Rates
Room per couple $90
Apartment per night $175
(up to 4 people)
Continental breakfast provisions included, lunch/dinner available
Visa, MC, AMEX, DD, Eftpos

Location
2 hours or 160km north of Sydney. Map 5.

Facilities
Seven rooms with king/twin single, queen or twin singles, cable TV, fans (one with RC AC), shared bathroom facilities. One-bedroom apartment (queen), lounge (cable TV, sofa bed), kitchen, bathroom, RC AC. Bar, restaurant, gaming lounge.

Other
Suitable for children
Restaurant, bar open seven days

Manager details
Corey Crooks
▪ info@thealbion.com.au
▪ www.thealbion.com.au

Billabong Moon
Pokolbin

393 Hermitage Road, Pokolbin ▪ 02 6574 7290, 0415 709 880
www.beautifulaccommodation.com/billabongmoon

48

Rates
Whole cottage per couple
from $235-$510
Full breakfast provisions included
Visa, MC, AMEX, DD, Eftpos

Location
2½ hours or 200km north
of Sydney. Map 5.

Minimum stay
Two nights at weekends

Facilities
Five open-plan one- and
two-bedroom cottages with lounge
(fire, LCD TV, DVD, CD), dining,
kitchen, RC AC, WiFi, BBQ. Some
with spa bath, hot tub or garden
bath. Pool, chipping/putting green.

Other
Disabled facilities

Host details
Andy and Jenny Birtchnell
▪ relax@billabongmoon.com.au
▪ www.billabongmoon.com.au

Harmonious bushland haven

It's too easy to rave about the seductive qualities of Billabong Moon. This Hunter Valley property strikes a wonderfully resonant tone for every note of presentation, design, privacy and service. Think contemporary Australian architecture infused with a Japanese sensibility for uncluttered interiors.

A Zen-like trance of peace and tranquillity descends like a veiled curtain after you have dropped the bags, settled in with a Pokolbin red and begun to hear the wind and the birdsong around you.

There are five cottages and two guest rooms on this 25-acre estate, not that you would know it. Each cottage is carefully screened away in its own private communion with the surrounding landscape. For example, Billabong sits like a Kyoto temple before a sublime lake and Treetops is at bird height, featuring an amazing outdoor claw-foot bath.

The standard of service and appointments is first-class. There are four-poster beds, Australian antiques and hearty breakfast hampers to cook in your kitchen.

The Pokolbin area is synonymous with superb shiraz and semillon wine, with many cellar doors to visit. But we also recommend indulging in the treats at Billabong Moon, such as its famous red wine bath or the celebrated gourmet barbecue packs.

Bracken Ridge Vineyard Estate
Pokolbin

447 Old North Road, Pokolbin ▪ 0401 288 840
www.beautifulaccommodation.com/brackenridge

Life among the vignerons

Bracken Ridge Vineyard Estate's villas are at the heart of one of Australia's great wine growing regions. The local map reads like a guide to the better shelves of the local wine shop, with these villas in the centre of the action.

Bracken Ridge is a working estate with four attractive villas, a converted stables and a homestead, allowing you to sample the life of a vigneron. While you could be forgiven for feeling as if you've settled into the French provinces, watching kangaroos nibble the grass between the vines at sunset is an only-in-Australia experience.

The villas can sleep from two to eight people. Most have romantic timber-lined lofts, some reached by a spiral staircase.

Each villa is fully self-contained and you can choose between breakfast supplies or a cheese platter on arrival. The interior style is simple, unaffected and very comfortable, making superb use of picture windows to look across the estate to Brokenback Ridge.

The country-style homestead has three bedrooms, a wonderful kitchen an entertainment lounge with wood fire and a pool.

Bracken Ridge would make an ideal venue for an unforgettable wedding with a marquee on the expansive lawns with everyone able to nestle down happily afterwards.

Rates
Villa per couple $180-$225 (up to 2 people, $125 per extra couple)
Homestead per night $450-$750 (up to 6 guests)
Full breakfast provisions included (first morning) or cheese platter and bottle of wine on arrival, gourmet platters available
Visa, MC, DD

Location
2½ hours or 200km north of Sydney. Map 5.

Minimum stay
Two nights

Facilities
Four villas, one stables and one homestead: two or three bedrooms (some loft), lounge (fire, TV, DVD, iPod dock), dining, kitchen, bathroom (some with spa), RC AC, BBQ. Homestead with two queen, one twin singles, lounge (fire, TV, DVD), kitchen/dining, two bathrooms, RC AC, BBQ.

Other
Suitable for children

Manager details
Barbara Cowley
▪ info@brackenridgevillas.com
▪ www.brackenridgevillas.com.au

Elfin Hill Studios and Villa

Pokolbin

250 Marrowbone Road, Pokolbin ▪ 02 4998 7543
www.beautifulaccommodation.com/elfinhill

50

Rates
Villa per couple from $180-$300
Studio rooms per couple
from $140-$230
Continental breakfast included,
full breakfast available
Visa, MC, DD, Eftpos

Location
2½ hours or 200km north
of Sydney. Map 5.

Minimum stay
Two nights at weekends

Facilities
One villa (loft queen bedroom,
lounge/dining, kitchenette,
bathroom, RC AC) and six
hotel-style studio rooms (queen
bed, ensuite, TV, RC AC). Central
guest lounge and dining pavilion
(TV, DVD, CD, BBQ). Pool.

Host details
Marie and Mark Blackmore
▪ relax@elfinhill.com.au
▪ www.elfinhill.com.au

Scenic Pokolbin paradise

Elfin Hill is the Pokolbin district's
longest-running accommodation
venue. It is easy to see why it has
thrived for almost 40 years – it
combines a tradition of superb
service with a breathtaking hillside
location in one of Australia's most
celebrated winemaking regions.
Everyone from couples to friends on
a cellar door tour will find a cosy bed
and a wonderful breakfast awaiting
them here.

Elfin Hill has two choices of
accommodation. There is a gorgeous
contemporary villa with a loft
bedroom, kitchen and private patio
that overlooks a neighbouring
vineyard. In the late afternoon
sunshine it is idyllic.

There are also six hotel-style studio
rooms – all beautifully renovated with
comfy beds and garden views from
their big picture windows.

Up to 22 guests can stay and larger
travelling parties always love the
lounge and kitchen pavilion. There
is even a pool for splashing in on
a summer's day.

The Pokolbin Valley setting is flooded
with birdsong throughout the day and
Elfin Hills' majestic garden has seats
for meditating on the view. You can
order up special picnic baskets to
take along on your explorations.

Hunter Valley Cooperage Bed and Breakfast
Pokolbin

Lot 41, Kelman Vineyards, Pokolbin ▪ 02 4990 1232, 0427 752 010
www.beautifulaccommodation.com/huntervalleycooperage

Love among the vines

The Hunter Valley Cooperage Bed and Breakfast earned its place in *Beautiful Accommodation* from the moment we first visited. It has a winning formula: put a five-star B&B in the middle of a gorgeously landscaped vineyard and winery in the Pokolbin district of the Hunter Valley. Then add all sorts of goodies such as complimentary port, chocolates, gourmet breakfasts, a Gold-Class standard movie theatre and hosts who love to share winemaking lore with fellow wine lovers. No wonder *Gourmet Traveller* raves about this gem.

Since our last visit, things have only got better. Gay and Warren Cooper have added a new accommodation option to the mix with the Champagne Suite, which adds to their beautiful Vineyard Rooms and Scandinavian-influenced Retreat.

Champagne is richly appointed with exquisite Turkish rugs, Chinese vases and items that reflect the hosts' love of treasures from Istanbul and Asia. Couples will relish the double Kaldewei bath, double showers and sinks. This huge suite – it's 12 metres wide with floor-to-ceiling glass – opens onto a deck and garden of Manturian pear trees and the vineyard.

The Coopers are mainstays of the Pokolbin district and can tell you about all the best cellar doors to visit, places to see and fooderies that are running hot.

Rates
Room per couple from $270-$370
(up to 2 people)
Full breakfast included
Visa, MC, DD, Eftpos

Location
2½ hours or 200km north
of Sydney. Map 5.

Minimum stay
Two nights at weekends

Facilities
One suite and three rooms (ensuite, LCD TV, DVD; suite with lounge); one self-contained retreat (two queens, kitchen, bathroom, lounge/dining). All with RC AC. Guest lounge/dining (fire), movie theatre. Tennis, boules, golf driving range. WiFi. Massage.

AAA Star Rating
★★★★★

Member
BBFNSW

Host details
Gay and Warren Cooper
▪ coopers@cooperage.com.au
▪ www.huntervalleycooperage.com

Grapevines Boutique Accommodation
Pokolbin

1941 Broke Road, Pokolbin ▪ 02 4998 6766
www.beautifulaccommodation.com/grapevines

Rates
Studio per night from $155-$240
(up to 2 people; $60-$70 per extra
person per night)
Two-bedroom villa from $310-$570
(up to 4 people, $60-$100 per extra
person per night)
Full breakfast provisions included
Visa, MC, AMEX, DD, Eftpos

Location
2½ hours or 200km north of
Sydney. Map 5.

Minimum stay
Two nights at weekends

Facilities
Studios: queen, ensuite, lounge
(TV), kitchenette, patio, RC AC.
Villas: two queen bedrooms, each
with ensuites (deluxe villa also
with second bathroom), lounge
(TV, DVD; deluxe with fire, Austar),
dining, kitchen, patio, RC AC.
Deluxe also with annex (twin
singles), sun deck and connects
with second two-bedroom villa.

AAA Star Rating
★★★★ and ★★★★☆

Other
Suitable for children
Disabled facilities (studio villa)

Host details
Michael Griggs and Mary Booth
▪ stay@grapevines.com.au
▪ www.grapevines.com.au

Hunter heartland estate

Grapevines has a perfect Pokolbin
location. It is superbly positioned on
a sun-drenched ridge, overlooking a
landscape painted with vineyards and
pastures. These comfortable villas
are filled with original artworks and
blessed with fine linens and fluffy
towels. The attentive hosts pride
themselves on tailoring itineraries
to suit their guests' interests such
as vineyard tours and walks. Anyone
from couples escaping the kids to
friends celebrating a special life event
will love this peaceful retreat.

The deluxe villa is a party host's
delight with a stunning wooden sun
deck that looks across to the
Barrington Tops. The outside table
can seat 14, enabling you to
celebrate in unforgettable style.

You can expand the deluxe villa
into a four-bedroom, four-bathroom
mini-mansion by connecting it with a
neighbouring two-bedroom villa,
enabling a party of up to 12 to relax in
supreme comfort. Then there are the
delightful studio villas that are perfect
for couples.

Grapevines is a short walk from the
Hunter Valley Gardens (check out the
unique collection at the Wine Glass
Gallery, run by Grapevines' owners)
and the famous Harrigans Irish Pub.

All the best Hunter Valley dining spots
are a few minutes' drive and the
walks around the Pokolbin vineyards
and bushland are quite magical.

Kinsale Cottage
Pokolbin

551 De Beyers Road, Pokolbin ▪ 0412 931 191
www.beautifulaccommodation.com/kinsale

Hunter Valley homestead

You have to love a Hunter Valley place that has a specialised wine fridge in the kitchen. It's just so in tune with the whole vibe of this valley.

However, the thoughtfulness at Kinsale Cottage extends beyond providing an ideal place to park your cellar door treasures. There is play equipment for kids, a grand 10-seat dining table and a kitchen full of Smeg appliances for your holiday's masterchef creations.

Owner Vanessa Edmondson has brought a very sure aesthetic sense to the whole design and layout of this 'cottage', which in reality is a large three-bedroom, two-bathroom house on a 110-acre property.

Dark timber, white walls and red accents in throws, cushions and artwork create a brilliantly integrated and warmly welcoming ambience.

Kinsale has two large living areas, both with flat-screen TVs and DVDs so the kids can have their own retreat while the grown-ups converse over local wine and cheese before the gas-log fire.

Two of the area's best restaurants are in the neighbourhood. Across the road, Andrew Clarke's two-hat Rock Restaurant serves up extraordinary Australian-French fusion and the award-winning Muse is a short drive away. *Bon appétit!*

Rates
Whole house per night from $360-$480 (up to 4 people, $180 to $240 per extra couple) Accommodation only, full breakfast provisions and private chef by prior arrangement Direct deposit, no credit cards

Location
2½ hours or 200km north of Sydney. Map 5.

Minimum stay
Two nights

Facilities
One three-bedroom house (one king with ensuite, two queen), two lounge rooms (both with TV, DVD, CD and one with gas log fire), kitchen, dining, second bathroom, RC AC, BBQ.

Other
Suitable for children

Owner details
Vanessa Edmondson
▪ nesseddo@bigpond.net.au
▪ www.beautifulaccommodation. com/kinsale

Manzanilla Ridge

Rothbury

442 Talga Road, Rothbury ▪ 02 4930 9082
www.beautifulaccommodation.com/manzanillaridge

Rates
Whole cottage per couple from
$250-$350 (extra guests $75-$100
per person; up to 6 people)
Full breakfast provisions included,
barbecue hampers available
Visa, MC, AMEX, DD, Eftpos

Location
2½ hours or 200km north
of Sydney. Map 5.

Minimum stay
Two nights at weekends preferred

Facilities
Four cottages: two with three
bedrooms; two with two. Each
with kitchen, RC AC, plasma TV,
DVD/CD, iPod docking station, fire,
outdoor heated spa, gas BBQ.

AAA Star Rating
★★★★☆

Member
BBFAA

Other
Suitable for children
Disabled facilities

Hosts details
Dominic and Jane Peacock
▪ manzanillaridge@austarnet.com.au
▪ www.manzanillaridge.com.au

Spas beneath the stars

Manzanilla Ridge commands its
upland position with a quiet majesty.
A screen of forest surrounds this
idyllic bushland kingdom, which is
dotted with cottages that feel more
like homesteads in their generous
size. Don't try to resist the primal urge
to fire up the spa, uncork a bottle of
shiraz and begin to relax into an
afternoon of country bliss.

The four superbly appointed cottages
– two with three bedrooms, two with
two bedrooms – are discretely dotted
around the property, ensuring
absolute peace and privacy.

They are wonderfully fitted out for
a fun stay with big return verandahs
that feature barbecues, bubbling
spas and outside dining settings.

Hosts Dominic and Jane can prepare
gourmet barbecue packs of fresh
local produce for you on request.
Inside are wood fires, cathedral
ceilings and chef's kitchens with
everything you could need. Get the
kids busy with the breadmakers so
that you wake to fresh bread to go
with your Gaggia-made coffee.

Manzanilla is superb in all seasons.
Days start with a full hamper of
breakfast provisions. Then you can
laze on the verandah or tour the local
boutique Lovedale winemaking area.
The hosts can arrange transfers for
guests who fly in to Newcastle.

Heritage Retreat
Allynbrook (near Dungog)

840 Allyn River Road, Allynbrook ▪ 02 4938 9663
www.beautifulaccommodation.com/heritageretreat

Sensational old school charmer

Magic happens when a property's owners fall passionately in love with their estate, committing their lives and treasure to realising their restoration dreams. That's the story at Heritage Retreat, where Ron and Elinor Scott have turned their prodigious design talents to an 1881 school house and principal's residence.

The result is a deluxe guest experience in rooms that faultlessly combine classic lines with modern treats such as glass baths and gourmet kitchens.

There are three beguiling options. The School House is an extraordinary melange of New York loft elements including exposed walls and groovy fittings (we love the Italian glass bath and waterfall). In the French suite, a brick round arch connects the bedroom with a gorgeous bathroom, featuring a claw-foot tub set on a stunning checkerboard floor. A big gourmet kitchen, courtyard dining area and a set of boules complete the provincial French picture.

The River Wing basks in the soothing babble of water over rocks and adding to this water setting is the deckside spa bath. You can even pop out to your own private croquet lawn for a hit.

Nearby are wonderful Hunter Valley walks, various golf courses and a selection of cellar doors to visit and sample their wines.

Rates
Whole suite per couple
from $220-$330
Full breakfast provisions included
Visa, MC, DD, Chq

Location
3 hours or 210km north
of Sydney. Map 5 and 6.

Minimum stay
Two nights at weekends preferred

Facilities
Three suites: each with queen bed, lounge (fire, LCD TV, DVD, CD), dining and kitchen, RC AC; one with outdoor undercover spa.

Member
National Tourism Accreditation

Host details
Ron and Elinor Scott
▪ enquiries@heritage
retreat.com.au
▪ www.heritageretreat.com.au

Yeranda at Barrington Tops and Noonameena

Main Creek

117 Skimmings Gap Road, Main Creek ▪ 02 4992 1208
www.beautifulaccommodation.com/yeranda

Rates
Whole cottage per couple from
$100-$160 ($40-$60 per extra
adult; $11-$22 per child)
Accommodation only
Weekly rates available
Direct deposit, no credit cards

Location
3 hours or 220km northwest
of Sydney. Map 5 and 6.

Minimum stay
Two nights

Facilities
Three self-contained cottages
(one to three bedrooms) all with
lounge (wood fire), kitchen,
bathroom. Camp fire, BBQ. One
five-bedroom homestead (sleeps
up to 12) with two lounge rooms
(wood fires), dining, kitchen, AC.

Other
Suitable for children

Host details
Ros and Kevin Runciman
▪ ros.runciman@gmail.com
▪ www.yeranda.com.au/
elouera.htm

Mountaintop eco-cottages

The mystically beautiful Barrington
Tops plateau has a magnetic
attraction for those who want to
check into the ancient world of
Gondwanaland. This is a land of
valleys, waterfalls, starry nights and
trees and ferns that have held on for
100 million years. At Ros and Kevin
Runciman's three secluded eco-
cottages you can travel back to
this land that time forgot.

Ros and Kevin have created
something special with these
cottages, which reflect their passion
for connecting dwellings with the
surrounding landscape.

A profound place awareness shines
through in every detail, from the local
stone and timber used in their

construction to the ultra-light tread
of their carbon footprints.

Elouera is perfect for a family getaway
with older kids. It has two queen-size
beds and twin singles, a fire-lit lounge
(with a great sound system), a full
kitchen and a funky detached
shower house.

Each cottage has an outdoor firepit
for cooking and after-dinner
sing-alongs under the crystal clear
stars. For bigger parties, Ros and
Kevin also have the five-bedroom
Noonameena House down the road.

Trips to the scenic highlights of the
Barrington Tops are easy. But there
is plenty to see and do on this
57-hectare, officially designated
wildlife refuge.

Banjos Bushland Retreat
Vacy

Summerhill Road, Vacy ▪ 02 9403 3388
www.beautifulaccommodation.com/banjos

Bushy mountain high

Finding a place that will keep your crowd busy, active and very comfortably housed in a pristine bushland setting can seem impossible – until you stumble upon Banjos Bushland Retreat. We did and instantly loved the place.

It has three impressive lodges scattered across a 20-acre estate, set within a 1000-acre nature reserve. It's a five-star, AAA-rated property surrounded by bushland that is teeming with birds and wildlife.

The lodges are separate from each other, meaning you can enjoy yours in serene seclusion or come as a group of up to 18 and have the estate all to yourselves. The lodges range in size from two to four bedrooms (with extra roll-out beds if needed) and have

been architect-designed to maximise both space and light.

Each bedroom is indulgently large and all have their own ensuite. The splendid kitchens and outdoor barbecue decks invite guests to play Masterchef, complete with the option of organising either supplies or catering ahead of your visit. But you can also take it easy and eat at the nearby restaurant.

There is so much good, wholesome family fun to be had at the on-site recreation facility including tennis, mini-golf, billiards, ping pong and bushland strolls, not to mention the playground and the spa and sauna. Get a group and go – you'll love it.

Rates
Lodge per adult/child per night from $120-$130/$64 (up to 12; $105/$58 per extra adult/child) Accommodation only
Visa, MC, DD, Chq

Location
2½ hours or 187km north of Sydney. Map 5 and 6.

Minimum stay
Two nights at weekends

Facilities
Three lodges (two, three or four bedrooms, king/twin singles, all with ensuite, RC AC), lounge (fire, TV, DVD, CD), dining, kitchen, laundry, BBQ. Tennis, mini golf, spa, sauna, billiards, table tennis.

AAA Star Rating
★★★★★

Other
Suitable for children
Disabled facilities
AAA Eco-Friendly Accredited
Accredited Tourism Business Australia

Owner details
Jenny and Malcolm Patterson
▪ bookings@banjosretreat.com.au
▪ www.banjosretreat.com.au

North Coast

○ SYDNEY

North Coast

The New South Wales North Coast is a holiday planner's dream.
Just about anywhere you stick a pin on the map from Port
Stephens to Tweed Heads, you are bound to strike somewhere
with wonderful beaches, beautiful bays or nature reserves –
or perhaps all three. You can go back to an old favourite or
discover somewhere new. So get your pin out, close your eyes,
pop it on the map and set off for a serendipitous stay in some
beautiful accommodation.

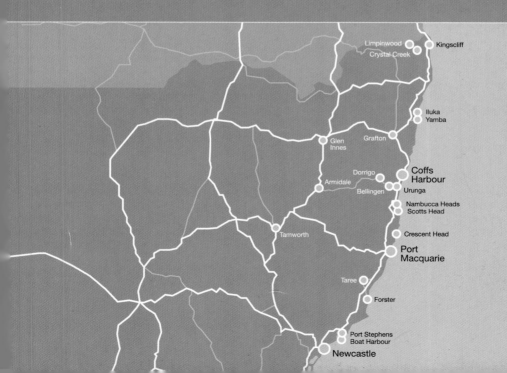

Limpinwood
Kingscliff
Crystal Creek

Iluka
Yamba

Grafton

Glen
Innes

Dorrigo
Coffs
Harbour

Armidale
Bellingen
Urunga

Nambucca Heads
Scotts Head

Crescent Head

Tamworth
Port
Macquarie

Taree

Forster

Port Stephens
Boat Harbour
Newcastle

Crescent Head is a tiny village with a huge reputation among surfers worldwide for its 300-metre right-hand break, which has been attracting board riders since 1958.

Port Stephens is larger than Sydney Harbour and resplendently beautiful. Its huge bay runs inland for more than 20kms and is speckled with elegant places to stay. Nelson Bay is the local 'capital' – if an unpretentious little town of 8000 can take that title – and a favourite spot for holidaying families, scuba divers, fishing fanatics and whale watchers. The Fly Point marine reserve is much loved by snorkellers and divers, and you can hand-feed the remarkable eastern blue gropers there.

Hawks Nest, across from Nelson Bay, is a quiet village (and sometime holiday haven of former Prime Minister John Howard). The area has prolific wildlife including a rare coastal dingo

population. The view to Jimmy's Beach from the Yacaba headland is breathtaking.

The Forster/Tuncurry inlet north of Hawks Nest is a busy holiday town in season with fantastic family-friendly beaches and superb fishing. The climb up the Cape Hawke in Booti Booti National Park will test your legs but the outlook is phenomenal.

Port Macquarie's beaches are picture postcard pretty and will keep you splashing with pleasure, whether you like paddling in the shallows or riding the waves. Take a camel safari over the sands at Lighthouse Beach. The Camden Haven Music Festival in May is an eclectic and superbly run regional music treat.

Crescent Head is a tiny village with a huge reputation among surfers worldwide for its 300-metre right-hand break, which has been attracting board riders since 1958. It is a designated National Surfing Reserve with 60km of protected coastline. Each May, the Malibu Classic draws big-board riders in their droves. Hathead National Park has wonderful walks and unspoiled beaches.

The Trial Bay Gaol at Arakoon was an internment camp for German prisoners during World War I. Now you can explore the State Conservation Area there before toddling into South West Rocks for coffee and the morning papers.

Accredited Visitor Information Centres

Newcastle
3 Honeysuckle Drive, Lee Wharf
02 4929 2588
www.maritimecentre-newcastle.org.au

Port Stephens
Cnr Victoria Parade &
Teramby Road, Nelson Bay
02 4980 6900
www.portstephens.org.au

Port Macquarie
Cnr Clarence and Hay Street
02 6581 8000
www.portmacquarieinfo.com.au

South West Rocks
Ocean Avenue
02 6566 7099
www.macleayvalleycoast.com.au

Coffs Harbour
Cnr Pacific Highway &
McLean Street
02 6648 4990
www.coffscoast.com.au

Bellingen
29-31 Hyde Street
02 6655 1522
www.waterfallway.com

Kyogle
Cnr Summerland Way &
Anzac Drive
02 6632 2700
www.visitkyogle.com.au

Tweed Heads
Cnr Bay and Wharf Street
1800 674 414
www.destinationtweed.com.au

One of Australia's best dive spots is just offshore – the 125-metre long Fish Rock Cave. Up the road is the laid-back fishing village of Macksville and nearby Taylors Arm is famously the source of Slim Dusty's 1957 hit, *A Pub With No Beer*. Nambucca Heads is another fantastic holiday town with patrolled beaches and unusual local exhibits such as the Frank Partridge VC Military Museum.

Bellingen is well worth a detour inland, through valleys covered in rainforest and spliced by rivers and creeks with great swimming holes. The Old Butter Factory Co-Op has good food and local artwork. Dorrigo's Rainforest Centre provides an accessible walk through the local ecosystem.

Coffs Harbour has the Big Banana and it is the big town of the north coast. It has all the attractions that fun-hunting kids, shopaholics and party hounds need to stay entertained. In September, the city hosts the International Buskers and Comedy Festival.

If you prefer more placid surrounds, Iluka and Yamba lie across the Clarence River's coastal estuary. And for complete privacy, Toumbaal Plains House is within Yuraygir National Park. Up near the Queensland border is Kingscliff, another surfers' paradise without the big buildings and neon lights. It has lakes, beaches and walking trails. Inland Crystal Creek has a sublime mountain landscape.

Port Stephens Luxury Apartments

Port Stephens

Locations on enquiry, Port Stephens ▪ 1300 679 559
www.beautifulaccommodation.com/portstephensapartments

A private port of call

Port Stephens quickly becomes a favourite of everyone who detours off the Pacific Highway and follows their way to the sea. It has an extraordinarily beautiful coastal landscape with dramatic headlands, islands offshore, little bays and beaches for picnics, and plenty of places for walking and swimming. You can have your own holiday haven here whenever you like thanks to Port Stephens Luxury Apartments.

These four self-contained apartments are located in two sensational resorts. Three are at Pacific Blue at Salamander Bay, which has the largest pool in the southern hemisphere. Two are swim-in, swim-out apartments and one has its own plunge pool for complete privacy.

This a true resort with everything necessary to heal the inner and outer 'you' including a Japanese steam room, gym, tennis courts and a lap pool, as well as the Body and Soul day spa and Azure restaurant.

The fourth apartment is at Cote D'Azur in the heart of Nelson Bay. It is a spacious two-bedroom, two-balcony apartment with some spectacular views.

Both properties are ideally placed for exploring the Port Stephens area. You can pop out for groceries, fish and chips or beach swims, and there are diving, fishing and whale-watching tours.

Rates
Whole apartment per night
$94-$450 (2 to 6 people)
Accommodation only, full breakfast provisions available
Visa, MC, AMEX, DD, Eftpos

Location
2½ hours or 200km north of Sydney. Map 5.

Minimum stay
Three nights

Facilities
A range of one- to three-bedroom apartments all with lounge (LCD TV, DVD), dining, kitchen and one to three bathrooms. RC AC. Pool, BBQ, off-street parking.

AAA Star Rating
★★★★☆

Other
Suitable for children

Manager details
Richard Knuppe
▪ info@portstephens.net.au
▪ www.portstephens.net.au

Beach House 7

Boat Harbour (near Nelson Bay)

26 One Mile Close, Boat Harbour ▪ 0407 616 921
www.beautifulaccommodation.com/beachhouse7

Rates
Apartment per night from
$350-$850 (up to 6 people)
Accommodation only
Visa, MC, DD, Chq

Location
2½ hours or 200km north
of Sydney. Map 5.

Minimum stay
Three nights

Facilities
One house: three bedrooms
(two queen, twin singles; master
with spa ensuite), lounge (gas
fire, TV, DVD, CD), dining, kitchen,
second bathroom (bath). Two
balconies (BBQ), laundry. Pool.

Other
Suitable for children

Manager details
Glenyss de Vylder
▪ enquiries@boatharbour.biz
▪ www.bh7.com.au

Summit of holiday success

Stunning, stunning, stunning! Do we need to say it again? This new find for *Beautiful Accommodation* perfectly illustrates what we are on about – discovering Australia's best places for you to unwind and enjoy.

Beach House 7 is surrounded by Tomaree National Park and has views over One Mile and Samurai beaches that will have you transfixed on your seat on the deck. The house has been cleverly designed to maximise all the advantages of its elevated site and sunny aspect.

The interior is groovy, relaxed and totally liveable. It flows over two levels, each with its own bathrooms and living spaces. This makes the property ideal for an upstairs-downstairs spread between kids and adults. You can all join together around the oval dining table on the second level for family meals that have been prepared on the huge marble benches in the kitchen.

If the weather turns cool, light up the fire for warmth and flickering radiance. The three wonderful bedrooms are beautifully set with colourful fabrics and fine bed linens. Fluffy Egyptian cotton towels complete the bathrooms.

There is a sensational infinity pool on Beach House 7's estate. Patrolled surf beaches, sheltered harbours, places to eat and bush walks are all nearby.

The Outlook on the Beach

Boat Harbour (near Nelson Bay)

2/4 Ocean Parade, Boat Harbour ▪ 0407 616 921
www.beautifulaccommodation.com/theoutlook

Stunning view with rooms

Boat Harbour looks like something a beach holiday theme park designer invented for their showroom. It's a gorgeous little bay that has been nibbled into the sandstone ramparts that face the Pacific.

At the head of the bay is one of the prettiest and quietest beaches we know – and that is where The Outlook on the Beach gets its name. It is just 20 metres to the sand and rock pools from your front door. Families with young kids love this place because of the safe waters and easy amble back to get sandwiches or another bottle of water.

The apartment is tailor-made for holidaying families or a bunch of friends away together. There are three queen bedrooms, a couple of bathrooms (always handy for extra showers), and climate control air-conditioning.

From the lounge and expansive deck, you look straight down to the beach below, which is an ideal vantage point for firing up the barbecue and uncorking a bottle of sparkles. The kitchen has granite benches and all you need for slapping together summer smorgasbords.

Nelson Bay is just a few minutes' drive away for shopping, restaurants, cafes and more. There are dolphin and whale-watching tours in season.

Rates
Apartment per night from $180-$390 (up to 6 people)
Accommodation only
Visa, MC, DD, Chq

Location
2½ hours or 200km north of Sydney. Map 5.

Minimum stay
Three nights

Facilities
One apartment: three bedrooms (queen, one with ensuite), lounge (TV, DVD, CD), dining, kitchen, second bathroom (spa). Balcony (BBQ), laundry, RC AC. Secure parking.

Other
Suitable for children

Owner details
Glenyss de Vylder
▪ enquiries@boatharbour.biz
▪ www.boatharbour.biz

Flynns On Surf Beach Villas

Port Macquarie

25 Surf Street, Port Macquarie ▪ 02 6584 2244
www.beautifulaccommodation.com/flynnsonsurf

Rates
Whole villa per night from
$110-$350 (up to 6 people)
Accommodation only
Visa, MC, DD

Location
5 hours or 395km north
of Sydney. Map 6.

Minimum stay
Two nights at weekends preferred

Facilities
19 one-, two- or three-bedroom
villas, each with lounge (LCD TV,
Austar), dining, kitchen, balcony,
WiFi, fans, ducted RC AC, garage.
Gas- and solar-heated pool, BBQs.

AAA Star Rating
★★★★

Other
Suitable for children

Host/Manager/Owner details
Richard and Caroline de Waal
▪ enquiries@flynns.com.au
▪ www.flynns.com.au

Private beachside estate

If the children are happy, busy and
safe on their holiday, parents are likely
to be relaxing too. Flynns on Surf –
a collection of villas in its own private
precinct – has been tailor-made to
ensure both these desirable
outcomes. Kids can scoot up and
down in front of the villas in absolute
security, play on the grassy koala
reserve behind the estate, or splash
in the heated pool. Finding friends
and playmates is easy, which leaves
parents to relax into a book on a
banana lounge by the pool.

The estate has 19 villas available
in one-, two- and three-bedroom
configurations. The interiors are
contemporary without being fussy

or overdesigned. Private rear decks
look out over the koala reserve or
gardens. A koala hospital is nearby,
with tours each day at 3pm – just slip
in through the back gate.

There are poolside communal
barbecues and each villa has a
lock-up garage, air-conditioning, WiFi,
a gigantic 50" plasma TV in the main
lounge and a 33" screen in the
master bedroom.

The surf beach is a 200-metre walk
away and there are shops for coffee,
takeaways and icecreams up the
street. In short, all the ingredients are
here for a memorable family break.

Sun Worship Luxury Eco Villas
Crescent Head

9 Belmore Street, Crescent Head ▪ 1300 664 757, 0459 260 369
www.beautifulaccommodation.com/sunworship

Clean, green seaside holiday

The Sun Worship villas show how eco-designed buildings can be both stunningly beautiful and thoroughly liveable. These five Crescent Head holiday homes place a tiny resource footprint on our planet, making them world-class examples of green housing. They use recyclable building materials, such as rammed earth walls, and employ passive heating and cooling design to maintain a perfect living temperature.

The villas' interior layout is superb for holiday living (and temperature-controlling airflow). Doors and wall panels can be opened up, providing the sensation of being in an even larger indoor-outdoor space. The intelligent design enables up to 10 people (and your dog too!) to be comfortably accommodated, depending on the villa.

But being green doesn't mean any loss of amenities. Every villa has a bubbling spa on the deck, huge plasma TVs and DVD players (with recent movies), washing machines, dryers and WiFi. Fluffy white towels and crisp linen sheets are included, so all you need to bring are your togs.

Crescent Head is a peaceful beachside town that has escaped the ravages of overdevelopment. Surfers love the famous Point Break but there is also a quiet tidal lagoon for kids to paddle in.

Rates
Whole eco villa per night from $150-$300 (up to 2, $10/$5 per extra person/child per night)
Accommodation only
Visa, MC, DD, PayPal, Chq

Location
5½ hours or 435km north of Sydney. Map 6.

Minimum stay
Two nights

Facilities
Five villas: each with one or two queen bedrooms and one bunk room (two double/single bunk beds), lounge (LCD TV, DVD), dining, kitchen, one or two bathrooms, private courtyard spa, BBQ, toilet and shower, WiFi, laundry.

Other
Suitable for children
Pets welcome

Owner details
Cinde Fisher
▪ info@sunworship.com.au
▪ www.sunworship.com.au

OceanScape Luxury Beachfront Villas

Scotts Head

2 Sea Breeze Place, Scotts Head ▪ 0416 293 256
www.beautifulaccommodation.com/oceanscape

Rates
Villa per night from $250-$325
(3-5 guests)
Accommodation only
Direct deposit, no credit cards

Location
6 hours or 480km north
of Sydney. Map 6.

Minimum stay
Two nights

Facilities
Two villas: one- and two-bedroom
(all bedrooms with spa ensuite).
Each villa with lounge (Austar TV,
DVD, CD; two-bedroom villa with
media room), dining, kitchen,
laundry. Under-floor heating,
garages, broadband internet.

Owner details
Jon Holcombe
▪ mail@oceanscape.com.au
▪ www.oceanscape.com.au

Dramatic coastal villas

The old real estate maxim location, location, location is what you get at OceanScape: two beautiful villas perched above the dramatic shoreline of Wakki Beach. At night, the hypnotic roll of waves below will have you drifting off into a dreamy sleep. By day, you can choose between the eastern and western aspects for sunsets and sunrises.

OceanScape has been designed from the ground floor up for a relaxed, contemporary beach holiday lifestyle. The open-plan spaces flow into each other, creating lovely breezeways and a grand sense of space.

Big picture windows bring in the views to every room and cast magnificent hues of light in the evenings and mornings.

The downstairs villa has two double bedrooms, a huge chef's kitchen and its own media centre for games and cable TV viewing. Upstairs is a one-bedroom villa with phenomenal views in every direction. Both villas are generously appointed, including double wash basins and spas in the bathrooms.

These villas make an ideal choice for an extended family or a group of old friends who relish spending some time together in a glorious location. There are plenty of local activities to indulge in such as kayaking, fishing, surfing and bushwalking.

Casa Belle Country Guest House
Bellingen

90 Gleniffer Road, Bellingen ▪ 02 6655 9311
www.beautifulaccommodation.com/casabelle

Tuscany by Bellingen

It's very hard to beat this Tuscan-style hilltop mansion that overlooks the gorgeous Bellingen valley, near the alternative town of Bellingen. The friendly and attentive hospitality of hosts Suzanne and Fritz is a hallmark of a stay at Casa Belle and after 14 years, their guestbooks overflow with superlatives.

There is also an eco-consciousness here that extends to natural pigments on the walls, filtered rainwater for bathing, sun-dried linens to sleep on and zero use of pesticides and chemical fertilisers.

The architectural melange of a Moorish courtyard, princely bedrooms, flagstoned floors and Italianate touches everywhere works perfectly in this sub-tropical climate.

On cool nights there is an open fire in the impressive guest lounge and during the heat of the day the colonnades and interior are cloisters of cool. There are furnishing highlights dotted throughout the Casa – a cross-framed curule seat here, a Bolivian bell there – that make exploring this wonderful estate a delight.

The bedrooms are sumptuous and offer luxuries like L'Occitane toiletries and two have spa baths. Generous breakfasts, private dinners and home-baked afternoon tea complete this utterly gracious picture.

For the ultimate indulgence, enjoy a massage or facial using organic products in the privacy of your suite.

Rates
Room per couple from $235-$250
Full breakfast and afternoon tea included, dinner by prior arrangement
Visa, MC, Eftpos

Location
6½ hours or 525km north of Sydney. Map 6.

Facilities
Three suites with queen or king, all with ensuite (two with spa), TV, DVD/CD, private patio. Guest lounge (fire), dining room. Free WiFi.

AAA Star Rating
★★★★☆

Member
BBFAA

Other
Pets by arrangement
Disabled facilities

Host details
Fritz and Suzanne Dimmlich
▪ enquiries@casabelle.com
▪ www.casabelle.com

Clouds End

Dorrigo (near Bellingen and Coffs Harbour)

Whisky Creek Road, Dorrigo ▪ 0401 572 275
www.beautifulaccommodation.com/cloudsend

Rates
Whole house per night from
$170 to $200 (up to 2 people, $30
to $50 per extra person per night)
Accommodation only
Visa, MC, DD

Location
6½ hours or 545 km north of
Sydney, one hour southwest
of Coffs Harbour. Map 6.

Minimum stay
Two nights

Facilities
One house: three queen
bedrooms (one with ensuite),
lounge (fire, LCD TV, DVD, VCR,
CD), dining, kitchen, bathroom.
BBQ, laundry, WiFi.

Other
Suitable for children

Host/Manager/Owner details
Beth and Kelvin Henwood
▪ bookings@cloudsend.com.au
▪ www.cloudsend.com.au

Panoramic mountaintop retreat

Cloudsend beckons you to quit the
city, move to Dorrigo and settle in to
a cloistered life of meditation, novel
writing, painting and cooking.
The views from this cosy wooden
farmhouse are utterly beguiling.
On a clear day, you can see over
the rainforested hills and far away
to the distant ocean.

The house has an irresistible
wrap-around verandah with a table
and deckchairs for gazing, gossiping
over coffee or simply settling in with
a good book.

Through the French door, off the
verandah, is a dining room with its
own bay window and more stunning
views. The interior glories in the use
of local timber, a spacious design
and cathedral ceilings.

Bedrooms are serene in the simplicity
of their wooden furnishings and restful
hues. Upstairs is a loft the kids will
love, which is fitted with a dormer
window daybed. A claw-foot bath
complements the main bathroom.

Twitchers love Cloudsend for its
inexhaustible supply of bird species
including satin bowerbirds, wompoo
fruit doves and peregrine falcons.
Perhaps the birds love the sanctuary
of Cloudsend's 22 hectares, which
include Open Garden-feted English
hedge gardens and a pond.

If you must leave, Dorrigo is just a
10-minute drive away for the papers,
supplies or a pub meal.

Diggers Beach House
Coffs Harbour

11 Sandon Close, Coffs Harbour
www.beautifulaccommodation.com/diggers

Family holiday mansion

Bringing friends and family together is what holidays should be about – when you finally have the time to share books, gossip over a long lunch, play board games, watch movies or splash together in a pool or the surf. For big get-togethers – say 10-14 people – you need a place where your mob can join up for meals and fun but also spread out for individual peace and serenity. Sounds like a big ask, but not at Diggers Beach House.

This coolly contemporary mini-mansion has six spacious bedrooms, plenty of bathrooms and an ideal position above one of Coffs Harbour's best beaches.

The site design couldn't be better suited to keeping your gathering fed, entertained and rested. A huge kitchen-dining area (with wood fire) opens onto a floodlit central pool and heated spa. Then there is a home cinema/rumpus room for movie screenings (it even has its own bar and makes Gold Class look crowded). The bedrooms are quiet, spacious havens and there is a formal lounge to entertain friends and family.

Coffs Harbour is a real playground, with plenty of shopping and dining options within a few minutes' drive. The tranquil half-moon of Diggers Beach is a short stroll away.

Rates
Whole house per night from $250-$1000 (up to 14 people)
Accommodation only
Visa, MC, DD

Location
6 hours or 530km north of Sydney. Map 6.

Minimum stay
Two to seven nights

Facilities
Six-bedroom house (king/twin singles, master with ensuite) with lounge (wood fire, TV, DVD, CD), dining, kitchen, two bathrooms, movie theatre/rumpus room (bar), laundry, RC AC, garage. Pool, spa.

Other
Suitable for children

Details
▪ glenn@inh.com.au
▪ www.stayz.com.au/32770

Toumbaal Plains

Sandon River (near Yamba)

Location on enquiry, Sandon River ▪ 02 9417 6881
www.beautifulaccommodation.com/toumbaalplains

Rates
Whole house per night $400-$600
(up to 6 people)
Accommodation only
Visa, MC, DD

Location
3½ hours or 300km south of
Brisbane; 8 hours or 675km north
of Sydney. Map 6.

Minimum stay
Three to seven nights (seasonal)

Facilities
One house: three bedrooms (king
with ensuite, king and king/twin
singles), lounge/dining/kitchen
pavilion (wood fire, TV, Austar,
DVD), internal courtyard (wood
fire), second bathroom (soaking
tub). Laundry. Airfield.

Other
Suitable for children

Owner details
Alec and Kath Waugh
▪ travel@blueskies.com.au
▪ www.toumbaalplains.com

National park pleasure pavilions

One of our goals at *Beautiful Accommodation* is to find iconic places to stay like Toumbaal Plains, which has more than earned its right to feature in these pages. This multi award-winning property combines a daring contemporary architectural design with a setting of absolutely pristine splendour on a sliver of private land within Yuraygir National Park near Yamba.

Unspoilt Sandon Beach is nearby and your only neighbours are the local kangaroos and emus who come out to feed in the evenings. Artists, poets, romantics and stressed executives: pack your bags and prepare for paradise here.

The design and build quality of Toumbaal is sensational and it would make a brilliant setting for a small wedding. It comprises two pavilions – one for the three bedrooms; the other for the kitchen-lounge-dining – which are linked by a grassy inner courtyard that features a stunning fireplace.

You can slide open the walls to link the interior to the outdoors, providing a magnificent sense of space and light. The views are incredible, particularly while you soak at sunset in the double-ended pedestal tub with a bottle of bubbles beside you.

Yuraygir is NSW's largest coastal national park and has walks through beach and hinterland terrains. Sandon Beach has wonderful swimming and paddling places.

Amarco-Iluka
Iluka (near Yamba)

2/38 Marandowie Drive, Iluka ▪ 02 6646 6210
www.beautifulaccommodation.com/amarco

Riverside village refuge

Do you ever dream of finding a serene place to stay in a little riverside village, set on an idyllic coastal peninsular, far from the madding crowd? The river would be near enough to walk over and toss in a line, and the sunsets would be ethereal showcases of reds, oranges, purples and yellows. If so, stop dreaming and start booking at Amarco-Iluka.

This is a two-storey, three-bedroom, two-bathroom home, complete with two separate living areas, a ground-floor patio and upstairs verandah with Clarence River views. There is also a big kitchen and a courtyard barbecue area out the back, and you can arrange for full breakfast provisions to be included by prior arrangement.

Taken as a whole house, it would leave space to spare for a big family seeking a quiet holiday refuge or a party of seniors on a tear away from the grand kids. There is also the option to take just the ground floor, with lounge, kitchen, bathroom and king bedroom. The interior is modern and thoroughly practical, making it ideal for those who don't want too much trendy fuss and feathers.

Here you have the opportunity to enjoy profound silence at night, gaze at stars not backlit by neon, and walk pristine beaches or wonderfully preserved forests.

Local activities include river cruises, coffee plantation tours, surfing and golf at nearby courses.

Rates
House per night $290-$440
(up to 6 people)
Ground floor per night $185-$340
Accommodation only
Visa, MC, AMEX, DD, Eftpos, Chq

Location
4 hours or 280km south of
Brisbane. Map 6.

Minimum stay
Three nights

Facilities
One house: three bedrooms (king/twin singles, queen, twin singles), two lounges (TV, Austar, DVD), dining, kitchen (kitchenette/bar upstairs), two spa bathrooms. Patio, verandah, laundry, RC AC.

AAA Star Rating
★★★★☆

Member
Accommodation Association of Australia
AAA Eco Friendly Accreditation
National Tourism Accreditation

Other
Suitable for children

Host/Manager/Owner details
Anne and Graeme Lockyer
▪ stay@amarco-iluka.com.au
▪ www.amarco-iluka.com.au

Valley View Hideaway Cottage

Crystal Creek (near Murwillumbah)

160 Upper Crystal Creek Road, Crystal Creek ▪ 02 6679 1505
www.beautifulaccommodation.com/valleyview

Rates
Cottage per night from
$240-$260 (up to 2 people,
$90 per extra couple)
Full breakfast provisions included
Visa, MC, DD, Eftpos

Location
1¾ hours or 145km south of
Brisbane; 50 minutes or 50km
southwest of Gold Coast airport.
Map 6.

Minimum stay
Two nights

Facilities
One cottage with two master
bedrooms (each with king and
ensuite with double spa), lounge
(gas-log fireplace, TV, DVD/CD),
dining, kitchenette, covered patio
(BBQ). RC AC, fans. Undercover
parking.

Owner details
Donna and Stewart Baericke
▪ hideaway@crystalcreek.com.au
▪ www.crystalcreek.com.au

Crystal-clear contemporary style

Crystal Creek near Murwillumbah
is one of our favourite places. It
flows through a fertile terrain with
myriad green trees rooted in rich
volcanic soils.

The region is centred on the
dramatic peak of Mount Warning
(or Wollumbi, which means 'cloud
catcher' in the local Aboriginal
language). It is the core of a vast
volcanic caldera that erupted 23
million years ago.

Valley View Hideaway Cottage is
nestled in one of this amazing
landscape's most picturesque
settings. The Hideaway was
completed in 2009 and it is a
state-of-the-art stay for one or two
couples seeking a stylish and
thoroughly indulgent base for
exploring the Tweed and surrounds.

It has Crystal Creek frontage, allowing
you to play spot the platypus and
wander through its beautiful
sub-tropical garden and paddocks.

The residence is breathtaking and
we particularly like the two distinctive
Asian-influenced bedrooms with
four-poster beds and ensuites with
double spas and views. No need to
argue over who gets the best room
– they are identical apart from the
decor. This hobby farm even has
a collection of animals.

Murwillumbah thrives on its mix
of farmers and hippies, offering
everything from art to great dining.
The region also has many inspiring
walks through the world heritage-
listed national parks.

Crystal Creek Rainforest Retreat

Crystal Creek (near Murwillumbah)

201 Brookers Road, Upper Crystal Creek ▪ 02 6679 1591
www.beautifulaccommodation.com/crystalcreekretreat

Rainforest of dreams

Honeymooners and romantics: pay attention. We have found a divine sanctuary for you at Crystal Creek Rainforest Retreat.

Here is a collection of exquisite havens planted in absolute privacy around a 250-acre rainforest reserve. It is even surrounded on three sides by a World Heritage-listed national park. These hideaways have each been architect-designed to immerse you in ultimate eco-conscious luxury.

Every line of sight – from the soft leather sofas to the sumptuous king beds and sunken double spas – leads your eyes to dazzling leafy greens. Just sit, relax and watch as the forest reveals its secrets to you

in your luxurious perch. Who needs the HD plasma TV in the living area when you have this unfolding nature documentary before you?

You can choose between six different styles, ranging from the Creek Side Cabins up to the new Luxury Mountain View Lodges, which have their own plunge pools. Each has polished timber floors, panoramic glazing and pitched roofs that lend an incredible sense of space and light.

Thanks to the truly impressive selection of gourmet meals and hampers available for guests to prepare at their leisure, you hardly need to leave your pleasure pavilion.

Rates
Cabin, bungalow and lodge per couple from $365-$645 Accommodation only, breakfast and dinner provisions available Visa, MC, DD, Eftpos, Chq

Location
1¾ hours or 145km south of Brisbane; 50 minutes or 50km southwest of Coolangatta airport. Map 6.

Minimum stay
Two nights

Facilities
A range of cabins, bungalows and lodges, each with king, lounge (fire, TV, DVD, iPod dock; sound piped to all rooms), dining, kitchen, bathroom (double spa), RC AC. Pool, lodges also with pool. Games room (DVD library, WiFi).

Member
Accommodation Association of Australia

Other
Disabled facilities
Prepared meals available

Host details
Mark van Renen
▪ ccrr@optusnet.com.au
▪ www.ccrr.com.au

Limpinwood Lodge

Limpinwood (near Murwillumbah)

531 Zara Road, Limpinwood ▪ 02 6679 3805
www.beautifulaccommodation.com/limpinwood

Rates
Chalet per night $395
(up to 2 people)
Continental breakfast provisions
included, dinner served to chalet
by prior arrangement
Visa, MC, DD

Location
1¾ hours or 126km southeast
of Brisbane; 50 minutes or 55km
southwest of Gold Coast airport.
Map 6.

Minimum stay
Two nights

Facilities
Three chalets, each with king bed,
lounge/dining (fire, TV, Austar,
DVD), kitchen; two with spa on
deck, one with spa in gazebo;
bathroom (two with double
shower). BBQ, RC AC, fans.
Shared, covered entertainment
area (fire, pizza oven, BBQ).

Other
Disabled facilities

Owner details
Robyn and Bob Rowney
▪ info@limpinwoodlodge.com.au
▪ www.limpinwoodlodge.com.au

Lodged in loving bliss

Sometimes you need a getaway that is the complete package, a place you can arrive at and know everything will be taken care of – including you.

Limpinwood Lodge is all about lifting burdens from shoulders – no driving around to find somewhere to eat at night, no finding somewhere else for breakfast. You can feel the weight of city concerns falling away as you nose your car up the Numbah Valley Road into a spectacularly beautiful landscape of forests and farms.

Limpinwood has three chalets that have been purpose-built to enable couples to escape for a few days and nights of romantic bliss. All three have their own secluded outlook onto the nine-acre estate with names

that allude to their views: Rainforest, Pinnacle and Valley View.

Each has its own discrete charms such as a four-poster bed or a funky woven-cane daybed. All have a spa (one in a pavilion), open fires, cable TV and kitchenettes for preparing your complementary breakfast, which includes fresh-baked hot bread. We also recommend taking one of Robyn and Bob Rowney's comfort food dinner packages to enjoy on your private deck.

Nearby is historic Tyalgum village, which has the gorgeous Flutterbies Cafe, galleries, shops to browse and a classical music festival is also held every September.

Ming Apartments
Kingscliff (south of Tweed Heads)

236 Marine Parade, Kingscliff ▪ 07 4638 4861, 0408 384 861
www.beautifulaccommodation.com/ming

Orient-inspired seaside apartments

If you love the Gold Coast sunshine, its warm sandy beaches and tepid water temperature but want to avoid all the high-rise, razzle-dazzle, read on. The Ming Apartments at Kingscliff is just 10 minutes' drive from the airport but serenely located on the appropriately named Dreamtime Beach. Here, life is low-rise and very family friendly.

The owners' love of China is subtly displayed in the Ming's elegant works of art, furniture and porcelain without being overpowering. The design is ideal for families with children of any age.

The three-bedroom ground-floor apartment opens onto a patio and lawn for the kids to scamper on.

Upstairs is a four-bedroom apartment with wonderful views over Dreamtime beach, and the same spacious proportions and high-end fittings as the lower level.

The top floor of Ming Apartments has an extraordinary entertainment area with ocean and parkland views, a billiard table, bar, table tennis and an entertainment system.

You can find coffee and good food nearby on Kingscliff's Marine Parade. And, of course, golfing, the hinterland and the bright lights and shopping of the Gold Coast are all nearby.

Rates
Apartment per night from
$128-$445 (6-8 guests)
Use of fourth bedroom $150
(flat fee); use of rooftop
entertaining room $300 (per stay)
Accommodation only
Visa, MC, DD

Location
1½ hours or 110km south of
Brisbane; 10 minutes from Gold
Coast airport. Map 6.

Minimum stay
Three to seven nights (seasonal)

Facilities
Two apartments: three and four
bedrooms. Both with lounge (TV,
DVD, CD), dining, kitchen, patio or
balcony (BBQ). Entertainment
room (billiards, table tennis, bar, AV
system). Parking.

Other
Suitable for children

Owner details
Philippa Adsett
▪ enquiries@ming
apartments.com.au
▪ www.mingapartments.com.au

Byron Bay
& Surrounds

The stretch of seashore from Brunswick Heads to Byron Bay and Ballina is arguably one of the grooviest on Australia's east coast. Its balmy weather, warm sands, great surf and outrageously beautiful mountain hinterland draw everyone from backpackers to celebrities. They all have their own reasons for coming – partying, meditation retreats, spa pampering or quiet summer holidays with the kids. Everyone finds their groove in this idyllic piece of northern New South Wales. This is sunshine on a stick.

Brunswick Heads

Nimbin

Ewingsdale

Byron Bay

Bangalow

Suffolk Park

Newrybar

Broken Head

Tintenbar

Lennox Head

Lismore

Alstonville

Ballina

The region's beautiful beaches, perfect waves and soft, warm sand help to keep holiday-makers happy over the long summer months.

Byron Bay. It's a name that evokes memorable times and places for everyone who visits. Back in the late 1960s, the region was discovered by surfers and then lovingly embraced by the Flower Power generation of hippies – most of them escaping regimented lives in the city. That rebellious, fun-seeking vibe still lingers in the hills and shores but it now has an incredible range of places to stay, eat and shop.

The whole Byron Bay area has become a magnet for artists, musicians and writers – and their fans. One of Australia's best-known crowd-pullers for musicians and music lovers alike is The East Coast Blues & Roots Music Festival at Byron each Easter.

This extraordinary spectacle draws talent from around the world, ranging from Grace Jones and BB King to Trombone Shorty and The Cat Empire. The town loves its music and there are plenty of places to drink and listen all year-round, such as the Byron Bay Brewery and Buddha Bar. The Byron Bay Writers Festival in August is a great place to hear your favourite authors and collect autographs.

The region's beautiful beaches, perfect waves and soft, warm sand help to keep holiday-makers happy over the long summer months. For those who want to be near the Byron buzz but not right in the middle, Suffolk Park to the south is a quiet little village with some fabulous

beaches. Settle in here for some 1960s seaside holiday ambience. Brunswick Heads is equally relaxed as it sprawls along its pretty river estuary and beachfront. Torakina Beach has placid waters to paddle in for families with young kids. The town hosts a Fish and Chips Festival with lots of fireworks each January.

Inland from Byron Bay is a patchwork landscape of farms, forests and plantations. The result is a dazzling array of textures and shades of green, which helps explain the region's attraction for artists. Picturesque villages are dotted through the hills. Bangalow has a verandah-fronted main street that is lined with cafes, alternative lifestyle shops and

therapists. If you and the family are near Bangalow in May, take your junior Mark Webbers along to The Billy Cart Derby for some thrills and spills.

Newrybar offers a glorious prospect over the plains to the sea and has the very chic Harvest Cafe for grazing or long, lingering meals. Try one of their Naked Native cocktails to quench your thirst.

Another local hamlet, Federal, has the Village Gallery, which features work by local silversmiths and jewellery makers. Up the road is a town that has become a byword for alternative north coast lifestyles – the incense-scented town of Mullumbimby. Stop by the Crystal Castle, which has soothing grounds

and everything you need for some alternative healing.

Ballina is a brilliant town for those who are seeking a quieter vibe than there is in busy Byron. Nearby Lennox Head has a surf break that draws surfers from around the world (and they are sometimes joined in the waves by local dolphins).

Between June and November each year, whales romp in the seas along the coast and there are plenty of tour operators to take you out spotting. There are regular markets, car boot sales and swap meets all along the coast with fresh produce, bric-a-brac, antiques, food and music. The Ballina Market, held every third Sunday, has food, gifts, fashion and gadgets.

Byron Bay
80 Jonson Street
02 6680 8558
www.visitbyronbay.com

Ballina
Cnr River Street
& Las Balsas Plaza
1800 777 666
www.discoverballina.com

Brunswick Heads
7 Park Street
02 6685 1003
www.brunswickheads.org.au

Murwillumbah
Cnr Alma Street
& Tweed Valley Way
02 6672 1340
www.destinationtweed.com.au

Tweed Heads
Cnr Bay and Wharf Street
1800 674 414
www.destinationtweed.com.au

Barefoot at Broken Head

Broken Head (near Byron Bay)

6/137 Broken Head Reserve Road, Broken Head ▪ 0411 888 448
www.beautifulaccommodation.com/barefootbrokenhead

Rates
Whole house per night $1400-$2200
Weekly rates from $7500-$15,000
(up to 12 people)
Accommodation only
Direct deposit, Chq, no credit cards

Location
60 minutes or 70km south of
Coolangatta; 25 minutes or 26km
north of Ballina. Map 6.

Minimum stay
Three to five nights (seasonal)

Facilities
One house: three pavilion
bedrooms (each with king, single,
double daybed on verandah and
ensuite), lounge pavilion (cable TV,
DVD, CD, piano), kitchen/dining,
laundry. iPod docks in all rooms,
WiFi. RC AC. Reading/reflection
pool, lap pool, BBQ. Garage (bikes,
surfboards).

Other
Suitable for children
Pets by arrangement

Owner details
Timothy James
▪ barefoot6@bigpond.com
▪ www.beautifulaccommodation.
com/barefootbrokenhead

Barefoot in paradise

Heaven must be rather like Barefoot
at Broken Head – surrounded by
rainforest, a short stroll down a
private path from one of the world's
best right-hand surfing breaks and
unbelievably luxurious. What a reward
for a life well-lived, but fortunately, you
can have it now. Plus, you are only
minutes away from groovy Byron
when you need some action after
blissing out at what is undoubtedly
one of Australia's most superb
beachfront hideaways.

Barefoot integrates the best of
Balinese architectural design with
stylish contemporary pizzazz. It
comprises three separate bedroom
pavilions arrayed around a central
lounge pavilion, which breathes in the
superbly landscaped tropical garden.

A gourmet kitchen and lounge
complete the compound. Each
bedroom pavilion is simply exquisite
– two have netted daybeds on their
entrances (anyone for an afternoon
nap?) and all offer sumptuous
ensuites, their own plasma TV and
air-conditioning. An iPod-linked music
system is also wired throughout the
property. The stunning 'reading and
reflection pool' has four infinity edges
to create a millpond reflection of the
gardens. This flows seamlessly into
a 20m lap pool.

This is a superlative choice for the
ultimate beach holiday, to celebrate a
special occasion or hold an intimate
wedding for up to 70 guests.

Brunswick Pavilions

Brunswick Heads (near Byron Bay)

26 Fawcett Street, Brunswick Heads ▪ 0410 340 365
www.beautifulaccommodation.com/brunswickpavilions

Brunswick Heads pleasure pavilions

It's easy to see why Brunswick Pavilions won the Master Builders Association Excellence in Regional Building Awards 2010 for this stunning renovation. It combines architectural ingenuity with superb artisanship, and together with its pitch-perfect styling, it makes a holiday space that works brilliantly.

There are two pavilions here – Mango Tree and Bamboo Grove – which can be taken separately (each sleeps up to four people) or together for a laid-back reunion of friends or family.

Mango Tree and Bamboo Grove are nearly identical in layout and appointments, so there won't be any arguments about who has the better place. Each is dashingly decorated with splashes of red, polished

wooden floorboards and plenty of space to lounge around. The kitchens are fully equipped with everything from coffee makers to dishwashers and there is a laundry for salty and sandy clothes.

Each pavilion has a 42-inch plasma TV with an SD card slot so you can check out your holiday photos whenever you like. The uniting element is an eight-metre pool and a brilliant sundeck that connects the two pavilions.

Brunswick Heads is a wonderful secret. Rather like Byron in its early days, perhaps it is Byron's quiet cousin – close to the action, but hidden away. This is the ideal family entertainer.

Rates
Whole pavilion per night
from $200-$350
(each sleeps up to 4 guests)
Accommodation only
Visa, MC, DD

Location
2 hours or 148km south of Brisbane; 15 minutes or 17km from Byron Bay. Map 6.

Minimum stay
Three nights

Facilities
Two pavilions: each with two bedrooms (king and king/twin singles), lounge (plasma TV, Austar, surround sound, DVD, CD, iPod dock), dining, kitchen, deck with lounge and dining, BBQ, WiFi. Shared pool, sun deck, laundry.

Other
Suitable for children

Owner details
Annie and Rory O'Halloran
▪ bookings@byronparadiso.com.au
▪ www.byronparadiso.com.au

Apartments Inn Byron

Byron Bay (Ewingsdale)

20-22 Fletcher Street, Byron Bay ▪ 02 6620 9600
www.beautifulaccommodation.com/apartmentsinnbyron

84

Rates
Whole apartment per night
from $180-$750 (for 2-6 people)
Accommodation only
Visa, MC, DD

Location
55 minutes or 66km south of
Coolangatta; 35 minutes or 38km
north of Ballina. Map 6.

Minimum stay
Two nights at weekends preferred

Facilities
A range of studio and studio deluxe
rooms and one-, two- and three-
bedroom apartments, all with
ensuite, plasma TV, DVD, iPod
dock, RC AC. Apartments with
kitchen, laundry. Pool, internet.

Other
Suitable for children
Disabled facilities

Manager details
Alan Junor
▪ innfo@apartmentsinn
byron.com.au
▪ www.apartmentsinn
byron.com.au

Cool Byron vibe

There are two ways to do Byron:
the hippy backpacker way or the
luxuriously chilled-out Apartments
Inn Byron way. Both are equally valid
experiences but if you crave respite
from a hectic urban life, we
recommend the latter. This elegantly
finished property is one of Byron's
newest upmarket apartment choices,
combining a central location with
in-house facilities that would make
many five-star hotels blush.

The style is funky-modern offset by
charming contrasts such as a rustic
dining table that could be from a local
farmhouse kitchen. Works by local
artists grace the walls. The open-plan
kitchen-dining-lounge area is brilliantly

designed for laid-back beach holidays
for couples, a bunch of friends or a
family with kids. Just pull the lunch
makings out of the stainless steel
fridge, lay out a buffet on the marble
bench and spread out in comfort.
The bedrooms are unobtrusively
stylish and calmly serene.

You could easily stay here without
leaving the property – just lounge
around on the deckchairs beside
the pool, order up a chai latte or slip
downstairs for a meal. But that would
mean missing the delights of Byron's
main beach and groovy shopping,
which are all an easy stroll from
Apartments Inn Byron.

Byron Cove Beach House

Byron Bay (Ewingsdale)

10 Kendall Street, Byron Bay ▪ 02 6680 7595, 0429 043 391
www.beautifulaccommodation.com/byroncove

Sunny days by Belongil

Whatever happened to those relaxed guesthouses by the sea with whitewashed bedrooms and verandahs for afternoon drinks followed by a sunset barbecue? They turned into sensational stays like Byron Cove Beach House, which has all that plus a plunge pool, steam room, sauna and landscaped grounds.

Even better, here you are just a short amble along a bush track from the iconic Belongil Beach. It is a great spot for swimming or long walks in the morning or evening light.

Byron Cove's owners Donna and Tramain Cassar have created exactly the right holiday vibe here, complete with tactile wooden floors, plantation louvres and crisp white ensuites.

The attractively understated bedrooms are dressed in white linen and decorated with groovy original artworks and comfy furniture. All five bedrooms have an ensuite, plasma TV and individual air-conditioning. It's a little bit Bali, a little bit Mediterranean, which makes it very Byron Bay. Each morning, Donna offers guests a healthy continental breakfast buffet with fruit, toast and espresso coffee or tea.

Byron Bay is a lazy eight-minute walk along the beach and nearby there are plenty of great places for coffee and meals, including the hip Utopia cafe. The other way up the beach leads you to the brilliant Treehouse for gourmet pizzas and cocktails.

Rates
Room per couple from
$150-$350 (up to 2 people,
$50 per extra person)
Continental breakfast included
Visa, MC, AMEX, DD, Eftpos

Location
55 minutes or 66km south of
Coolangatta; 35 minutes or 38km
north of Ballina. Map 6.

Facilities
Five guest rooms, each with king
or king/twin singles, ensuite, TV,
mini fridge, RC AC. Breakfast
room. Plunge pool, steam room,
sauna, BBQ. Laundry.

Other
Disabled facilities

Owner details
Donna and Tramain Cassar
▪ byroncoveguesthouse@gmail.com
▪ www.byroncove.com.au

Byron Retreat

Byron Bay (Ewingsdale)

Location on enquiry, Ewingsdale ▪ 1300 660 422
www.beautifulaccommodation.com/byronretreat

Rates
Whole house per night $200-$500
(up to 6 people; extra 2 people
by arrangement)
Accommodation only
Visa, MC, DD

Location
45 minutes or 65km south of
Coolangatta; 35 minutes or 38km
north of Ballina. Map 6.

Minimum stay
Two nights

Facilities
One house: three bedrooms (two
with queen and ensuite, third
with queen and two singles by
arrangement; all with RC AC),
lounge (fire, TV, DVD, VCR
with library, CD), library, dining,
kitchen. Pool, BBQ, laundry, cot
and high chair.

Other
Suitable for children
Pets by arrangement

Owner details
Melissa and Ian Burgess
▪ relax@byronretreat.com
▪ www.byronretreat.com

Garden of delights

You will know Byron Retreat was the
right choice for your family holiday or
getaway with friends as soon as you
enter its gorgeous sub-tropical
garden. There is the shimmering blue
pool that you will all romp around in,
deck chairs for lazing away the
afternoon with a magazine and an
iced tea, and the barbecue setting
for evening get-togethers. Just pick
your bedrooms and hop straight into
holiday mode.

Byron Retreat is a charming folly.
It comprises two, two-storey pavilions
that are linked by a light-filled atrium
with a quietly burbling fountain.

Curved staircases wind up to each
of the mezzanine floors, lending a
Spanish mission feel.

Tiles are brilliantly used throughout
the property, notably in the funky
bathrooms and the Mexican-
influenced barbecue terrace.

The owners welcome kids and their
pets, and they have provided a cubby
to play in, DVDs to watch and a toy
cupboard to explore.

The generosity of spirit extends
to everyone, with goodies such as
Sanctum toiletries in the bathrooms
and local Ewingsdale plunger coffee
in the arrival hamper.

Ewingsdale is serenely quiet but just
a few minutes from all Byron's best
beaches, shopping and places to eat.

Sojourn at Byron

Byron Bay (Ewingsdale)

42A Bay Vista Lane, Ewingsdale ▪ 02 6684 7083
www.beautifulaccommodation.com/sojournatbyron

Panoramic Byron-hinterland B&B

Get ready to change your view of what a B&B can be at the sophisticated Sojourn at Byron. This emphatically contemporary property is set in a stunning Byron landscape of rolling hills and farmland dotted with contented sheep and cattle. For pure bliss, just loll in the infinity pool and survey the magnificent scenery below you.

Sojourn's owner-operators, Helen and Peter McHugh, have brought a well-integrated sense of style to its design and layout. As you enter the lobby, a wall of windows frames the distant hills and pasture in a surreally beautiful sequence of vignettes. Afternoon tea is served as you arrive.

The three guest rooms are secluded havens with big posturepedic beds fitted with crisp linen. Ensuite spa bathrooms are perfect for some 'you' time with a flute of bubbles and a splash of organic Sanctum spa product to nourish your skin.

It's hard to believe at Sojourn that Byron is just minutes away. You can slip out for a meal, live music, the beach or some boutique browsing before returning to your own private country estate. The morning breakfast choice will appeal to everyone from those seeking a hearty breakfast to homemade muesli, organic fruit and espresso coffee.

Rates
Room per couple from $180-$260
Full breakfast included
Visa, MC

Location
55 minutes or 66km south of Coolangatta; 35 minutes or 38km north of Ballina. Map 6.

Minimum stay
Two to four nights

Facilities
Three rooms (one king/twin single; two queen), each with spa bathroom, TV, DVD, RC AC, fans, patio or balcony. Guest lounge (wood fire), dining. WiFi, pool with decks, BBQ.

AAA Star Rating
★★★★☆

Other
AAA Eco-Friendly Accredited
Disabled facilities

Host details
Helen and Peter McHugh
▪ helen@sojournatbyron.com.au
▪ www.sojournatbyron.com.au

BlueGreen House

Byron Bay (Newrybar)

320 Piccadilly Hill Road, Newrybar ■ 02 6687 2366, 0438 446 287
www.beautifulaccommodation.com/bluegreenhouse

88

Rates
House per night from $350-$950
(up to 4 or 2 adults and 6 children)
Studio from $150-$300 (up to 2)
Accommodation only
Visa, MC, DD

Location
55 minutes or 66km south of
Coolangatta; 35 minutes or 38km
minutes north of Ballina. Map 6.

Minimum stay
Three to seven nights

Facilities
One house: two bedrooms
(master with spa ensuite), lounge
(wood fire, TV, DVD, Austar),
dining, kitchen opening to
entertaining and pool terrace,
second bathroom (bath). Heated
pool, BBQ. One studio: one
bedroom, ensuite, kitchenette,
living and gazebo.

Other
Suitable for children
Pets by arrangement
Disabled facilities

Host details
Simon and Dolores Kilpin
■ info@bluegreen-house.com.au
■ www.bluegreen-house.com.au

Magic holiday kingdom

Every child (or child at heart) should
have the privilege of staying at the
BlueGreen House near Byron Bay.
There is magic in the air here. Why?
Perhaps it is the painterly farm estate
set on five verdant acres, stocked
with adorable animals and with a
beautiful lake as its centrepiece.
Then there is the artistic sensibility
that completes every line of sight
within the house and the landscaped
views it commands.

BlueGreen is the brainchild of artist
Dolores and landscaper Simon,
which explains its delicious
ambience. The house is idyllically set
on five manicured acres of trim lawns,
garden nooks, a pool, a lake with a
viewing platform, and pasture with
alpacas and ponies.

Kids love the space to run, swim and
connect with nature. The grand estate
house is wonderfully appointed and
proportioned, and it offers treats such
as handmade terrazzo spa and baths,
a lavish master bedroom with
sensational views over the estate
and a stunning indoors-outdoors
kitchen-dining-barbecuing zone that
flows out to the poolside patio.

The accommodation options at
BlueGreen are very flexible with plenty
of space for up to six adults or an
extended family.

All the delights of Byron Bay and
Bangalow are nearby. But we know
that once you enter this magic
kingdom, leaving will be the last
thought on your mind.

Byron Plantation
Byron Bay (Newrybar)

Old Byron Bay Road, Newrybar ▪ **0413 123 000**
www.beautifulaccommodation.com/byronplantation

Palatial whitehouse in the hills

Byron Plantation provides a majestic resort-style farmstay in one of the district's most verdant nooks. It is perched on a ridge near Newrybar and five minutes' coffee run from the idyllic and very hip village of Bangalow. The views of the ocean across the macadamia nut plantations are inspiring and will have you looking up from your book in awe as you relax poolside.

The homestead was completed in 2006 and features a flowing interior layout with extraordinary panoramas from every window. Antique curios dot the stylish interior, nicely offsetting the modern comforts.

There are two bathrooms and four big bedrooms, two with French windows

that open onto the grand wraparound verandah. A couple of families or a party of friends exploring the Byron area will find plenty of room to spread out in absolute comfort here.

The 40-hectare property could also make an ideal setting for a spectacular wedding party, with a reception at Kassia Picone and Tristan Grier's Harvest Cafe in Newrybar.

Byron Bay is a 12-minute drive away through a green and undulating landscape. Do check out Bangalow, which is the only intact Federation-period village on Australia's east coast. Enjoy wandering the streets looking for lattes, antique shops and artists' galleries.

Rates
Whole house per night from
$471-$1150 (up to 8 people)
Accommodation only
Direct deposit, no credit cards

Location
10 minutes or 16 km southwest of Byron Bay; 55 minutes or 70km south of Coolangatta. Map 6.

Minimum stay
Three to seven nights

Facilities
One house: four bedrooms (king and/or king singles; fans), lounge (log fire, plasma TV, DVD, Bose sound system), dining, kitchen, two bathrooms. WiFi, laundry, BBQ, fans, undercover parking. Pool and pergola.

Other
Suitable for children

Host/Manager/Owner details
Tony Gilding
▪ stay@byronplantation.com.au
▪ www.byronplantation.com.au

The Old Church at Byron Bay

Byron Bay (Newrybar)

14 Brooklet Road, Newrybar ▪ 0402 245 957
www.beautifulaccommodation.com/theoldchurch

Rates
Whole church per night from
$150-$625 (up to 12 people)
Accommodation only
Midweek specials available
Visa, MC, DD

Location
10 minutes or 16km southwest of
Byron Bay; 55 minutes or 70km
south of Coolangatta. Map 6.

Minimum stay
Two nights

Facilities
One church: four bedrooms (two
queen, one double, one large attic
with queen, extra beds if required),
lounge, dining and entertainment
area (TV, Austar, DVD, iPod docks,
CD), kitchen, bathroom (additional
shower and two toilets), separate
rumpus. Gas heaters, WiFi, BBQ.

Other
Suitable for children
Disabled facilities

Owner details
Kylie Baxter
▪ info@theoldchurchbyronbay.com
▪ www.theoldchurchbyronbay.com

Divine right to pleasure

Bonding time with your clan members
requires somewhere special to make
it truly memorable. So where better to
congregate than the stunning,
converted Old Church in the Byron
Bay hinterland? This brilliant
renovation took eight years to
complete and creatively uses the vast
space of the old structure to make a
playground for guests today.

Down where the pews once stood
is an astounding living space with a
refectory dining table that can seat
12 and there are also deep leather
chesterfield lounges. The atmosphere
is unique with cathedral ceilings and
peaked church windows that flood
the floor with light. Feeding your flock
is easily done in the gigantic chef's
kitchen, which includes a huge

Beaumatic oven and miles of bench
space. Get everyone cooking
together here.

The four bedrooms are divinely
uncluttered retreats from the main
house and there are two bathrooms
to keep everyone polished. A
separate games room and barbecue
deck overlooking the heavenly garden
complete this paradise.

The Newrybar neighbourhood is
delightful. Around the corner is the
acclaimed Harvest Cafe, where head
chef Joseph Griffin does wonders
with local produce. Olivia Newton-
John's Gaia Retreat and Spa is
nearby for pampering. All the
beaches and fun of Byron are
just minutes away.

Oceanstyle
Byron Bay (Suffolk Park)

164A Alcorn Street, Suffolk Park ▪ 0419 922 426
www.beautifulaccommodation.com/oceanstyle

Quiet coastal cottage

Sometimes you need to squirrel yourselves away from the hoi polloi and make room for each other in a tranquil setting. If you need that in the glorious Byron Bay district, then book in for some private seaside time at Oceanstyle.

This thoroughly unpretentious cottage is opposite Tallows Beach in the peaceful village of Suffolk Park, about five minutes' drive from all the buzz of Bryon Bay.

Oceanstyle's design is simplicity itself: a coastal cottage set among the trees with a return deck for breakfast or afternoon tea. The interior has been completely renovated with an emphasis on minimising clutter and maximising comfort.

There is a big comfy lounge to stretch out on before the plasma TV, a vast bed with a curving wooden bedhead and a well-equipped kitchen for DIY catering. Everywhere the soothing hum of distant waves suffuses the atmosphere like an aural lullaby. Passing into a dreamy sleep has never been easier.

Suffolk Park is a wonderful find in the Byron area: a secluded oasis of sleepy beach houses and streets that see the occasional passing car.

Tallows Beach is just across the road and offers miles of beachcombing prospects. It's just a short stroll for the papers, coffee, a meal and groceries. Relax.

Rates
Whole cottage per night
from $160-$300
(up to 2 people; $60 cleaning fee applies)
Accommodation only
Visa, MC, DD

Location
55 minutes or 66km south of Coolangatta; 35 or 38km minutes north of Ballina. Map 6.

Minimum stay
Two nights

Facilities
One beach cottage: one bedroom (king), lounge (TV, DVD, movies and games), dining and kitchen, bathroom, laundry, AC, heaters.

Owner details
Catherine Zanevra
▪ info@oceanstyle.com.au
▪ www.oceanstyle.com.au

SYDNEY

South Coast & Snowy Mountains

South Coast
& Snowy Mountains

Most people travel between Sydney and Melbourne one of the boring ways: flying over it at 700km per hour or driving on cruise control down the inland freeway. If you take those routes, you miss exploring the breathtaking coastline from Kiama to Merimbula. And almost anywhere you turn inland, you will strike gorgeous uplands such as Kangaroo Valley or cosy alpine villages like Dalgety and Guthega. This is the road less travelled. And all the better for it.

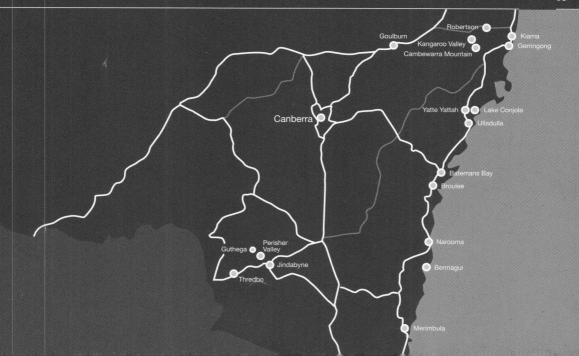

Batemans Bay has an exquisite combination of sensational surf beaches and the beautiful Clyde River estuary, which just begs you to jump aboard a boat and cast a fishing line.

Pack the car and take the trip of a lifetime along the New South Wales south coast to the Victorian border. The 400km stretch from Kiama to Eden glories in superb beaches, historic towns and beautiful valley hinterlands.

Getting to Kiama is easy on the Grand Pacific Drive, which weaves its way around the coastline. Kiama is a beach holiday paradise for families. And, yes, do take them to the famous Blowhole, which shoots up to 60 metres in the air. Nearby Gerringong is a hilltop village with stunning coastal vistas. Surfers love nearby Werri Beach for its uncluttered waves.

Turn inland towards Berry and you will soon reach the stunning scenery of Kangaroo Valley. The National Trust-listed village of Kangaroo Valley is thoroughly charming. Stop for a beer outside the Friendly Inn and some chocolate fudge at the 1891 Fudge House. Canoe trips around the Kangaroo and Shoalhaven rivers are an eco-tour treat.

From high on Cambewarra Mountain, you can see an extraordinary panorama of Nowra and Shoalhaven. After you leave the hills, make a left at Nowra to reach the stunning natural spectacle of Jervis Bay. It has pristine beaches and frequent sittings of calving Humpback whales and Bottlenose dolphins. Nearby Lake Conjola is peaceful coastal waterway with a sensational surf beach.

Few seaside towns have such an inspiring natural setting as Mollymook, just south of Lake Conjola, beyond the unspoiled Narrawallee Creek Nature Reserve. Inland is the quaint town of Milton, which has monthly farmers' markets and a Scarecrow Festival in June. Nearby Ulladulla has fantastic beaches and a harbour full of fishing boats. Don't miss the Blessing of the Fleet festival at Easter.

Batemans Bay is a favourite resort town of Canberrans. It has a magical combination of surf beaches and the beautiful Clyde River estuary, which just begs you to jump aboard a boat and cast a fishing line. The Art Gallery at the Ulladulla Guest House has a unique collection of contemporary

Australian art. Broulee is a relaxed village for quiet family holidays, especially those with young kids. Your young pirates will enjoy exploring Broulee Island, which is connected to the main beach.

Narooma is a great little beach town to the south and a jumping off point for Montague Island, which has a large colony of Little Penguins (appropriately enough, the smallest penguin species). Merimbula is spread along the rim of a beautiful coastal lake, with quiet waters for young kids and surf beaches for everyone else. It draws fresh produce from farms and fisheries into the lively local restaurant scene.

A real beauty of Australia's east coast is the Great Dividing Range that separates coast from plains. If you cut inland from Merimbula through the dairy town of Bega and hop on the Snowy Mountains Highway, you will eventually reach Australia's alpine district, dotted with charming little towns like Dalgety.

Most people think of snow, skis and chalets when Perisher or Thredbo are mentioned. However, the Snowy is equally seductive when it is covered with wildflowers and the weather invites hiking or fly-fishing for trout. Guthega in Kosciuszko National Park looks over this landscape. See the country on horseback with a Snowy Wilderness ride at Jindabyne.

Batemans Bay
Cnr Princes Highway &
Beach Road
1800 802 528
www.eurobodalla.com.au

Gerringong
Shop 2/131 Fern Street
02 4234 0211
www.kiama.com.au

Kangaroo Valley
10 Marshall Street
02 4465 1175
www.shoalhaven.nsw.gov.au

Kiama
Blowhole Point Road,
off Terralong Street
02 4232 3322
www.kiama.com.au

Merimbula
2 Beach Street
02 6945 1129
www.sapphirecoast.com.au

Narooma
Princes Highway
1800 240 003
www.eurobodalla.com.au

Robertson
The Old Cheese Factory,
Illawarra Highway
02 4885 1133
www.robertsoncheesefactory.com

Ulladulla
Civic Centre, Princes Highway
02 4455 1269
www.shoalhaven.nsw.gov.au

Wollongong
Princes Highway, Bulli Tops
02 4227 5545
www.visitwollongong.com.au

Yarrawa Hill

Robertson (near Bowral and Moss Vale)

Lees Road, Robertson ▪ 02 4885 1643, 0413 482 775
www.beautifulaccommodation.com/yarrawahill

Rates
Whole house per night from
$357-$475 (up to 6 people;
minimum stay $950)
Accommodation only
Direct deposit, Chq, no credit cards

Location
2 hours or 124km south
of Sydney. Map 2.

Minimum stay
Two nights

Facilities
One house with three suites
(queen, ensuite, study, kitchenette;
master with fireplace, second with
conservatory), lounge (wood fire,
TV, DVD, CD), dining, kitchen
(wood fire), library. Laundry, BBQ.

Other
Pets by arrangement

Manager details
Michael Robinson
▪ yarrawa@gmail.com
▪ www.yarrawahill.com

Scene-stealing star

It is easy to see why Yarrawa Hill
frequently features in magazines
like *Home Beautiful* and *Highlife*.
This is a breathtakingly eclectic mix
of Australian design vernacular and
was built to incorporate antique
fittings and furnishings collected by
the owners from travels in Indonesia,
Africa and further afield.

Yarrawa Hill is set in a forested estate
of 156 acres and uses its hillside
location atop the Illawara Escarpment
to bring a beautiful landscape of
trees, sky and coastal views into
every corner.

There are three living spaces: the
West Wing has the central living,
dining and main kitchen, and is joined
by a library walkway to the East Wing,
which offers two guest suites, each

with their own ensuite and study,
and a glass conservatory.

Downstairs is another self-contained
suite with its own fireplace, lounge,
study and ensuite. From every room,
decks offer vantage points for wildlife
spotting and view gazing.

Yarrawa Hill would make an ideal
retreat for groups of writers, book
club members, wine aficionados or
anyone who wants to be able to
retreat in seclusion or reunite with
family and friends.

The village of Robertson is 4km away
and there are endless spots to
explore nearby, including Budderoo
National Park and many waterfalls,
lookouts and walking trails.

The Dairy @ Cavan

Kangaroo Valley (Barrengarry)

Cavan Road, Kangaroo Valley ▪ 0412 666 767
www.beautifulaccommodation.com/thedairy

Land of milk and honey

It's easy to see why The Dairy @ Cavan has won tourism awards and building design industry plaudits. The owners have taken a 1920s heritage-listed dairy and turned it into an uber-chic den for escapees from the city.

Conservation consultants advised on how to retain the integrity of the structure while making it an abode of light and luxury. We love every aspect of this conversion and can only envy the generations of cows that enjoyed the sensational views here.

The Dairy is set up for a couple to arrive, relax and melt into the surrounding landscape, which features extraordinary views across Kangaroo Valley to the sandstone escarpments beyond.

The interior is utterly bewitching: it brilliantly uses period materials – corrugated iron, original fencing and beautifully polished timbers – to create a breezy inside-outside living space. A spa is brilliantly positioned for maximum scenic effect. There could be no finer place to sit back with a glass of red at sunset or a morning plunger of coffee than on the outside terrace here. And at night, light the fire and snuggle in for an evening together.

Kangaroo Valley has something for everyone, from hiking and canoeing to country pubs and markets.

Rates
Whole cottage per night from $250-$310 (up to 2 people)
Accommodation only
Direct deposit, no credit cards

Location
2 hours or 155km south of Sydney; 2½ hours or 195km north of Canberra. Map 2.

Minimum stay
Two nights

Facilities
One cottage: one bedroom (queen), lounge (wood fire, TV, DVD, CD), dining, kitchen, laundry. RC AC.

Owner details
David Cochrane
▪ david.cochrane@ oakleighproperties.com.au
▪ www.thedairycavan.com.au

The Heavens Mountain Escape

Kangaroo Valley (Barrengarry)

94 Paddington Lane, Barrengarry ▪ 02 4465 1400, 0411 445 523
www.beautifulaccommodation.com/theheavens

Rates
Cabin per night from $215-$340
(2-4 people)
Full breakfast provisions included
Visa, MC, Eftpos

Location
2 hours or 155km south of Sydney;
2½ hours or 195km north of
Canberra. Map 2.

Minimum stay
Two nights

Facilities
Three cabins: two one-bedroom,
one two-bedroom. All with spa
bathroom, lounge (gas fire, TV,
DVD), kitchen, laundry, RC AC, BBQ.

Member
Accommodation Association
of Australia

Owner details
Jan and Rob McGregor
▪ info@theheavens.com.au
▪ www.theheavens.com.au

Up in the heavens

Up, up where the air is clear pretty much describes The Heavens. This gorgeous 160-acre property perches on a plateau on Kangaroo Valley's sandstone walls.

To say the views from this idyllic spot are breathtaking is a simple understatement – you will sit transfixed on your deck happily tracking the flight of distant eagles and the Gang-Gang species of cockatoo. Waking in your warm bed to gaze across the cloudtops is, well, heavenly.

There are three accommodation options. We particularly like the two self-contained, one-bedroom pavilions, which are named Aurora and Inanna and feature superbly realised contemporary designs.

The interiors of these curvaceous cottages are spacious and use recycled Australian hardwoods that have been revivified by local woodworkers.

Every room glories in the sensational panoramas, and the deck is a wonderful spot to sit with some binoculars and a pot of tea and play bird twitcher for a while. At night, there is a flickering gas fire to keep you cosy before you retire to the huge king-size bed. There is also a quaint two-bedroom cottage for families and friends to share.

The Kangaroo Valley-Berry district is renowned for its antique shops, farmers' markets, cafes, galleries and hikes to waterfalls. Have fun!

Barefoot Springs Bed and Breakfast
Cambewarra Mountain, Beaumont (near Kangaroo Valley)

155 Carrington Road, Beaumont ▪ 02 4446 0509
www.beautifulaccommodation.com/barefoot

Garden of delights

The quality of a B&B's garden often reflects a deeper attention to the comfort and care of its guests. That's certainly true at the impeccably maintained Barefoot Springs, which has an admirable garden and recently refurbished guest accommodation. This boutique property is located high on Cambewarra Mountain with spectacular views in every direction.

You can choose between wandering up a delightful garden path to one of the three studios or staying in the Queen Room in the grand main house. All are designed for couples but the studios can accommodate three if required.

The studios will appeal to those who like a secluded hermitage with a crackling fire, a deep spa with a view and a kitchenette. In the big house, the Queen Room is an uncluttered boudoir with ensuite that is quietly cordoned off in its own space.

All guests are welcome to gather on the magnificent terrace or, if wintry, in the dining room for Kay's delectable breakfasts. Her dinners, which feature seasonal dishes created from fresh local produce, are also a treat.

In the local area you can peruse local markets, visit wineries, play golf, hike, canoe and more.

Rates
Studio per couple from $215-$275
Room per couple from $195-$240
Full breakfast included, dinner by prior arrangement
Visa, MC, DD, Eftpos

Location
2 hours or 162km south of Sydney. Map 2.

Minimum stay
Two nights at weekends preferred

Facilities
Three studio cottages (two queen, one king; foldaway bed available), fire, TV, DVD, double spa bathroom, kitchenette, balcony/patio. RC AC. In-house ensuite queen room. Wifi, guest lounge/dining, fire.

AAA Star Rating
★★★★☆

Member
BBFAA

Other
Pets by arrangement

Host details
Tim and Kay Johnston
▪ info@barefootsprings.com.au
▪ www.barefootsprings.com.au

Spring Creek Retreat

Kiama

41 Jerrara Road, Kiama ▪ 02 4232 2700
www.beautifulaccommodation.com/springcreekretreat

Rates
Whole house per night from
$1500- $2000 (up to 12 people)
Cottage per night from $225-$295
Accommodation only, catering by
prior arrangement
Visa, MC, DD, Eftpos

Location
90 minutes or 140km south of
Sydney. Map 2.

Minimum stay
Two to seven nights (seasonal)

Facilities
One house: five ensuite bedrooms
(three with spa), two lounges
(both with fire), dining, laundry.
Three cottages (one or two
bedrooms), kitchen, lounge,
bathroom (two with spa). BBQ. All
with TV, CD, AC. Parking.

AAA Star Rating
★★★★☆

Other
Horses/pets welcome (cottages)

Owner details
Susan and Jack Stoertz
▪ springcreekretreat@hotmail.com
▪ www.springcreekret.com

Country house weekend away

Spring Creek Retreat's grand rooms,
magnificent views and expansive
estate beckon you to gather family or
friends together for a country house
party. You can even bring your horse
and dogs. We can already picture the
glowing rooms, the quiet clink of
champagne glasses and the tinkling
laughter of conversation among old
friends. With space for up to 24
guests in the main house and the
three outlying cottages, Spring Creek
is an ideal venue to celebrate a
wedding anniversary, significant
birthday or another special occasion.

The house has the glamour of a
Federation design with the
convenience of a contemporary build.
It has five spacious ensuite bedrooms
with wonderful views and private
patios. Your guests will love the room

to relax in the two enormous fire-lit
lounges and there is also the option
to plan ahead and arrange for a
private chef to cook up a banquet
in the house's kitchen.

The cottages enjoy similar space and
style, and they come in one- and
two-bedroom configurations.

Spring Creek Retreat commands
an enviable position overlooking the
Kiama hinterland and its manicured
gardens offer stunning vistas and
a plethora of bird life.

All this is just a few minutes' drive
from the beaches of Kiama and the
cute towns of Berry and Berrima.

Bellachara Boutique Hotel
Gerringong (near Kiama)

1 Fern Street, Gerringong ▪ 02 4234 1359
www.beautifulaccommodation.com/bellachara

Bella, bella, bella!

If you are within 1000 kilometres of Gerringong, we have found an ideal place for you to gather friends and family to indulge. Bellachara Boutique Hotel is one of the most relaxed yet utterly stylish stays on the east coast.

The rooms have a funky décor of chocolate leather lounges, creamy walls, stainless steel kitchen gear and bathrooms stacked with fluffy towels. There are 52 luxuriously appointed rooms – enough for a wedding or conference – with goodies like Playstation2 consoles and heavenly beds. There is even a kids' club open on weekends and school holidays.

We love the whole property design and the obvious thought that has gone into the guests' experience.

The pool area is lined with shaded banana lounges and overlooked by a deck, making it a great spot for parents to linger over coffee and a magazine while keeping an eye on the littlies.

There is a glorious day spa (see our review on page 270) for some indulgent you-time and a restaurant that won the 2010 Best Restaurant within a Deluxe Hotel award.

Kiama and Gerringong are blessed with superb beaches to swim, paths to walk and historic places to see.

Rates
Room per couple from $195-$350
Full breakfast included
Visa, MC, AMEX, DD, Eftpos

Location
1¾ hours or 130km south of Sydney. Map 2.

Minimum stay
Two nights at weekends (spring/summer)

Facilities
A range of Garden, Balcony and Spa rooms (king/twin singles, lounge, plasma TV, Playstation 2, kitchenette; some with spa) and one Pool Suite (kitchen). Two pools, tennis court, Jaks Corner kids' club. Restaurant, conference and event facilities. Day spa.

Other
Suitable for children
Disabled facilities
Restaurant open six days (seven days in January)

Owner details
Gregg Currie
▪ hello@bellachara.com.au
▪ www.bellachara.com.au

Driftwood

Lake Conjola

14 Prior Street, Lake Conjola ▪ **0412 292 822, 0407 950 768**
www.beautifulaccommodation.com/driftwood

Rates
House per night from $180-$400
(up to 6 people)
Accommodation only
DD, Chq, Pay Pal, no credit cards

Location
3 hours or 218km south
of Sydney. Map 2.

Minimum stay
Two nights

Facilities
One house: two bedrooms
(queen, twin king singles, double;
master with TV/DVD), lounge
(wood fire, TV/DVD, CD), dining,
kitchen (espresso machine),
bathroom (laundry). Large deck,
BBQ.

Other
Suitable for children
Pets by arrangement

Owner details
Virginia Hewitt and
David Norton-Smith
▪ dnortons@optusnet.com.au
▪ www.driftwood
lakeconjola.com.au

Lady of the lake

Just thinking about Driftwood and
its sublime lakeside setting makes us
want to return for a stay. This property
has been in the owner's family since
her dad purchased it back when
pounds, shillings and pence were
currency. Since then, love and
attention has been lavished on
Driftwood, turning this charming
cottage into an oasis of serenity,
style and total comfort.

Driftwood's inner authenticity shines
through in the artwork, the nautical
overtones and the quietly integrated
decor of elegant lamps, plump-
cushioned sofas and cosy bedrooms.
We love the elegant principal
bedroom, which has tall French
doors that open to the deck

and lake view, making it a splendid
setting for morning toast and coffee
brewed on the espresso machine.

The main lounge has a boldly fluted
open fireplace that projects radiant
warmth throughout the room and
Driftwood's country-style kitchen is
a real charmer and well-equipped
to prepare for a dinner party.

The real pleasures here are the
simple ones – walking a few steps to
the water's edge for a swim, a sunset
stroll around the lake, a seafood
barbecue with friends – these are
the lasting memories that a stay
at Driftwood will bring.

Milton Country Cottages

Yatte Yattah (near Milton)

83 Egans Farm Lane, Yatte Yattah ▪ 02 4456 5299, 0417 467 880
www.beautifulaccommodation.com/miltoncottages

Tinker, tailor, potter, guest

Milton Country Cottages has received state and national tourism awards and also earned rave reviews in publications such as the *Sun Herald*. You'll quickly see why when you arrive at this charming artist's retreat near the historic (and quite hip) little town of Milton.

The property is the brainchild of the renowned potter Kees Staps and his wife Carol. Kees' works feature on the property, and he can provide guests with lessons. This is the only accommodation option in New South Wales that includes a ceramics studio and gallery.

There are three cottages set apart from each other, so you don't need to rub shoulders with anyone if you prefer peace and quiet.

The interiors feature a gorgeously eclectic melange of furnishings: a winged armchair here, a leather sofa there, and a blonde timber dining table to share a meal. But it all comes together in a serenely relaxed tableau that is sunlit by the huge picture windows.

A gourmet breakfast is provided and there is an excellent massage service that will visit your cottage on request.

The birdlife in the garden is prolific and Lake Conjola is a very pleasant 2.5km amble from the house. Just remember to take your fishing rod. Milton is a fun place for browsing and coffee.

Rates
Cottage per night from
$150-$250 (up to 2 people)
Full breakfast provisions included
Visa, MC, DD, Eftpos

Location
3 hours or 210km south
of Sydney. Map 2.

Minimum stay
Two nights at weekends preferred

Facilities
Three one- and two-bedroom cottages with lounge (fire), two with spa and one with spa pavilion. Kitchen or kitchenette, RC AC, BBQ. Laundry facilities.

Member
BBFAA, Accommodation
Association of Australia

Other
Suitable for children
Pets by arrangement
Disabled facilities
Gallery open seven days

Host details
Carol Joyce and Kees Staps
▪ enquiries@miltoncountry
cottages.com.au
▪ www.miltoncountry
cottages.com.au

Ulladulla Guest House

Ulladulla

39 Burrill Street, Ulladulla ▪ 02 4455 1796
www.beautifulaccommodation.com/ulladullaguesthouse

Rates
Room per couple from $128-$298
($50 per extra person)
Accommodation only
Visa, MC, AMEX, DC, JCB, DD, Eftpos

Location
3 hours or 220km south
of Sydney. Map 2.

Minimum stay
Two nights at weekends

Facilities
Luxury and Executive rooms (spa);
self-contained units (one or two
bedrooms). French restaurant,
room service. Gallery. Pool, spas,
sauna, exercise equipment.
Conference facilities.

AAA Star Rating
★★★★★

Member
Accommodation Association
of Australia

Other
Suitable for children
Pets welcome
Restaurant: open Thurs-Tues
Gallery open seven days

Contact details
▪ info@guesthouse.com.au
▪ www.guesthouse.com.au

Cote d'Azur, Ulladulla style

Don't be deceived by the old-fashioned elegance implied in the name Ulladulla Guest House. Yes, it's certainly a guest house but one you might expect to find at Cap d'Antibes rather than on the NSW south coast.

Its French restaurant, Elizans, has won a swag of awards for its cuisine and wine list, it has a permanent art gallery that is recognised as one of the finest regional showcases in Australia, and the ambience is one of sophisticated European relaxation. All this is set within a striking sub-tropical garden that is a pleasure to explore.

The lounge at the Guest House nicely illustrates the tone of the whole place:

an elegant room featuring plush sofas, a library of books, hanging lights, tiffany lamps and a wood fire for cold nights. It makes the ideal setting for an aperitif before embarking on a degustation menu at the acclaimed in-house Elizans.

Afterwards you can retire to your beautifully presented abode; the rooms include self-contained units (where your well-behaved dog is welcome too) and luxury suites with spas. There is even an in-house spa.

The art gallery is a magnificent creation that features work by Meagan Jacobs, Graeme Nilsson and Judy Trick, and an ever-changing compendium of regional artists.

Corrigans Cove
Batemans Bay

204 Beach Road, Batemans Bay ▪ 02 4472 6111
www.beautifulaccommodation.com/corriganscove

Swell time by the seashore

Corrigans Cove sounds like an anchoring spot for jaded pirates. How happy they would have been to find this easy-going resort during their travels. It offers a sparkling selection of one-, two- and three-bedroom apartments that are arranged in a sweeping arc facing Corrigans Beach. Many have a seascape view and all share a cooling flow of ocean breezes. It makes an ideal escape away for everyone from couples on the run to families needing a self-contained place for their holidays.

The interiors at Corrigans are very comfortable, thoroughly stylish and practical. Plush sofas invite you to sit back and watch the cable TV after a hard day relaxing on a banana lounge by the solar-heated pool or playing the local golf course.

There are stainless steel kitchens for preparing a picnic lunch or evening meal of fresh seafood from Batemans Bay.

Every apartment has washing machines and driers. Complimentary, serve-yourself continental breakfasts are provided in the restaurant, which also offers delicious meals on Fridays and Saturdays.

Batemans Bay is a great holiday destination that is much loved by those who discover it. There are fabulous beaches, plenty of places to eat and drink, and lots of activities for the kids.

Rates
Whole studio/apartment per night from $140-$420 (up to 6 people) Continental breakfast included
Visa, MC, AMEX, Eftpos, Chq

Location
4 hours or 275km south of Sydney; 2 hours or 145km east of Canberra. Map 1.

Minimum stay
Two nights at weekends preferred

Facilities
A range of studio, one-, two- and three-bedroom apartments, each with lounge (TV, DVD), dining, bathroom (some with spa; three with two bathrooms), laundry (apartments), RC AC. Pool. Restaurant.

AAA Star Rating
★★★★☆

Other
Suitable for children
Restaurant: dinner Fri and Sat

General Manager details
Vicki and Geoffrey Tolhurst
▪ relax@corriganscove.com.au
▪ www.corriganscove.com.au

Boots On Broulee Dunes

Broulee

5/39-41 Imlay Street, Broulee ▪ 02 4471 6444
www.beautifulaccommodation.com/bootsonbroulee

Rates
Whole unit per night from
$250-$350 (up to 7 people)
Accommodation only
Visa, MC, DD, Eftpos, Chq

Location
4 hours or 298km south
of Sydney Map 1.

Minimum stay
Two to seven nights (seasonal)

Facilities
One three-bedroom unit (queen,
double and three singles), lounge,
dining, kitchen, two bathrooms
(one with spa), laundry, BBQ,
electric heating, secure
undercover parking.

Manager details
Fraser Gray Real Estate
▪ frasergray.rentals@bigpond.com
▪ www.beautifulaccommodation.
com/bootsonbroulee

Hang your boots beachside

Broulee one of the lesser-known
wonders of the New South Wales
south coast, which is fortunate for
holidaymakers who find their way to
this quiet beach haven.

The township nestles between
bushland and two glorious beaches,
and there is Broulee Island Nature
Reserve to explore.

Blessed with the sounds of distant
waves and birdsong, Boots on
Broulee Dunes is a three-level
townhouse with views over the dunes
of South Broulee beach and easy
access to the waves via a path.

Boots has three blissful bedrooms
and the master has a double spa
bath to spoil you after a busy day
of bush walks and body surfing.

Upstairs is a lounge, dining and
kitchen, with views over the dunes
from a spacious front balcony as well
as from a sheltered courtyard at the
rear balcony.

Families will love Boots, but its
intimacy and style will equally appeal
to a couple seeking a romantic
seaside interlude. And the name
Boots? The secret lies in a piece
of artwork in the lounge.

The local area is ideal for beach
fossicking and bush walks through
the pristine environment. Foodies
will love the region's Clyde River
oysters, Lake Coila prawns and
organic fruits, vegetables and
herbs found at local markets.

The Bower at Broulee
Broulee

2352 George Bass Drive, Broulee ▪ 02 4471 8666
www.beautifulaccommodation.com/thebower

In the bower of love

When a bowerbird seeks a mate, he builds a tunnel-like nest – or bower – and fills it with colourful curios to catch his love's attention. This design inspired Sue and Mark Berry's brief to their architect when they planned their ultra-contemporary accommodation at Broulee.

The Berrys wanted their 'bowers' to be romantic bush havens that resonate with the surrounding landscape. The result? A dazzling collection of cathedrals of light and air that soon have couples swooning in relaxed delight.

The Bower at Broulee mimics the bower design, although its comfort level is something else altogether.

The fire-lit lounges are flooded with light by day and have the airy grandeur of bush basilicas. As you relax into a sofa with some chilled bubbles, it is like being at some vast gallery of Australian landscapes.

Gorgeous double spas off to the side beckon lovers to soak away their cares and reconnect in utter privacy. And further down the bower is a sublime bedroom with king-size bed.

Broulee is near some of the south coast's best beaches and the gorgeous little 1850s gold town of Mogo. Here you can let your inner bowerbird out of its cage and hunt for antiques and bric-a-brac.

Rates
Whole Bower per night
from $250-$500
Full breakfast provisions
included (first night)
Mid-week packages available
Visa, MC, AMEX, DD, Eftpos

Location
4 hours or 298km south
of Sydney. Map 1.

Minimum stay
Two nights

Facilities
One- and two-bedroom Bowers,
each with king bedroom, kitchen,
lounge (wood fire, TV, DVD/CD),
bathroom (double spa), deck
(BBQ), laundry, WiFi.

Owner details
Sue and Mark Berry
▪ recharge@thebower.com.au
▪ www.thebower.com.au

Amooran Oceanside Apartments and Motel

Narooma

30 Montague Street, Narooma ▪ 02 4476 2198
www.beautifulaccommodation.com/amooran

Rates
Room per night $106-$265 (up to 2)
Apartment per night from
$155-$400 (up to 4 people)
Accommodation only
Visa, MC, AMEX, DC, DD, Eftpos

Location
8½ hours or 685km northeast of
Melbourne; 4½ hours or 350km
south of Sydney. Map 1.

Minimum stay
Two nights at weekends preferred

Facilities
Studio, spa, family rooms and
one- to three-bedroom apartments,
all with cooking facilities, Austar,
DVD, RC AC, WiFi. Pool, BBQs,
laundry, off-street parking.
Conference facilities.

AAA Star Rating
★★★★

Member
Accommodation Association
of Australia

Other
Suitable for children
Disabled facilities

Host details
Libby and John Burbidge
▪ enquiries@amooran.com.au
▪ www.amooran.com.au

Ocean view apartments

Narooma has been a real surprise
during the search for generous stays
in wonderful places for *Beautiful
Accommodation*. This seaside holiday
town combines a majestic coastal
location with intriguing natural
wonders such as Montague Island,
which has the state's largest colonies
of fur seals and Little Penguins. We
have found a place with sensational
ocean views and a perfect Narooma
location – Amooran Ocean
Apartments and Motel.

Amooran is a resort-style property
with 29 apartments ranging from
studios to three-bedroom units. It
also has a lovely outdoor pool and
barbecue area. All units have been
refurbished to a four-star level with
plasma TVs, Austar cable, WiFi and
stylish furnishings.

Many rooms have spas, balconies
and spectacular views of Montague
Island. We love how you can just step
out the door and be on the stunning
Narooma golf course, which sweeps
around a dramatic coastal headland.
Executives who tire of strategising in
the conference room can pop out for
a quick round between sessions.

Generous breakfasts are available
for all guests and group catering
can also be arranged.

There is plenty to do in the region
including whale watching, scuba
diving, fishing, kayaking, golf and
bowls, as well as some of the most
picturesque cycling and walking trails
you'll find in the region.

Bantry1villa
Merimbula

1/80 Lake Street, Merimbula ▪ 03 9815 1212, 0400 194 493
www.beautifulaccommodation.com/bantry1villa

Headland of content

Merimbula is one of our favourite coastal towns. It has a dazzling combination of lakes, surf beaches and bushland. It also supports a vibrant local foodie culture that relishes serving up fresh flathead, local beef, cheeses and creams from nearby Bega, and fat oysters from Pambula.

That all makes it well worth the trip from Sydney or Melbourne to stay in Bantry1villa, which is in town's premier residential precinct and overlooks the glorious spectacle.

Bantry1 is thoroughly adaptable, with three king-size bedrooms, all with ensuites. You can take the top floor as a couple or the whole place as a group of six.

The owners Marion and Tony Carden are avid spotters of emerging artists and the walls of Bantry1 are a testament to their taste and discernment. It all creates a wonderfully fresh and vibrant holiday mood. The lounge is a favourite spot with sensational sea views, richly stained floorboards and comfy sofas to seat your whole crew.

The location is Merimbula-perfect, overlooking the old wharf and aquarium, which has a sunny, sheltered restaurant (ideal for a chocolatey morning cappuccino with the papers).

The gorgeous and child-friendly Bar Beach is a short stroll down the cliff.

Rates
Whole villa per night from $230-$495 (up to 6 people)
Specials for couples available
Accommodation only
Direct deposit, Chq, no credit cards

Location
6 hours or 455km south of Sydney; 7 hours or 580km northeast of Melbourne. Flights daily from Sydney and Melbourne. Map 1.

Minimum stay
Three to seven nights (seasonal)

Facilities
One house with three ensuite bedrooms (queen upstairs, king and king twin singles downstairs), lounge (TV, DVD, RC AC), dining, kitchen, upstairs deck, laundry. BBQ, garage.

Other
Suitable for children

Owner details
Marion and Tony Carden
▪ marioncarden@gmail.com
▪ www.bantry1villamerimbula.com

Robyn's Nest Guest House & Cottages

Merimbula

188 Merimbula Drive, Merimbula ▪ 02 6495 4956
www.beautifulaccommodation.com/robynsnest

Rates
Room per couple from $165-$285
Cottage per night $199-$250
(up to 2; $20 per extra person)
Full breakfast/provisions included
Visa, MC, AMEX, DD, Eftpos

Location
6 hours or 455km south of Sydney;
7 hours or 580km northeast
of Melbourne. Map 1.

Minimum stay
Two nights (cottages only)

Facilities
Rooms: king, queen and king/twin
singles, ensuite, RC AC; Guest
lounge and dining (fire). Cottages:
one or two bedrooms, lounge,
dining, kitchen, one or two
bathrooms (some with spa), RC
AC, BBQ. Pool, spa, sauna, tennis.

AAA Star Rating
★★★★☆ / ★★★★★

Member
BBFAA, Accommodation
Association of Australia
Eco-Friendly Star Accreditation

Other
Suitable for children (cottages)
Disabled facilities

Host details
Robyn and Michael Britten
▪ enquiries@robynsnest.com.au
▪ www.robynsnest.com.au

A nest of indulgence

Robyn's Nest immediately appealed to our inner comfort hound. As you travel from Sydney, Melbourne or Canberra, this imposing Merimbula property makes an ideal stopping point for rest, relaxation or a complete holiday. The atmosphere is homey and inviting, reflecting host Robyn Britten's genuine love of gorgeous florals, rich burgundy fabrics and divinely detailed interiors.

The facilities are ideal for holiday-makers or conference delegates using the 40-seat meeting centre. You can play tennis, do laps in the pool, take a spa or sauna, or wander down to the private jetty for some quiet reflection or fishing.

The main house has six sumptuous guest suites (all with ensuites and individual air-conditioning) and there are 14 self-contained one- or two-bedroom cottages in the superbly landscaped gardens.

Everyone is welcome to devour a full breakfast in the Lodge or prepare their own in a cottage. Bird lovers will also twitch with pleasure here as they try to count the 56 species that flutter around the local waters.

The location is ideal: a stroll to the boardwalk that leads around the lake to the town centre. A peaceful wander towards town will soon have you sipping a latte over your newspaper or booking in for a deep-sea fishing tour.

Alpine Habitats
Crackenback

Corner of Alpine Way and Wollondibby Road, Crackenback ▪ 02 6457 2228
www.beautifulaccommodation.com/alpinehabitats

Snowy Mountains high

Alpine Habitats is showing the way of the future with its 18 ecologically sensitive 'habitats', which co-exist with a profoundly beautiful yet fragile eco-system.

When you stay here, you tread lightly on the landscape with absolutely no sacrifices in luxury or comfort. The innovations include ethanol-burning fireplaces, renewable electricity use, passive solar architecture, worm farm waste management and low visual impact.

The self-contained habitats are aesthetically elegant and seem to have grown organically from their alpine hillsides. The views from the airy interiors or the expansive decks are breathtaking, whether it is spring flowers or winter snow drifts.

A spare simplicity of interior design makes each habitat thoroughly pleasing. Lying back on the leather lounges or the king bed listening to the bird calls and whispering wind is a thrill for the soul.

The location is ideal whether you are there for the snow, the wilderness walks or the calm. Flip a coin to decide between Perisher and Thredbo each day.

Two of the Snowy's great fooderies are within walking distance: the Thredbo Valley Wild Brumby Distillery (phenomenal comfort food and schnapps – try the butterscotch) and the award-winning Crackenback Cottage Restaurant – pop over for breakfast, lunch or dinner.

Rates
Habitat per night from $190-$580 (up to 4 people) Accommodation only
Free Distillers Platter for *Beautiful Accommodation* bookings
Visa, MC, DD, Eftpos

Location
6 hours or 495km southwest of Sydney; 2½ hours or 210km south of Canberra. Map 1.

Minimum stay
Two nights

Facilities
18 Habitats, each with one or two bedrooms (king/twin singles), lounge/dining (LCD TV, DVD/CD, Ecosmart fireplace), kitchen, bathroom, balcony (BBQ). Floor heating.

AAA Star Rating
★★★★☆

Other
Suitable for children
Disabled facilities

Manager details
Rocky Harvey
▪ info@alpinehabitats.com.au
▪ www.alpinehabitats.com.au

Guthega Alpine Inn

Guthega (Kosciusko National Park)

35 Guthega Road, Guthega ▪ 02 6457 5383
www.beautifulaccommodation.com/guthega

Rates
Summer: Room per couple
from $188-$277.
Full breakfast included,
dinner and breakfast available
Winter: Room per couple
from $299-$719
Dinner, full breakfast included
Visa, MC, DD, Eftpos

Location
6 hours or 495km south
of Sydney; 3 hours or 210km
south of Canberra. Map 1.

Minimum stay
Two nights (winter)

Facilities
10 guest rooms (a range of
configurations), each with ensuite,
some with balcony. Guest lounge
(wood fire), bar (pool table),
restaurant, TV lounge, spa, sauna,
gym. Central and hydronic heating.

Other
Suitable for children
Restaurant open seven days
(bookings required in summer)

Host details
Jenny and Nick Kennedy
▪ stay@guthega.com
▪ www.guthega.com

Climb every mountain

Relaxing with a mug of steaming
hot chocolate on the terrace at the
Guthega Alpine Inn instantly reveals
why so many people love this
mountain hideaway. A sweeping vista
of hills and valleys lies before you –
snow-covered in winter, green and
vibrant in summer. Behind you is the
most enchanting chalet in the
Kosciusko National Park.

The Inn has all the elements of a
great chalet: an inviting lounge that
is rosy with firelight, a superb
restaurant and bar to sate your
hunger pangs, a sauna to soak heat
into the bones, comfortable guest
rooms, and space for ski gear or
hiking packs.

The Guthega's dining room rates a
special mention. Its fans ski in from
Perisher for lunch and guests dream
about its dinner all day, which can
include beef from the owner's farm.
Its liberal breakfasts (included in the
tariff) set you up for a day of activity.
You can even get a scrumptious
packed lunch made for your summer
hiking or fishing expeditions.

Snow fun is the focus here in winter,
with ski runs for all levels, a relaxed
family vibe, and lifts to Perisher.
When the snow has melted, guests
are drawn to the trout fishing,
mountain biking and the many
sublime alpine walks.

Marritz Alpine Inn
Perisher Valley

Location on enquiry, Perisher Valley ▪ Reservations: 02 9239 5500 Lodge: 02 6457 5220
www.beautifulaccommodation.com/marritz

Snowy, sainted Marritz

When the days grow shorter and a winter chill seeps into the night air, snow lovers' thoughts turn longingly to Marritz Alpine Inn at Perisher. Soon its doors will open for the snow season and all the delights of this exquisite Xanadu on the slopes will be at guests' beck and call.

You don't even need to know *piste* from *randonnée* to enjoy Marritz, which has the only indoor heated pool in Perisher. Just sit back in your bathers with a mug of hot chocolate and watch the action on the slopes.

Marritz has 24 rooms to suit every budget, from no-expense-spared to those seeking style on a budget.

The pick of the lot is the amazing Tower Suite, which commands 360-degree views from its lounge-dining eyrie. On moonlit evenings, the snowy landscape is simply ethereal. In all rooms, you can lie back in the warmth of your bed and gaze at the snow blanketing outside.

The spirit of The Marritz is that of a cosy European chalet. There is a bar and lounge (with log fire) and a gallery restaurant that draws crowds from elsewhere. And the best part for skiers is that Marritz is only 250 metres from the main slopes.

Rates
Room per person $200-$400
Tower Suite per person $200-$465 (minimum 2 adults per room)
Dinner and breakfast included
Visa, MC, AMEX, DC, DD, Eftpos

Location
5½ hours or 490km southwest of Sydney; 2½ hours or 210km southwest of Canberra. Map 1.

Minimum stay
Two nights (two adults per room)

Facilities
24 rooms/suites. Guest lounge, bar (fireplace), restaurant (fireplace) open to public. Indoor heated pool, sauna, billiards room. Free luggage pickup to/from Skitube. No overnight parking (leave your car at Bullocks Flat and catch the Skitube).

Other
Suitable for children
5% discount for direct bookings

Contact details
▪ marritz@mulpha.com.au
▪ www.marritzalpine.com.au

Snowy View Cottage
Dalgety

5199 Snowy River Way, Dalgety ▪ **0414 377 082**
www.beautifulaccommodation.com/snowyview

Rates
Cottage per night from $145-$190
(up to 2 people, $20/$15 per extra
person/child per night)
Accommodation only
Direct deposit, Chq, no credit cards

Location
6 hours or 445km south
of Sydney; 2 hours or 163km
south of Canberra. Map 1.

Minimum stay
Two nights

Facilities
One cottage: two bedrooms
(queen and double), lounge
(wood fire, sofa bed, TV, DVD, CD),
dining, kitchen, bathroom, laundry.
Underfloor heating, RC AC. BBQ.

Other
Suitable for children

Host details
Mary Shipway
▪ maryshipway@skymesh.com.au
▪ www.beautifulaccommodation.
com/snowyview

Rocky mountain high

We are huge fans of the Snowy View
Cottage in all seasons. In winter, the
distant snowy landscape makes the
cosy wood-fired lounge a perfect
spot to snuggle while your comfort
food cooks. In warmer months, the
exquisite garden – part of Open
Gardens Australia – draws you
outside with its intoxicating blend
of scents, colours and textures. It
is hard to believe all this is just five
years old.

A fully integrated design ethic
permeates the property, which was
influenced by an American small-
home design book that captured host
Mary Shipway's heart. The roomy
two-bedroom cottage was built from
locally found recycled materials that
create an organic feel of having been
there longer than its five years.

The bedrooms are lusciously refined
havens of comfort and simplicity with
wonderful views from picture-window
doors. A diverse range of artworks,
antiques and curios draw the eye and
interest to the corners and walls of
these delightful rooms. Considerate
attention to guests' needs is evident
everywhere, even including a
milkshake maker for the kids.

Nearby is the mountain village of
Dalgety for coffee, papers and pub
meals. This is a very genuine Snowy
hideaway that resonates the
generosity and passion of its owner.

Snowy Wilderness Resort

Jindabyne

2911 The Barry Way, Ingebyra via Jindabyne ▪ 1800 218 171, 0414 544 503
www.beautifulaccommodation.com/snowywilderness

High country heaven

If you want the quintessential high-country experience, Snowy Wilderness Resort is the real deal. It's a 7200-acre reserve and sanctuary for the wild mountain horses known as Brumbies. Think Russell Crowe in *The Silver Brumby* with warm beds and good plumbing. Here, you can don your Akubra hat and Drizabone oilskin jacket, hop on a horse or quad bike, and ride the range.

The Resort's facilities are magnificent, with options whether you are a party of 10 (try the Homestead) or a couple seeking absolute solitude (try a one-bedroom lodge or the cottage). You can even camp under the stars – a real thrill for the kids. There is also a two-bedroom apartment available on nearby Lake Jindabyne.

The Homestead is completely in sync with its gorgeous lakeside setting and location. It brilliantly uses local stone and timber to create a wonderfully organic feel with a fire-lit lounge-dining area and bedrooms with tranquil vistas. As with the lodges, the Homestead has broadband and a laundry. There is even a stunning marquee available for weddings or events.

All the accommodation is self-contained but no stay here would be complete without sampling owner Justin MacIntosh's high country cuisine. How about local duck cooked in a camp oven or a breakfast of scrambled eggs infused with black truffles?

Rates
Homestead, cottage and lodge per couple from $175-$375 (2 to 4 people, $60/$25 per extra person/child 3-12 years per night) Accommodation only, dinner and catering by prior arrangement Visa, MC, DD, Eftpos, Chq

Location
5¾ hours or 490km southwest of Sydney; 2½ hours or 210km southwest of Canberra. Map 1.

Minimum stay
Two nights

Facilities
One- and two-bedroom Lodges (king), four-bedroom Homestead (king, two queen, double, twin singles) one-bedroom Cottage (queen). All with lounge (fire, TV, DVD, CD) dining, kitchen, BBQ. Two-bedroom apartment in Jindabyne. Function marquee.

Other
Suitable for children
Pets by arrangement
Horse riding and quad bikes available seven days

Owner details
Justin and Delia MacIntosh
▪ info@snowywilderness.com.au
▪ www.snowywilderness.com.au

Heart of the Country
& the ACT

The Great Dividing Range splits New South Wales into two very distinctive climatic and cultural zones. On the eastern side is the coast, often with a sub-tropical climate. To the west lie the vast spreading plains of the inland that run up to the edge of Australia's interior deserts. The landscape and lifestyle of country NSW is very different from its urbanised cityscapes. Here in the wheat belt of NSW there are farmstays, grand old pubs and spectacular natural scenery.

If Parliament is sitting, make sure you stop by Parliament House at about 2pm to see the bear pit of Question Time.

As you follow the Great Western Highway through the Blue Mountains (see Sydney and Surrounds, page 22), you eventually reach the steep descent to Lithgow and the western foothills of the mountains. Make a detour to Hassans Walls for phenomenal views of the mountain range and the Hartley Valley. Kids will love riding the steam train along the Zig Zag Railway.

Governor Lachlan Macquarie established Bathurst in 1815 as the first administrative centre of inland New South Wales. It retains many impressive buildings, including the ominous sandstone walls of the Bathurst Gaol and the copper-domed Bathurst Court House.

The 1870s mansion Abercrombie House is an astonishing testament to the wealth generated in the local area. It has more than 40 rooms and a ballroom with a 30-foot ceiling.

If you are heading further west, slip off the Great Western Highway to Peel Road and the Castlereagh Highway to Mudgee. It has developed a thriving wine industry over the past 40 years and is noted for its rich cabernet sauvignon, shiraz and chardonnay. Wineries such as Moothi Estate are part of the monthly Mudgee Progressive Lunch.

Dubbo is a transport hub for the central west of NSW, with roads linking Melbourne tourists to their Gold Coast holiday haunts and far western towns like Bourke with the big smoke of Sydney. The Western Plains Zoo in Dubbo has an amazing collection of animals including African elephants and bison. Get up early and participate in the morning feeding. Narromine, to the west, offers some of the best gliding in Australia at its local club.

"The back o' Bourke" is old NSW jargon for a long way away but this historic Darling River town is a fascinating destination worth a closer look. Check out the town's history at The Back O'Bourke Exhibition Centre. You can see ancient Aboriginal rock art at nearby Mount Gundabooka National Park.

Accredited Visitor Information Centres

Albury
Railway Place
1300 252 879
www.visitalburywodonga.com.au

Australian Captial Territory
330 Northbourne Avenue, Dickson
02 6205 0044
www.visitcanberra.com.au

Bungendore
2/38 Ellendon Street
02 6238 1422
www.visitqueanbeyan.com.au

Dubbo
Cnr Macquarie & Erskine Street
02 6801 4450
www.dubbo.com.au

Snowy Region
Kosciuszko Road, Jindabyne
02 6450 5600
www.environment.nsw.gov.au

Mudgee
84 Market Street
02 6372 1020
www.visitmudgeeregion.com.au

Parkes
Henry Parkes Centre,
Newell Highway
02 6862 6000
www.visitparkes.com.au

Tenterfield
157 Rouse Street
02 6736 1082
www.tenterfieldtourism.com

Wagga Wagga
183 Tarcutta Street
1300 100 122
www.visitwagga.com

If you head south from Dubbo, the Newell Highway passes into fertile sheep and wheat growing country. As you head to Parkes, a gigantic radio telescope juts out of the farmland – the star of the hit Australian movie, *The Dish*. It has a wonderful cafe and brilliant educational displays.

Wagga Wagga has superb Botanic Gardens and the kids will be thankful if you detour slightly north to Junee for the Junee Licorice & Chocolate Factory. Albury is the centre of a vibrant net of small communities on the Murray River and Lake Hulme. There are plenty of water activities such as riding paddle steamers, skiing and fishing.

Canberra is a must-see for anyone interested in Australia's intricately planned capital. American architect Walter Burley Griffin beat 136 other applicants in 1911 with his design for the city. His original plans are in the National Archives of Australia.

If Parliament is sitting, make sure you stop by Parliament House at about 2pm to see the bear pit of Question Time. There are plenty of fascinating things to do, including checking out 400 portraits of prominent Australians at the National Portrait Gallery.

Historic Bungendore, on the outskirts of the ACT, is a relaxed old country village. It has craft shops and wineries to visit, including one of Australia's highest vineyards, Lark Hill Winery.

Albury Suites
Albury

537 and 539 Schubach Street, Albury ▪ 02 6023 6023, 0407 218 744
www.beautifulaccommodation.com/alburysuites

Rates
Whole apartment per night from
$170-$180 (up to 2 people,
$15 per extra person per night)
Accommodation only
Visa, MC, DD, Eftpos

Location
3½ hours or 315km northeast
of Melbourne. Map 1.

Facilities
A range of two-bedroom
apartments, each with lounge
(plasma TV, DVD), kitchen, dining,
bathroom and powder room,
laundry, courtyard (BBQ), RC AC,
internal garage.

Other
Suitable for children

Owner details
Michael Kean
▪ michael@alburysuites.com.au
▪ www.alburysuites.com

Country townhouses with room

Albury Suites provide an answer to
that nagging problem of where to stay
in a large regional country town if you
want contemporary style. These
modern townhouses were completed
in 2007 and they are immaculately
cared for by the owner, Michael Kean.

The East Albury location – near the
town's main Dean Street shopping
precinct – makes it ideal for either
inquisitive travellers on a longer
stay or professionals who have
business in town.

One of the most striking features of
these townhouses is their sheer
space. The two bedrooms are palatial
in size, with plenty of room to unsling
the bags, spread out your maps
or set up your mobile office.

There are full kitchens and laundries,
plus courtyards with barbecues and
internal garages. And at day's end,
you will relish flopping down on one
of the big comfy sofas with a glass
of local shiraz in one hand and the
remote control for the 42-inch plasma
TV in the other.

The local area is quiet and
convenient. Step out for dinner
at a local pub, order in, or grill a
steak in the privacy of your courtyard.
Afterwards, take an evening
constitutional walk over to the
wonderful Albury Botanic Gardens.

Albury Dream Cottages
Albury

727 –731 Wood Street, Albury ▪ 0427 257 900
www.beautifulaccommodation.com/alburydreamcottages

Albury Homes in the Albury heartland

These beautifully renovated 1940s red-brick bungalows are classic country town homes, with established gardens, lots of space and splendid architectural detailing.

The owners have thought of everything to make them perfect retreats for families who need to hop off the highway or gather at a central point. There are toys and play equipment for the kids and adults will love soaking in the backyard hydrotherapy spa.

Magnolia and Melrose are side by side, which allows groups of up to 11 to stay together. The bedrooms are attractive places to lay your head on crisp linen in peace and quiet.

You can cook up a meal for everyone in the fully equipped kitchens

or barbecue in the backyard. The convivial lounge rooms combine an Art Deco legacy with modern comforts and stained-glass windows by local leadlight artists.

Albury is the centre of a fantastically varied region. There are handsome streetscapes, historic buildings and notable Botanic Gardens. The Art Gallery is a hidden treasure; it has an important collection of works by former local resident Russell Drysdale as well pieces by Tom Roberts, Goya, Chagall and Renoir.

A visit to the new Albury Visitor Information Centre will unveil all the riches waiting to be discovered.

Rates
Whole house per night $180
(up to 2 people, $10 per extra person; children under 12 free)
Full breakfast provisions included
(first morning)
Visa, MC, DD

Location
3½ hours or 315km northeast
of Melbourne. Map 1.

Facilities
Two cottages: each with three bedrooms (one sleeps six, one sleeps five), kitchen, dining, lounge (TV, DVD, phone), central heating/AC; outdoor entertainment area, BBQ, outdoor heated spa, children's play centre.

AAA Star Rating
★★★★☆

Other
Suitable for children

Owner details
Jeanette and Brian Fealy
▪ jeanette@albury
dreamcottages.com.au
▪ www.albury
dreamcottages.com.au

Bishops Court Estate
Bathurst

226 Seymour Street, Bathurst ▪ 02 6332 4447, 0422 303 311
www.beautifulaccommodation.com/bishopscourt

Rates
Room per couple $270-$350
Full breakfast included, dinner
by prior arrangement
Visa, MC, AMEX, DC, DD, Eftpos

Location
3 hours or 205km west
of Sydney. Map 1.

Facilities
Historic home: six guest rooms
(king bed, ensuite or separate
private bathroom), guest lounge
(log fire, TV), library (TV), dining
room, grand chapel for functions.

Member
BBFAA
Amazing Country Escapes

Other
Disabled facilities
Functions catered

Host details
Christine Le Fevre
▪ christine@bishopscourt
estate.com.au
▪ www.bishopscourt
bathurst.com.au

By the Bishop blessed

Bishop Samuel Marsden spared
no expense when he built the now
historic Bishop's Court in Bathurst
in 1870, paying for this magnificent
ecclesiastical folly from his own deep
pockets. The old evangelical Anglican
could never have imagined the future
role of his diocesan palace: as a
luxurious stage for indulgence in food,
wine and love. This is one of NSW's
great stays, which you should visit at
least once in this life.

Every superlative is warranted here.
The bedrooms are vast suites with
glorious views over the 140-year-old
garden. In the bishop's former
bedroom, there is a marbled ensuite
bathroom with a huge tub for
meditative soaking.

We just love every corner of this
house, including the second floor
terrace lounge with treetop views over
the parkland gardens. Bishop's Court
is renowned as a venue for weddings
– it has its own private chapel, of
course – and other special events.
The breakfasts and dinners are simply
superb, with elegant options such
as dinner in the chapel lit by
countless candles.

Bathurst is a vibrant regional NSW
town with a fascinating collection
of historic buildings and a growing
reputation as a regional food and
wine centre of excellence.

Encore Apartments and Dalkeith Cottage
Bathurst

187 Piper Street and 190 Peel Street, Bathurst ▪ 02 6333 6000
www.beautifulaccommodation.com/encore

Another good time

Encore Apartments have done it again with the latest addition to their suite of Bathurst accommodation – the beautifully restored Federation era Delkeith Cottage. But don't be misled by the 'cottage' moniker, Delkeith is a three-bedroom, two-lounge, two-bathroom home with a chef's kitchen and space to lounge in comfort and privacy.

We adore the restrained use of feature furnishings – a big brass bed in one bedroom or the pair of comfy lounges in the family room – to accent lines of sight and room proportions. This is Federation style with a modern fling.

The nearby townhouse and one- and two-bedroom apartments that Encore is best known for are as comfortably

contemporary as Delkeith is cosily traditional. They make the perfect bases for anyone with business in Bathurst or who pauses on their travels to explore this historic NSW inland town.

We like the uncluttered, Asian-influenced interior designs of these apartments, which are thoroughly relaxed yet wonderfully stylish. All are equipped with kitchens, bathrooms with quality products and fluffy towels, LCD TVs and air-conditioning. You can just shut the door and relax.

Bathurst has some of the finest colonial era architecture in New South Wales, reflecting its status as the first big settlement beyond the Blue Mountains.

Rates
Apartment per night $165-$590
Cottage per night $310
Accommodation only, continental breakfast provisions available
Visa, MC, AMEX, DC, DD, Eftpos

Location
3 hours or 205km west of Sydney. Map 1.

Minimum stay
Two nights (three-bedroom townhouse and cottage only)

Facilities
Eight apartments (one- and two-bedrooms) one townhouse (three bedrooms), all with lounge (LCD TV, DVD, CD), kitchen, RC AC, laundry, balcony or courtyard. Cottage: three bedrooms, one ensuite, lounge (TV, DVD, CD), family room, second lounge (TV, DVD, CD), dining, kitchen, bathroom (spa), deck (BBQ), WiFi, RC AC, ducted heating, fans.

Other
Suitable for children

Manager details
Helen and Bernard Kenelly
▪ info@encoreapartments.com.au
▪ www.encoreapartments.com.au

The Old Stone House

Bungendore (near Canberra)

41 Molonglo Street, Bungendore ▪ 02 6238 1888
www.beautifulaccommodation.com/theoldstonehouse

Rates
Rates per couple from $220-$300
Full breakfast included
Visa, MC, AMEX, DC, Eftpos

Location
20 minutes or 30km east
of Canberra. Map 1.

Facilities
Four guest rooms (two queen,
two double; three with ensuite,
one with private bathroom),
three guest lounges (two with
wood fire; 'Snug' also with TV,
DVD), billiard room, conservatory,
breakfast room, conference and
home theatre room. Hydronic
heating.

Host details
John and Debbie Putt
▪ bookings@theoldstone
house.com.au
▪ www.theoldstonehouse.com.au

Golden stones, warm hearths

We have seen many gorgeous
historic homes but The Old Stone
House at Bungendore easily earns
a position in our Top 10.

Its stonework glows with a 140-year-
old patina and the congenial rooms
have seen many nights of revelry and
quiet rest. It makes a perfect
travellers' stepping stone to the tourist
attractions of Canberra or the coastal
pleasures of Batemans Bay.

Age has not wearied this marvellous
gem. Its comforts are modern yet
entirely sympathetic with the period.

There are four delightful guest rooms,
three with ensuites and one with its
own private bathroom (complete with
a claw-foot tub, chequered floor and
MOR body products).

Guests can enjoy several gorgeous
rooms: play snooker in the billiards
room, take tea in the sunny
conservatory, relax by the fire in one
of the lounges or put on a DVD in
the home theatre.

The property is equipped with
conference facilities, making it an
ideal retreat for executive team
strategising. Bridal parties love
the brilliantly photogenic garden,
which includes a cherry arbour
and Japanese garden.

Places to eat in town include divine
French food at Le Tres Bon, which
also offers cooking classes. For
breakfast, host Debbie offers a
sumptuous three-course feast.

The Brassey of Canberra
Canberra (Barton)

Belmore Gardens and Macquarie Street, Barton ▪ 1800 659 191, 02 6273 3766
www.beautifulaccommodation.com/thebrassey

A capital idea

The Brassey is as much a Canberra institution as Old Parliament House. Just about every Member of Parliament has been through its venerable doors at some time. It opened in 1927 – the year Federal Parliament relocated from Melbourne to its new Canberra capital – and functioned as a virtual government guesthouse for decades.

The location on 2.5 acres of beautiful gardens in Barton is right on the edge of the parliamentary precinct. It is a short walk from many of the national capital's iconic tourist sites.

A very sympathetic renovation has given The Brassey's spacious Heritage guest rooms a well-earned makeover, with high-backed lounge chairs and brass light fittings.

As befitting somewhere that parliamentarians would stay for months at a time, the rooms are generous in size and wonderfully peaceful at night.

Downstairs, the Belmore restaurant has a row of lovely arched French windows that bring in the light and views from the grounds. It's a very evocative setting to eat breakfast before you set off to see Canberra.

If you are playing tourist, ask The Brassey's front desk staff about packages that include visits to exhibitions at The National Gallery and The National Museum.

Rates
Room per couple $180-$260
Accommodation only, full breakfast and dinner available
Visa, MC, AMEX, DD, Eftpos,

Location
5 minutes or 2km from Canberra CBD; 2 minutes to Parliament House. Map 1.

Facilities
A range of Heritage and Garden Court rooms and two suites, all with ensuite, TV, broadband. Restaurant, bar. Conference facilities. Free off-street parking.

Other
Suitable for children
Disabled facilities
Restaurant open: Breakfast daily, Dinner Monday-Saturday

Manager details
Markus Gibson-Huck
▪ info@brassey.net.au
▪ www.brassey.net.au

Pericoe Retreat Bed and Breakfast

Dubbo

12R Cassandra Drive, Dubbo ▪ 02 6887 2705, 0407 896 828
www.beautifulaccommodation.com/pericoe

Rates
Suite per couple from $240-$280
Single rates available mid-week
Full breakfast included,
dinner available
Visa, MC, AMEX, DD, Eftpos

Location
5 hours or 400km northwest of
Sydney; 10 hours or 850km north
of Melbourne. Map 1.

Facilities
Four suites, each with queen,
ensuite (two with spa, two with
bath), TV, DVD. Two sitting rooms
(fire, one also with TV), RC AC.
Indoor/outdoor lounge and dining
with sun deck. Games room
(billiards table, bar). Pool, day/
night tennis court, gazebo. WiFi.

AAA Star Rating
★★★★★

Other
Suitable for children

Host details
Kem and Ross Irvine
▪ pericoe@pericoeretreat.com.au
▪ www.pericoeretreat.com.au

Inland country heaven

Dubbo is the longed-for overnight stop on runs between Melbourne and Brisbane – drivers are exhausted and everyone is hungry. You have two options: stay on the noisy motel strip or head to the serenity of Pericoe Retreat. You won't face this choice again once you have tried this immaculately presented five-star property (the only one with that rating in Dubbo).

Pericoe is the carefully nurtured project of Kem and Ross Irvine. They have made a place that will instantly appeal to tourists, families and business travellers. The rooms are lushly sumptuous with rich drapes, fine linens and spotless ensuites.

We love how you can make a suite of two bedrooms with a private sitting room (complete with a wood fire and TV) for a family or small party. And even better is Kem's food. She cooks up local beef, lamb, vegetables and fish for ravenous travellers – and you don't need to order in advance, which hints at the superlative service she offers.

There is a pool to splash in after a hot day in the car, a tennis court and billiards room. Dubbo's attractions including the zoo and the wonderful Japanese Garden, which was a gift from Minokamo city, are all just a short drive away.

Primo Cottages
Mudgee

9 and 12 Court Street, Mudgee ▪ 02 6372 6990, 0428 726 990
www.beautifulaccommodation.com/primocottages

127

Prime time for bliss

If you haven't explored the Mudgee wine district, try this: gather a bunch of good friends, get a people-mover and start visiting cellar doors. In the evenings, you can return home with your booty of wine to these two classic Mudgee cottages – Primo and Bliss.

We'll let the words of one Blissed-out guest last year capture the mood: "Beautiful house, beautiful fire, wonderful way to catch up with friends with a glass of wine!"

Bliss was built in the 1890s and has been superbly renovated. The interior has a quiet calm that is accented by its white walls and delightful furnishings that all hint at French country style.

There are three queen bedrooms and an inviting kitchen-dining area out the back for cooking up the generous supply of breakfast provisions.

Bliss is an adults-only house whereas at Primo, children are very welcome. Primo is an early 1900s red brick house with three comfortable bedrooms and two bathrooms. It has a colonial air that is highlighted by a broad, flagstoned front verandah.

The owners live elsewhere but are available for advice on your Mudgee stay. Nearby are bicycling tracks, parklands and the town centre, which has cafes, restaurants, galleries and shops to explore.

Rates
Cottage per couple $140 ($140 per additional bedroom used) Full breakfast provisions included
Visa, MC, DD, Chq

Location
3½ hours or 270km northwest of Sydney. Map 1.

Minimum stay
Two nights at weekends preferred

Facilities
Two cottages, each with three bedrooms (one with three queen; one with two queen and two king/twin singles), lounge (fire, TV, DVD, CD), dining, kitchen, two bathrooms, laundry, RC AC. BBQ.

Other
Suitable for children (Primo Cottage)

Owner details
Carolyn and Robert McKittrick
▪ bookings@primocottage.com
▪ www.primocottage.com

Mudgee's Getaway Cottages

Mudgee

Mortimer Street, Mudgee ▪ 1800 627 242, 02 6372 7272
www.beautifulaccommodation.com/mudgeesgetaway

128

Rates
Cottage/house per night
from $90-$1500
(rates are for 2 to 15 people)
Full breakfast provisions included
Visa, MC, DD

Location
3½ hours or 270km northwest
of Sydney. Map 1.

Minimum stay
Two nights at weekends

Facilities
Elington Manor: six bedrooms, six
bathrooms, multiple living spaces,
pool. Cottages with one to four
bedrooms; all with lounge, dining,
kitchen, RC AC.

Other
Suitable for children (except
Elington Manor)
Pets by arrangement

Owner details
Elizabeth Etherington
▪ info@mudgeesgetaway.com
▪ www.mudgeesgetaway.com.au

Lord of the manors

Mudgee is one of those wonderful
rural NSW towns with a real heartbeat
of civilised culture thumping away
at its centre. The town's valley setting
is enticing, the wine scene thriving
and the standards of accommodation
are sensational.

Mudgee's Getaway Cottages are
a prime example with six homes
on nine verdant acres in town.
The riverside location and freedom
to pluck your own vegies from the
gardens and collect fresh eggs are
a delightful bonus.

The absolute standout is Elington
Manor, a 1920s Federation home
that has been brilliantly transformed
into a dazzling stage for gatherings,
celebrations and corporate
brainstorming sessions, and a
private chef can be arranged.

It has six magnificent bedrooms:
five with king beds (including some
romantic four-posters) and all with
ensuite bathrooms. The central
kitchen and dining area is an
architectural coup, with an indoor-
outdoor mezzanine gallery living
room that leads to a deck for viewing
the glorious gardens (spot the
collection of farm animals from a
donkey to alpacas and more). Add
a marquee on the sprawling lawns
and you have the perfect setting
for a memorable wedding.

The town centre with its vibrant shops
and restaurants are a short walk from
your front door.

Welcome Cottage
Parkes

35 The Welcome Road, Parkes ▪ 02 6862 3768, 0428 623 768
www.beautifulaccommodation.com/welcomecottage

A haven off the highway

Parkes is a wonderful regional crossroads that fully repays spending time to explore and immerse yourself in its country town delights. Better still, you get to stay at one of the most beautifully situated properties in country New South Wales – Welcome Cottage.

The cottage name is apt as you arrive at this quiet haven, leaving highway angst far behind. Its sophisticated style is very city-meets-country, making it the only 4.5-star self-contained stay in Parkes.

The kitchen is a triumph, combining corrugated iron, clean-line bench tops and all the mod-cons. It has a AAA eco-tick rating and only natural cleaning products are used. Jill has stocked it with her scrumptious jams,

liberal breakfast supplies and a yummy welcome basket.

Hand-made soaps and fluffy towels make the spa bathroom a delight. The sunsets are simply awe-inspiring and extra friends can stay at the Saltbush Shed also on the property.

Yes, you know about The Dish at Parkes (the 3D tour to Mars is a must-see). But Parkes has other fabulous attractions: the annual Elvis Festival in January is a hoot (the King's last Cadillac is at The King's Castle), the Parkes Car Museum has an extraordinary collection and there is plenty to see in the region, including the Western Plains Zoo.

Rates
Cottage per night from $160-$175 (up to 2 people, $40 per extra person per night) Full breakfast provisions included (first 2 nights) Visa, MC, DD, Eftpos

Location
4½ hours or 360km west of Sydney; 8 hours or 730km northeast of Melbourne. Map 1.

Minimum stay
Two nights

Facilities
One one-bedroom cottage (queen), lounge (TV, DVD, CD), dining, kitchen, bathroom (double spa, underfloor heating), RC AC. Guest laundry. BBQ.

AAA Star Rating
★★★★☆
Eco-Friendly STAR Accreditation

Host details
Jill and Rob Bird
▪ welcomecottage@bigpond.com
▪ www.welcomecottage.com.au

Sylvan Park
Tenterfield

81 Logan Street, Tenterfield ▪ 02 6736 1136, 0439 362 630
www.beautifulaccommodation.com/sylvanpark

Rates
Whole house per night from
$250-$290 (up to 4 guests)
Accommodation only
Direct deposit, Chq, no credit cards

Location
3 hours or 272km southwest
of Brisbane; 8 hours or 710km
northwest of Sydney. Map 6.

Facilities
One house: two bedrooms (queen
and twin singles), formal lounge
(wood fire, flat-screen TV, DVD/
CD), reading room (library),
lounge (wood fire), dining and
kitchen. RC AC, ducted heating.
Parking.

Member
BBFAA

Agent details
Jenni Donges
▪ jenni.donges@raywhite.com
▪ www.sylvanpark.com.au

Classic Federation home

We suggest starting your stay at
stunning Sylvan Park in the bathroom.
Why? Because it exemplifies the
attention to style and guest comfort
found at this wonderful Tenterfield
property. Let your feet wander the
sparkling tiles, sample some of the
L'Occitane toiletries to freshen up,
and picture yourself soaking in that
huge claw-foot bath.

The 1903 house has been restored
to more than its original glory. It
sympathetically combines the classic
architectural motifs of Federation
Australia, including wide verandahs,
grandly spacious rooms and high
ceilings, with every modern comfort.

A huge gourmet kitchen provides for
the formal dining table, which just
begs to be set with some local wine
and a roast beef.

The bedrooms are a dreamy melange
of chocolate and cream with windows
that gaze across the home's half acre
of English gardens.

Tenterfield is a great town. The real
founding site of Australian Federation
brims with historic buildings and the
local district is rapidly becoming one
of New South Wales' most
interesting, and possibly least
explored, wine regions.

Little Bunda Cottages
Wagga Wagga

221 Coolamon Road, Wagga Wagga ▪ 02 6931 7016, 0412 257 482
www.beautifulaccommodation.com/littlebunda

A waylay in Wagga Wagga

Do yourself a big favour next time you are travelling between Sydney and Melbourne – detour along the Olympic Highway to experience Little Bunda Cottages in Wagga Wagga. You win three ways: break the long haul, stay in stunning accommodation and explore a vibrant regional city.

Little Bunda is a gift of love that was handmade by Jen and Greg Charleson. Their admirable philosophy is to source everything from local artisans (thus also minimising carbon emissions).

Mud bricks and Australian hardwoods provide natural insulation and pleasing aesthetics. The two bedrooms are sublime havens of minimalist beauty, with their sun-dried bed linen and graceful ambience.

Fine craftsmanship in the kitchen includes applebox and Tasmanian myrtle cabinetwork, and the quality appliances reflect the attention to detail throughout the cottages.

French doors open onto wraparound verandahs overlooking rolling paddocks and vineyards – the perfect place to enjoy an award-winning Charles Sturt University wine at sunset.

The Riverina is diverse and Wagga Wagga has many hidden treasures. The National Art Glass Collection has a dazzling range of displays, the September Jazz and Blues Festival attracts up to 60 bands, and Junee's Licorice & Chocolate Factory has some delectable treats.

Rates
Cottage per night $150 (2 people, $25 per extra person per night) Accommodation only, full breakfast provisions and hampers available
Visa, MC, DD

Location
5.5 hours or 460km southwest of Sydney or northeast of Melbourne. Map 1.

Minimum stay
Two nights

Facilities
Two-bedroom cottages (queen, twin singles), lounge (TV, DVD, CD, desk), dining, kitchen, spa bathroom, laundry, RC AC. BBQ.

AAA Star Rating
★★★★☆

Member
BBFANSW, Accommodation Association of Australia

Other
Suitable for children

Host details
Jen and Greg Charleson
▪ stay@littlebundacottages.com.au
▪ www.littlebundacottages.com.au

Brisbane & surrounds
& the Moreton Bay Islands

Brisbane is blessed with everything you need for a fun stay, from a delightfully relaxed vibe in town to the sheer natural beauty of its coastal hinterland. Dining al fresco at a city restaurant and taking in the best of modern art can be offset by side trips to spectacular national parks, vineyards and farm stays. And if you are looking to party or relax on the beach – or both – the Gold Coast and Sunshine Coast are within easy reach.

133

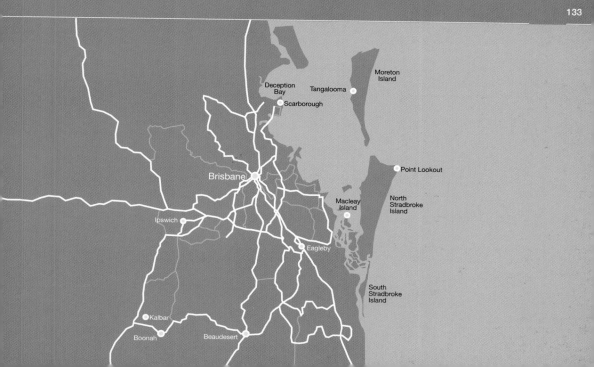

Romantics love the Mount Coot-Tha district, which has Brisbane's Botanic Gardens and one of Australia's best night cityscapes.

Queensland's capital retains much of the warm, sub-tropical ambience of a grand, old country town of the north. It meanders along the winding banks of its broad river, with each twist and turn revealing more of this wonderful city: gorgeous pockets of Queenslander architecture, galleries, boutiques and some of Australia's best al fresco dining. Brisbane's residents have made their city's name shine, too, retaining a tough but laconic country friendliness that made the whole nation proud during the floods of 2011.

Apart from boutiques and boardwalks, riverside restaurants and cafes, Brisbane has some important cultural icons including the Queensland Art Gallery and the Gallery of Modern Art, which has splendid post-1900 works. Unapologetic romantics love the Mount Coot-Tha district, which has Brisbane's Botanic Gardens and one of Australia's best night cityscapes. Kids and their families also throng to the Sir Thomas Brisbane Planetarium, where would-be astrophysicists can investigate black holes, cosmic collisions and extra-terrestrial life.

Adventure travellers will get a thrill from the rock climbing at the Kangaroo Point cliffs or the Story Bridge adventure climb. The latter involves two-and-a-half hours of spectacular views of the city and a full commentary on Brisbane's intriguing history.

Brisbane is a fine starting point to reach an astonishing variety of regions. Take your pick from the rich ecological treasures of the Moreton Bay islands, the upbeat holiday playground of the Gold Coast, the laid-back Sunshine Coast and its hinterland of small towns, rainforests and picturesque farmland.

Moreton Island, also known as Tangalooma, is Brisbane's easy-to-reach marine park. In just over an hour, visitors can be strolling on white beaches, snorkelling, frolicking with dolphins or watching feeding time with the pelicans. Marine biologists are on-hand to educate and entertain young naturalists with hands-on sessions exploring the island's diverse ecology.

The island's attractions include wildflower heaths, sand dunes, freshwater lakes, whale watching from June to October, coloured sands and rugged cliffs. You can also get with sand boarding, sea kayaking, four-wheel driving, sailing, windsurfing and diving among various shipwrecks.

In the lower reaches of Moreton Bay lies sublime Macleay Island. Its sheltered location, sandy beaches and mangrove foreshores are ideal for swimming, fishing, boating, picnicking and barbecues. Water taxis run seven days a week, connecting Macleay to other bay islands and the mainland.

To the south of Brisbane, the Mount Barney National Park is spiked with ancient volcanic peaks, caves,

rock pools, rare plants and World Heritage-listed Gondwana Rainforest. Reasonably fit, well-equipped bushwalkers will be rewarded with spectacular views from more than 30 routes to the mount's twin summits. Alternatively, sit back and admire Mount Barney while spending a few days at Barney Creek Vineyard.

Nearby Rathdowney flaunts its origins as a timber and dairy centre. In autumn, the Rathdowney Heritage Festival attracts thousands who come for the region's natural environment, Indigenous history and legacy of white settlement. A diverse range of accommodation and several national parks, including Lamington and Border Ranges, are a drive away.

Accredited Visitor Information Centres

Brisbane
Queen Street Mall
07 3006 6290
www.visitbrisbane.com.au

Brisbane International Airport
Level 2, International Terminal
07 3406 3190
www.southernqueensland.com.au

Brisbane Domestic Airport
Brisbane Domestic Terminal
07 3305 9233
www.southernqueensland.com.au

Rathdowney
82 Mt Lindsay Highway
07 5544 1222
www.rathdowney.org.au

Boonah
20 Boonah-Fassifern Road
07 5463 2233
www.scenicrim.qld.gov.au

City Treetops
Brisbane (Red Hill)

16 Glassey Street, Red Hill ▪ 07 3369 5930
www.beautifulaccommodation.com/citytreetops

Contemporary family retreat

We have found the perfect place for family get-togethers at City Treetops in Brisbane's delightful old Red Hill. Here is one of those rare places that genuinely welcomes real families – those with kids and pets in tow. It even has a 'secret' sleeping room that will bring out all the children's C.S. Lewis-inspired fantasies.

Two townhouses sit side-by-side on a ridge that offers a panorama of the district, complete with sprays of colour and palm trees. Each sleeps nine (or 18 as a package deal together). They are sensibly robust properties that haven't fussed with breakable bric-a-brac, hence

the welcome mat being laid out for kids and pets. That said, the beds are big and comfy, the style is contemporary, and there are plenty of decks, courtyards and balconies.

Catering to your crowd won't be a problem: the kitchens have bench space to spare and all equipment needed to prepare a family feast.

Brisbane's trendiest food and shopping district, Paddington, is very close. And you can easily get to theme parks on the coast, Suncorp Stadium and the Broncos Leagues Club.

Rates
Whole townhouse per night $264 (up to 4 guests, extra adult $25, extra child $15 per night)
Weekly rates available
Accommodation only
Visa, MC, DD

Location
5 minutes or 3km from the Brisbane CBD. Map 8.

Minimum stay
Two nights

Facilities
Two three-level townhouses: two bedrooms (queen, one also with sofa bed, AC in master) and 'secret bedroom' (queen, bunk, single); lounge (TV, DVD, CD), kitchen, dining room. BBQ, high chair, laundry, undercover parking.

Other
Suitable for children
Pets welcome

Owner details
Christine Butler and Mark Lowry
▪ petergrub@dodo.com.au
▪ www.accommodation brisbane-australia.com

Il Mondo Boutique Hotel

Brisbane (Kangaroo Point)

25-35 Rotherham Street, Kangaroo Point ▪ 07 3392 0111
www.beautifulaccommodation.com/ilmondo

Rates
Room and penthouse per night
from $159-$950
Continental breakfast included
Visa, MC, AMEX, DD, Eftpos

Location
Five minutes by car or ferry from
Brisbane CBD. Map 8.

Facilities
A range of hotel rooms,
apartments and penthouses, all
with ensuite, LCD TV, RC AC,
balcony. Apartments/penthouses
with lounge and kitchen. Breakfast
room, laundry, WiFi, internet kiosk,
conference facilities, free parking.
Pool, free bike hire. Restaurant.

AAA Star Rating
★★★★

Other
Suitable for children
Disabled facilities
Restaurant open: dinner Mon-Sat

General Manager details
Eleonora Ginardi
▪ reservations@ilmondo.com.au
▪ www.beautifulaccommodation.
com/ilmondo

Cool, calm city style

If only every CBD was as lucky as
Brisbane having somewhere like
Il Mondo on its doorstep. We admire
this boutique hotel for its location,
which is in a quiet pocket just across
the river from town near the Gabba.
The building stands proudly next
to Story Bridge and offers all the
convenience of city living, together
with an air of calm that is not found
in other grid-locked CBD choices.

You get a wonderful choice of options
here. Depending on the size of your
party, you can opt for hotel rooms,
one-bedroom self-contained
apartments or penthouses that can
sleep up to six people.

All rooms are decorated in a smoothly
contemporary melange of chocolate,
cream and white with funky little
cushions to add colour. Families are
made very welcome here with cots,
high chairs and rollaway beds
available for older kids. Downstairs
is a 20-metre lap pool and secure
parking for your car.

The local Kangaroo Point
neighbourhood has lovely riverside
walks. Nearby are the Beautiful
Beings day spa (see page 272) and
Stephanies Spas (see page 272 and
273) for pampering after a hard day
in the city.

To finish the day, dine at the very tasty
Italian-influenced restaurant, Pimento,
which services the hotel and also
provides takeaway and room service.

Sunset Waters
Macleay Island (near Brisbane)

126 Western Road, Macleay Island ▪ 03 9521 9250, 0425 714 753
www.beautifulaccommodation.com/sunsetwaters

Waterside holiday home

Since the last edition, our readers have fallen in love with Sunset Waters on Macleay Island – and we know why. This is one of those getaway locations with everything for the perfect holiday.

The two-storey home loves its waterway view and it has heaps of room for large families to play and relax. There is no finer end to a day than being perched up on one of the decks with a glass of wine in hand and the sun falling over the yardarm.

The bedrooms are a real highlight here, providing spacious and comfortable windows on the marine panorama below.

Adults will love stargazing from the blissful upstairs serenity of the master bedroom deck while the kids romp away downstairs or quietly bury themselves in a book or DVD. The kitchen is fully equipped, right down to scaling blades for your fishing catch. A timber walkway provides easy access to the foreshore.

If you have a boat, bring it along and tie it up to the property's private mooring. And don't forget your fishing rods, bathers and binoculars. The island lies within the Moreton Bay marine park, which is rich in birds, wildlife, dugongs and turtles.

Rates
Whole house per night
from $125-$275
Accommodation only
Direct deposit, no credit cards

Location
40-minute car/passenger ferry
from Redland Bay, which is 40
minutes or 40km from Brisbane.
Map 8.

Minimum stay
Two nights

Facilities
One house: three bedrooms (two
queen and one king/twin singles),
open-plan lounge (plasma TV,
DVD, CD), dining and kitchen.
Deck (BBQ), laundry.

Other
Suitable for children

Owner details
Debbie and Paul Wybrow
▪ debwybrow@gmail.com
▪ www.sunsetwaters.net

Tangalooma Beach Houses

Moreton Island (near Brisbane)

Location on enquiry, Moreton Island ▪ 0438 446 136
www.beautifulaccommodation.com/tangalooma

Rates
Whole house per night from
$600-$850 (up to 10 guests)
Accommodation only
PayPal, no credit cards

Location
One-hour ferry from Brisbane.
Map 8 and 9.

Facilities
A range of beach houses, each
accommodating up to 10 people.
All with lounges (TV, DVD, CD),
balconies, kitchen, two or three
bathrooms. Laundry.

Other
Suitable for children

Host details
Shaaryn and David Griffiths
▪ enquiries@tangalooma
beachhouse.com.au
▪ www.tangalooma
beachhouse.com.au

Spacious beach houses

Sometimes it's hard to imagine places like the gorgeous Tangalooma Beach Houses exist, beyond the freeways, traffic jams and stresses of city life. But they do – right here on magical Moreton Island.

The bright sea shines through every window, the calls of seabirds echo across the waters and you can hear the splash of dolphins happily following schools of fish. As day after wonderful day rolls past at Tangalooma, this alluring setting soon becomes your world.

The Tangalooma Beach Houses are perfect for large groups or family gatherings. Each can comfortably sleep eight to 10 guests, with separate living zones so that kids and adults can enjoyably pursue their own activities. Large all-weather beachside decks are ideal for long leisurely lunches that stretch into the evenings. The views from the decks are stunning and kids can play on the beach in full view of the houses.

You can scuba dive, snorkel and swim in the warm, clear blue waters. Sometimes you can watch as wild dolphins are fed and everyone will enjoy the rock pool walks, fishing, sand dune tobogganing and nature trails.

Moreton Island's charming lighthouse (the oldest in Queensland) and Blue Lagoon provide postcard-perfect photo opportunities.

Thistledown Country Retreat

Barney View (near Rathdowney)

'Roseland' 68 Harper Rd, Barney View ▪ 07 5544 3232
www.beautifulaccommodation.com/thistledown

Stunning country retreat

This gorgeous Barney View estate relishes its vista of verdant green, framed by the grandeur of Mount Barney. But the real treasure for guests lies within Thistledown's magnificently appointed spaces.

The elegant Roseland Homestead blends traditional Queenslander style with French provincial charm. Its charming gardens and secluded courtyard provide a peaceful setting for the Homestead and its two romantic guest rooms.

Tucked away in private gardens is the tranquil Thistledown Cottage, which is fully self-contained with a spa bathroom, cosy fire-lit lounge,

dreamy bedrooms and a scenery-soaked rear deck.

We suggest coming with a group of friends, or as a couple, and indulging in a grand hosted dinner. Dress up in your finest for an evening of candlelit silver service, and stunning food and wine.

Breakfast is served for all guests and casual dining options are available in the cottage, courtyard or outdoors in the superb gardens. With such a peaceful and restorative setting, the hosts have also made this the ideal place for life-coaching and residential retreats.

Rates
Homestead room per couple from $165-$185
Cottage per couple from $200-$250 (extra guests $35 per night)
Full breakfast included, dinner by prior arrangement
Direct deposit, no credit cards

Location
1½ hours or 110km south of Brisbane. Map 7.

Minimum stay
Two nights at weekends (cottage)

Facilities
One cottage with two bedrooms (double and twin singles), lounge (wood fire), kitchen and spa bathroom. Two Homestead rooms (queen, double). Breakfast room, lounge (wood fire), and grand dining room.

Host details
Micheline and John Guy
▪ info@thistledown
countryretreat.com.au
▪ www.thistledown
countryretreat.com.au

Barney Creek Vineyard Cottages
Rathdowney (near Beaudesert)

Seidenspinner Road, Mt Barney ▪ 07 5544 3285, 0419 737 167
www.beautifulaccommodation.com.au/barneycreek

Rates
Whole cottage per night
from $185-$300
Accommodation only,
meals by prior arrangement
Visa, MC, Eftpos

Location
1¾ hours or 122km south
of Brisbane. Map 7.

Minimum stay
Two nights at weekends

Facilities
Three cottages. Lakeside: queen,
lounge, kitchen, dining nook, spa
bathroom, AC. Garden: three
bedrooms (two queen, one twin
singles), lounge, kitchen, piano.
Hill Station: queen, lounge, spa
bathroom, kitchen. All with wood
fire, DVD, CD. Pool.

Other
Suitable for children (garden
cottage)

Host details
Barry Marshall and Jennifer Seale
▪ info@barneycreekcottages.com
▪ www.barneycreekcottages.com

Wine lovers' cottages

Barney Creek Vineyard Cottages
have only improved since our last visit
and the pristine mountain panorama
is as inspiring as ever.

Barry and Jennifer have worked hard
to make the award-winning Barney
Creek a sustainable and low carbon
emission property. The green theme
continues to the estate winery and
a cornucopic organic veggie garden
that guests are welcome to forage
like an edible library.

There are just three guest pavilions:
the tranquil and reflective Lakeside
cottage; the Hill Station, with its
marvellous views; and the quiet,
scented charm of the Garden

Cottage, which has three bedrooms
and is well-suited to families.

Each is thematically complete,
combining fabric, colour, timber and
stone to make an entirely comfortable
self-contained stay. Each cottage
also enjoys a serene privacy and
individual perspective on the
surrounding 40 acres and beyond.

We suggest ordering up one of
Jennifer's lunch platters or sumptuous
dinner packages, complete with a
selection of the property's organically
fertilised wines. A real treat.

Ocean View Estates Winery

Ocean View

2557 Mount Mee Road, Ocean View ▪ 07 3425 3900
www.beautifulaccommodation.com/oceanview

Tasteful vigneron's estate

As you wander the immaculate grounds of this very pretty estate, don't be surprised if thoughts of holding a vineyard wedding or a white-collar party start to surface in your mind. It happened for us. And why not? All the ingredients are here to turn any ordinary event into an extraordinary celebration of life and love.

There is a functioning winery with its own cellar door, a foodie's restaurant and two cottages for those who are tempted to stay on for a few days.

And what a place to indulge. Take in the pleasant green vistas over the lake with its wooden gazebo and up the distant slopes of budding vines. Then you can relax with a glass or three of estate-grown wine.

The passion that owner-winemaker Thomas Honnef has invested in Ocean View Estates is evident everywhere. Thomas, his wife Kate and their staff clearly love to share their wine, the beautifully matched food and their sublime surrounds with all those who make the scenic drive from Brisbane.

Forget hunting around from winery to winery in search of that perfect combination of food, drink and fun times... It's all here.

Rates
Whole cottage per night from $200-$300 (up to 4 guests) Accommodation only, breakfast by arrangement
Visa, MC, DD, Eftpos

Location
1 hour or 58km north of Brisbane. Map 7.

Facilities
Two cottages: one two-bedroom (queen and double with single upper bunk) and one one-bedroom (queen), lounge (wood fire, TV, DVD, CD, sofa bed), kitchenette, RC AC. Restaurant, cellar door. Lakeside gazebo.

Other
Suitable for children
Restaurant open Thursday to Sunday, or by arrangement
Disabled facilities

Owner details
Kate and Thomas Honnef
▪ info@oceanviewestates.com.au
▪ www.oceanviewestates.com.au

Sunshine Coast
& Hinterland
BRISBANE

Sunshine Coast
& Hinterland

Sun, sea, sand and sailing are catchwords for the Sunshine Coast,
which caters for water babies and landlubbers alike. Here you can
enjoy first-rate shopping and dining, discover amazing marine life,
walk majestic headlands and cycle on a national park oceanway.
In the hinterland, pretty towns dot the hills and valleys, and offer
all kinds of produce and artistic persuits. All this is set within a
landscape of extinct volcanic mountains, inland waterways and
some of Australia's most ecologically diverse state forests.

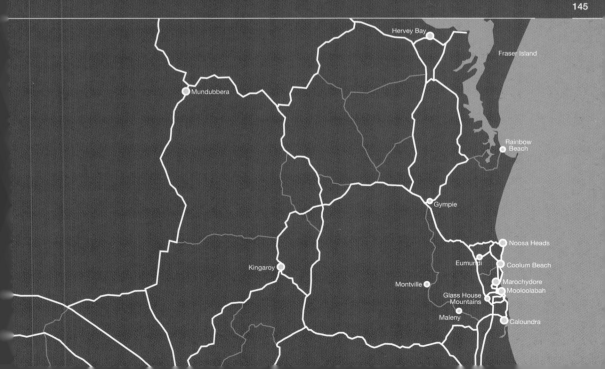

This region is virtually fail-safe for travellers, with more than 300 sunny days a year.

What's in a name?

The region has an ideal climate for being outdoors and loving life. Sunshine? This region is virtually fail-safe for travellers, with more than 300 sunny days a year. In summer, the average temperature ranges from 17 to 29 degrees, and the highs are tempered by sea breezes. Naturally, sunshine and beaches go together and there is an incredible choice here.

Caloundra's beaches are gorgeous stretches of warm sand that beg for a big towel, a sun umbrella and a good book. Surfers worship Moffat Beach for its breaks, but for less ambitious water-lovers there is protected swimming at Toowong lagoon. You can walk along the coastal path to Moffat Headland, with views to Point Cartwright in the north. Cafes with al fresco dining add a cosmopolitan buzz to the Moffat streetscape. Caloundra's markets make for fascinating Sunday excursions to pick through flowers, produce and bric-a-brac treasures.

The marina at Mooloolaba completes a waterfront picture-postcard scene and it is home to a fleet of trawlers. That means there is plenty of fresh seafood for visitors to enjoy at one of the area's sublime picnic spots, along with a bag of hot chips and a bottle of chilled white Stanthorpe wine. The harbour is the finishing point for yacht races from Sydney and Auckland, and it shelters all types of craft.

UnderWater World presents the region's diverse marine life and it is a rehabilitation centre for turtles, dugongs, dolphins and seals. Mooloolaba is a classic Aussie beach town, with sweeping lawns and tall pines in the foreground of a main street lined with shops, galleries, cafes, restaurants and spas.

Coolum has become a golfer's must-play with premier courses such as Mount Coolum and The Hyatt Coolum. Thrillseekers can go skydiving for stupendous views and the rare treat of landing on that extraordinary beach. For land-loving visitors, there are sensational vistas from the ancient volcanic dome of Mount Coolum, said to be the world's

Accredited Visitor Information Centres

Glasshouse Mountains
Cnr Reed Street & Bruce Parade
07 5438 7220
www.sunshinecoastvisit.com.au

Montville
198 Main Road
07 5478 5544
www.sunshinecoastvisit.com.au

Caloundra
77 Bulcock Street
07 5420 8718
www.sunshinecoastvisit.com.au

Mooloolaba
Cnr First Ave & Brisbane Road
07 5478 2233
www.sunshinecoastvisit.com.au

Sunshine Coast Airport
Friendship Avenue
07 5448 9088
www.sunshinecoastvisit.com.au

Coolum Beach
Cnr Tickle Park and David Low Way
07 5446 5910
www.sunshinecoastvisit.com.au

Noosa Heads
61 Hastings Street
07 5430 5000
www.visitnoosa.com.au

largest monolith after Uluru.

Just to the north lies charming Peregian Beach, with its village square of boutiques and cafes, and of course, the beach. Nearby Noosa Heads is becoming something of a world brand with famous Hastings Street running alongside a spectacular beach with azure waters. Visitors can walk, dive, paddle, ride or cycle through exquisite coastal landscapes.

At the top end of the Cooloola Great Sandy National Park, Rainbow Beach draws its name from the intriguing mineral sands. Vehicle ferries connect the town with Fraser Island.

In the Sunshine Coast hinterland, the pretty Blackall Range towns of Montville and Maleny are replete with art galleries, health food and organic produce stores, cafes and alternative therapies. Baroon Pocket Dam is a great base, with a sailing club, naval cadet unit, fishing club, accommodation and picnic facilities.

To the south, the Glass House Mountains are startling lava plug formations in the gently undulating landscape. And in Mary Valley, the town of Imbil is close to Lake Borumba, which is a great spot for swimming, boating, water-skiing and fishing. The Mary Valley Heritage Railway terminates in Imbil and traverses some magnificent valley landscape offering beautiful scenery.

Glass on Glasshouse

Glass House Mountains

182 Glass House-Woodford Road, Glass House Mountains ▪ 07 5496 9608, 0431 101 208
www.beautifulaccommodation.com/glassonglasshouse

Rates
Whole cottage per couple
from $250-$395 (extra guests
$70 per night)
Full breakfast provisions included
Visa, MC, DD, Eftpos

Location
50 minutes or 68km north of
Brisbane. Map 9.

Minimum stay
Two nights at weekends

Facilities
Three glass houses: one king
bedroom, spa bathroom, lounge
(LCD HD TV, DVD, entertainment
system, iPod dock, fire), kitchen
(espresso machine), WiFi, laundry.
RC AC, fans.

AAA Star Rating
★★★★☆

Other
Cafe open daytime, Wed-Sun

Owner details
Bill and Misao Rogers
▪ info@glassonglasshouse.com.au
▪ www.glassonglasshouse.com.au

Über modern rural retreat

A Bauhaus sensibility meets the Glass House mountains in this setting of utter tranquillity and über sophistication. The three Glass on Glasshouse cottages, designed by national award-winning architect Norman Richards, combine a location of extraordinary beauty – looking across to the 25-million-year-old volcanic cores of the Glass House mountains – with an unreservedly contemporary architectural genius.

Every room takes advantage of the brilliant views and is in harmony with the overall design. The floor-to-ceiling glass walls give these cottages a wow factor, dissolving the barrier between inside and outside.

The lighting is a feature, drenching selected spaces in a warm glow, and we love the incredible bathroom with its waterfall spa.

A true eco fireplace, which runs on ethanol from the nearby sugar cane fields, completes the integration of location with environmental consciousness. Kangaroos, wallabies and black cockatoos live their lives around you.

Cook for yourself, visit a local country pub or enjoy fine dining 25 minutes away. The world-renowned Australia Zoo is a 10-minute drive.

Mooloolah Valley Holiday Houses

Mooloolah Valley (near Caloundra)

93 King Road, Mooloolah Valley ▪ 07 5494 7109, 0408 224 668
www.beautifulaccommodation.com/mooloolah

Fantastical hippy hideout

Zany, delightful, warm, generous, stylish… that is the incredible spirit of Mooloolah Valley Holiday Houses and it flows straight from host Atalanta Moreau. We believe the best holiday accommodation reflects the passion and energy of the hosts, and that has never been truer than here.

With the new Piccaninny cottage, there are now three glorious timber-lined, hippy-happy, lead-lighted places on offer.

Their style is as eclectic as Atalanta herself, complete with brassy bedsteads, cow hide coverings, saddles on the ceiling, mosaic mermaids and serpents in the bathroom, hide-away lofts, and garden spas.

By some mystical alchemy, these elements come together to make a unified whole that is entirely charming and utterly comfortable. The place really sings when a group of families or old friends hire the lot and make its pool and terrace (complete with pizza oven and hide-and-seek gardens) their private playground.

The local area is full of activities including rainforest walks, picnic spots, horse riding, the Australia Zoo and the Chenrezig Buddhist monastery.

Rates
Whole house/cottage per night from $175-$375
Accommodation only, provisions and catering by prior arrangement
Visa, MC, DD

Location
70 minutes or 100km north of Brisbane. Map 9.

Minimum stay
Two nights

Facilities
Frangipani House (lounge, dining, fireplace, kitchen, spiral staircase, two double bedrooms, two singles and one cot). Jacaranda and Piccaninny cottages (lounge/dining, double and single beds, wood fire, kitchen). Outdoor spa, heated pool, pizza oven, BBQ.

Other
Suitable for children
Pets by arrangement

Host details
Atalanta Moreau
▪ info@mooloolahvalley.com
▪ www.mooloolahvalley.com

Bendles Cottages
Maleny

937 Montville-Maleny Road, Maleny ▪ 07 5494 2400
www.beautifulaccommodation.com/bendles

Rates
Whole cottage per couple
from $195-$285
Breakfast included (full, Sat-Mon;
continental Tue-Thu), platters and
hampers by arrangement
Visa, MC, DD, Eftpos

Location
1¼ or 92km hours north of
Brisbane. Map 9.

Minimum stay
Two nights at weekends, three
nights over public holidays

Facilities
Five cottages: each with queen
bed, lounge (wood fire, TV, DVD,
CD), spa bathroom, kitchenette,
verandah. Serviced daily. BBQ,
tennis court, gazebo.

Member
BBFAA

Host details
Tony and June Allison
▪ admin@bendles.com.au
▪ www.bendles.com.au

Garden of delights

The whole setting at Bendles
Cottages sighs of romance, discreet
trysts in the lush gardens and long
lazy afternoons sprawled across crisp
sheets. From the moment you pass
through the gorgeous old arched
bower out the front, you are entering
a princely garden of earthly delights.

The garden and cottages may be
set in the rustic paradise of Maleny
but the minute attention to the little
details of comfort will appeal to
urban sophisticates.

Your very private cottage has
scrumptious homemade cookies
baked and waiting for you. There is
a decanter of fine port to sip as you
sit on your balcony overlooking the
grotto gardens and sweeping lawns.

The breakfast, with treats like smoked
salmon and scrambled eggs, is
delivered to your hideaway on
Saturday, Sunday and Monday
mornings. During the week, you
receive continental breakfast goodies
to prepare at your leisure. The
balcony is a perfect breakfast nook.
Tennis anyone? Step out onto the
court if you're feeling active.

The hosts are only there as you need
them: to chauffeur you into town and
back for a meal at a local restaurant
(they'll tell you which ones are the
best) and to provide the daily
servicing of your cottage. This is a
perfectly presented, immaculately
maintained sanctuary.

Half Moon Hideaway
Maleny

599 Mountain View Road, Maleny ▪ 07 5494 3718
www.beautifulaccommodation.com/halfmoonhideaway

Family country hospitality

Here's the potted review of Half Moon Hideaway from our travelling notebook: "Very generous, stylish and excites all the senses… loved the dress circle views!" Clearly this property made an impression.

It is one of the great new finds of this edition. The hosts pay incredible attention to the details of comfort, such as sumptuous welcome hampers, full of wine, chocolates, cheeses, gorgeous soaps and more. They even have special guest dog hampers, which are full of treats, towels and a tennis ball, plus there are choccie frogs on the kids' pillows.

A refined style and generosity of spirit extends to every corner of the house.

The spa bathroom pavilion is country Australian but with a Japanese aesthetic sensibility. The bedrooms continue the unadorned simplicity and you need nothing more with the astounding Glass House Mountains vista from every window.

This is a great family stay. When the kids are not playing with the house toys or exploring the bedroom loft, they are welcome to visit the stables and collect farm eggs with the hosts. Meanwhile, grown-ups will welcome the chance to sit back in wonder at the panoramic views over the lake to the mountains beyond.

Rates
Whole cottage per night from $250-$320 (up to 2 guests, extra guests $10 per night)
Full breakfast provisions included
Visa, MC, DD, Eftpos

Location
1¼ hours or 92km or north of Brisbane. Map 9.

Minimum stay
Two nights

Facilities
One cottage with three pavilions: sleeping, with two bedrooms (queen and twin singles and loft with single); living (lounge with wood fire, TV, DVD, CD; dining, kitchen); bathing (spa). Deck.

Other
Suitable for children
Pets welcome

Host details
Gillian Leigh
▪ gillian@halfmoonhideaway.com
▪ www.halfmoonhideaway.com

Lillypilly's Country Cottages
Maleny

584 Maleny-Montville Road, Maleny ▪ 07 5494 3002
www.beautifulaccommodation.com/lillypillys

Rates
Whole cottage per night
from $209-$330
Full breakfast included, dinner
by arrangement
Visa, MC, AMEX, DC, Eftpos

Location
80 minutes or 100km north of
Brisbane. Map 9.

Minimum stay
Two nights at weekends

Facilities
Five cottages (queen bed,
kitchenette, lounge with fireplace,
DVD, CD, spa alcove, private
balcony). Pool. Massage available.

AAA Star Rating
★★★★☆

Member
BBFAA

Host details
Josef and Adele Gruber
▪ lillypillys@bigpond.com
▪ www.lillypillys.com.au

Gourmet mountain retreat

Some places just have it – the
sensual combination of style,
location, food and a genuine focus
on the guest's experience. Lillypilly's
is one of those places.

We think Lillypilly's works so well
because, as always, it comes down
to the people who run it. Josef
Gruber was a leading executive chef
at major Sydney hotels for more than
12 years and Adele is a sought-after
masseuse.

But we won't start with the fabulous
food and therapeutic touch you can
enjoy here. It is the five elegant
cottages that enthralled us with their
spellbinding views over Lake Baroon
and the Blackall Ranges.

Reclining in the spa alcove after
arrival with some of Josef's piping
hot scones, a pot of tea and the
sound of bird calls rising from the
ranges is a near-spiritual experience.
The self-contained cottages are
beautifully proportioned and
dressed with restful fabrics, hues
and timberwork.

The cottages make the perfect
setting for one of Josef's masterchef
presentations of progressive dining,
each course delivered in sequence
to the romantic privacy of your
cottage. The breast of free-range
chicken stuffed with herbs and pine
nuts, served with corn bread
and a *jus lie* is just one temptation.

Top of the Hill
Maleny

11 Hovard Road, Maleny ▪ 07 5494 3680
www.beautifulaccommodation.com/topofthehill

Hilltop foodie haven

Sometimes you just want to pack up the bags and get away to a place where it's all taken care of – from the gourmet meal at night to the full breakfast in the morning. But this special place must also lift the soul with its beauty, say, set atop a valley of drifting morning mists and flaring sunsets. We have found it near Maleny at Top of the Hill.

Food glorious food is central to the Top of the Hill experience. There are just six guest bungalows but the retreat has a commercial kitchen that serves a delectable Mediterranean menu against the stunning valley backdrop.

Groups of up to 45 love the combination of a unique setting and memorable gourmet pizzas from the wood-fired oven. BYO is fine (and they don't charge corkage). The terraced gardens are alive with birds and make for great breakout spots.

But we think couples who long to escape the rigours of family life and reconnect for a few pampered nights will most enjoy the Top of the Hill's full-service ethic. And everyone will love the bungalows for their serene vistas, best viewed from the bubbling comfort of your spa's sky window. Delicious.

Rates
Whole cabin per night per couple from $275-$370 (extra guests $125 per night)
Dinner and full breakfast included
Visa, MC, Eftpos

Location
1¼ hours or 92km north of Brisbane. Map 9.

Facilities
Six cabins: each with queen bed (two also with sofa bed), LCD TV, DVD/CD, spa, RC AC. Guest lounge and bar (gas fire), dining room, media room. Undercover entertaining area and deck (wood-fired pizza oven).

Host details
John and Gwenda
▪ getaway@topofthehill.com.au
▪ www.topofthehill.com.au

Spicy Oasis
Maleny (Curramore)

964 Kidaman Creek Road, Curramore ▪ 07 5435 8380, 0417 706 286
www.beautifulaccommodation.com/spicyoasis

Rates
Whole cottage per night
from $173-$257
Full breakfast provisions included,
picnic and BBQ packs available
Visa, MC, DD

Location
1¼ hours or 92km north of
Brisbane. Map 9.

Minimum stay
Two nights at weekends preferred

Facilities
Three villas: one with two queen
bedrooms; two open-plan villas
with one queen bed. All with
lounge (fire, TV, DVD/CD), dining,
kitchenette, ensuite (spa), BBQ.

Owner details
Irena Kalinacova and Tony Koda
▪ relax@spicyoasis.com.au
▪ www.spicyoasis.com.au

Grand Mediterranean glam

Picture yourself cresting a ridge
and finding below you a scene
from paradise: a secret valley
surrounding a shimmering lake, and
its shores are dotted with three villas
straight from the Arabian Nights.
Welcome to Spicy Oasis, a refuge
from the tribulations of city life in the
undulating beauty of Maleny.

The timeless sophistication of
Moroccan, Greek and Spanish
architectural styles inspired Irena
Kalinacova and partner Tony Koda
as they designed Spicy Oasis. A cool
Mediterranean ambience suffuses
every element of these grand villas,
from the original tiles in the bathrooms
to the recycled interior timbers and
gleaming whitewashed walls.

Tony and Irena are also respected
local natural therapists, providing
remedial massage and other
rejuvenating bodywork. It all makes
a perfect setting for a girls' getaway,
small wedding or couples' retreat.

The breezy, open-plan spaces have
all you need for a cosy stay, and you'll
find a brimming basket of breakfast
provisions ready for the morning.

Nearby Maleny provides a groovy
shopping and eating experience.
There are also cellar doors and
breathtaking picnic and walking
locations throughout the district.

Montville Country Cabins
Montville

396 Western Avenue, Montville ▪ 07 5442 9484
www.beautifulaccommodation.com/montvillecabins

Serene valley escape

Welcome to a natural amphitheatre that has as its focal point one of the most enchanting private lakes we have come across. In this gorgeous setting, nine charming cottages are sheltered within the manicured gardens, each with views over sweeping lawns down to the lake or across verdant rainforest.

The cottages each have their own character in various combinations, and guests can count on polished floors, a wood fire, spa bath, full kitchen and lovely views. You can also relax to the sound of rain on the roof even when it's not raining. Intrigued yet?

It's all thanks to a coin-operated eco-friendly rain-on-rooftop effect you can conjure at any time – instant romance on demand that will amuse the kids and also lull lovers to sleep.

Montville village is nearby for dining and shopping, and there are lots of craft shops and galleries to browse. Sumptuous seafood platters and barbecue hampers are available for those who want to stay in and indulge. With such a marvellous setting, accommodation and lakeside aspect, this is also a magical spot for intimate weddings.

Rates
Room per couple from $240-$300 (extra guests $55 per night; children over 6 years, $25) Continental breakfast provisions included, hampers available Visa, MC, AMEX, DD, Eftpos

Location
90 minutes or 116km north of Brisbane. Map 9.

Facilities
Nine cabins: each with king or queen bed (three also with queen sofa bed and two single beds), lounge (wood fire, TV, DVD, iPod dock), dining, kitchen, spa, BBQ.

Minimum stay
Two nights at weekends

Other
Suitable for children

Owner details
Christine and Anton Kardash
▪ info@montvillecabins.com.au
▪ www.montvillecabins.com.au

The Narrows Escape
Montville

78 Narrows Road, Montville ▪ 07 5478 5000
www.beautifulaccommodation.com/thenarrows

Rates
Cottage per couple from $260-$330
(extra guests $65 per night)
Full breakfast provisions included,
dinner provisions by arrangement
Visa, MC, DD, Eftpos, Chq

Location
1¼ hours or 99km north of Brisbane.
Map 9.

Minimum stay
Two nights at weekends

Facilities
Six one-bedroom cottages: five
with queen bed, one with king/
twin singles), open-plan dining/
kitchen/lounge (fire, spa, LCD TV,
DVD, CD, iPod dock). Deck (BBQ,
hammock), RC AC. Pool.

AAA Star Rating
★★★★☆

Member
Accommodation Association of
Australia, BBFQ

Host details
Joanne and Mark Skinner
▪ reception@narrowsescape.com.au
▪ www.narrowsescape.com.au

Stunning rainforest reverie

Any trip to Queensland inevitably
includes a rainforest tour as a sensory
highlight: the myriad shades of green
flickering in the immense quiet, the
secretive marsupials and the vague
scent of lemon and gum. At The
Narrows Escape you can go one
step further and stay in the midst
of a private forest valley.

Your personal rainforest tour begins
as you sip a complimentary aperitif
on the balcony hammock, listening to
the distant fall of water from the creek
that cuts through the valley. But this
highly commended property – a
leader in its area on *TripAdvisor* –
is anything but a bush camp.

Hosts Joanne and Mark Skinner have
gleaned the best bits from their own
five-star travels and applied them
here. There are cosy robes to slip
into, vast spa baths placed so you
can soak up the views, and endless
little treats, creams and soaps to test
and try. Romance and generosity of
spirit are on show everywhere.

The Skinners can organise day trips
to fabulous Fraser Island or lunch
and tastings at the famous Flame Hill
winery. This is a richly rewarding
eco-travel experience.

The Spotted Chook Ferme Auberge and Amelie's

Montville

176 Western Avenue, Montville ■ 07 5442 9242
www.beautifulaccommodation.com/thespottedchook

157

French provincial charmer

Hosts Jane and Leeroy's love affair with each other and provincial France began many years ago. Their time spent cycling through the French countryside has paid off in wonderful style and panache at The Spotted Chook and Amelie's. Perhaps that is why they have come to specialise in intimate wedding parties of fewer than 50 guests. Love is in the air here.

The sensual experience of a French country inn pervades every corner, from the vases of fresh roses to the frankly glamorous use of colour in each guest room. We think the Snowpea could have even inspired van Gogh during his Arles period.

The four rooms in The Spotted Chook guesthouse are immaculately presented and each has its own discrete charm including a big, deep bath and private verandah. The separate cottage, Amelie's, is a decadent treat that might have been designed just for you and your *amour*.

Food is never far from French thoughts. As part of this experience, we recommend pre-booking a dinner featuring a French-Australian fusion of tastes. This is gourmet cuisine served with passion. *Magnifique*!

Rates
Room per couple from $190-$270
Cottage per night from 290-$320
Continental breakfast included, full breakfast available
Visa, MC, AMEX, DC, DD, Eftpos

Location
1.5 hours or 116km north of Brisbane. Map 9.

Minimum stay
Two nights (cottage), two nights at weekends (guesthouse)

Facilities
Guesthouse: four ensuite rooms with AC, most with claw-foot bath and fire. Guest lounge, dining. Cottage: lounge/dining, king, kitchen, deck, double spa. AC.

AAA Star Rating
★★★★☆

Member
BBFAA

Other
Disabled facilities (Amelie's)

Host details
Jane and Leeroy Hutton
■ info@spottedchook.com.au
■ www.spottedchook.com.au

The Queen

Moffat Beach (near Caloundra)

19 Queen Of Colonies Parade, Moffat Beach ▪ 0417 775 918
www.beautifulaccommodation.com/thequeen

Rates
Whole house per night from
$269-$625 (up to 8 guests)
Accommodation only
Direct deposit or cheque,
no credit cards

Location
65 minutes or 94km or north of
Brisbane. Map 9.

Minimum stay
Three to seven nights (seasonal)

Facilities
Four bedrooms (one king with
ensuite, three king/twin singles).
Open-plan lounge/dining (LCD TV,
DVD, wood fire), kitchen, second
bathroom, outdoor covered
entertainment/living (BBQ,
kitchenette, outdoor bathroom,
laundry facilities). Fans.

Other
Suitable for children

Owner details
Brioney and Charles Kirby
▪ enquiries@thequeen.com.au
▪ www.thequeen.com.au

Clifftop ocean-view beach house

Many properties have regal
pretensions but few fulfil them as
extravagantly as The Queen. The
makeover of this quietly sumptuous
family home has turned it into a
breezy pleasure palace for families
and friends who want space, style
and a dazzling coastal panorama.

The location can't be outdone. Five
generations of the same family have
enjoyed this superb hilltop site near
Caloundra, where they camped
out before building The Queen in
the 1950s.

The northern aspect worships the
warm Queensland sun and it's only
a short stroll to the quiet, toddler-
friendly waters of Two Way Lake
and Moffat Beach.

The design just begs its lucky guests
to sit, eat, relax and talk. We love the
entertainment terrace, which is
devoted to the supreme holiday acts
of feasting and socialising. But there
are also plenty of nooks and
balconies to escape to for reading,
contemplating the vista or a quiet
afternoon nap. The comfy bedrooms
are tastefully completed in chocolate,
cream and white.

Down the street are cafes, a great
gelato stop and a traditional fish
and chippery.

Oceans Mooloolaba Beach
Mooloolaba

101-105 Mooloolaba Esplanade, Mooloolaba ▪ 07 5444 5777
www.beautifulaccommodation.com/oceansmooloolaba

Luxury seaside resort

With a bustling shopping strip, fab food and a brilliant beach, Mooloolaba is quickly becoming the 'it' destination for lovers of seaside glamour. And if you like your glam upmarket, Oceans Mooloolaba Beach, which was developed by luxury apartment leaders Juniper, has blossomed into one of the standard-setting resorts on the Sunshine Coast.

Every apartment and penthouse shares equally in the sweeping ocean views. All are superbly appointed with full marble bathrooms, luxury fittings and the finest furnishings and linens.

With a choice of two-, three- and four-bedroom apartments or penthouses, and some special extras (a wading pool for the kids, movie theatrette for the grown-ups), Oceans is a magnet for tired families in need of a break or groups with a special occasion to celebrate.

The location can't be bettered. Oceans is right on Mooloolaba Esplanade with the galleries, restaurants, boutiques and shopping all laid out below the apartments.

Nearby attractions include Eumundi Markets and Australia Zoo. This is the ultimate beach pad: surrounded in luxury, spoilt with beaches and immersed in Queensland sunshine.

Rates
Whole apartment/penthouse per night from $550-$2000
Accommodation only
Visa, MC, AMEX, DC, DD, Eftpos

Location
1 hour or 97km north of Brisbane. Map 9.

Minimum stay
Two to seven nights (seasonal)

Facilities
29 apartments and penthouses: each with two, three or four bedrooms, open-plan lounge, dining and gourmet kitchen. Daily servicing, 25m heated lap pool, spa, children's wading pool, gym, steam room, private cinema.

AAA Star Rating
★★★★★

Other
Suitable for children

Manager details
▪ stay@oceansmooloolaba.com.au
▪ www.oceansmooloolaba.com.au

Element on Coolum Beach

Coolum Beach

1808 David Low Way, Coolum Beach ▪ 07 5455 1777
www.beautifulaccommodation.com/elementoncoolum

Rates
Whole apartment per night
from $139-$499
Sub-penthouse per night
from $249-$749
Accommodation only
Visa, MC, DD, Eftpos

Minimum stay
Two nights at weekends

Location
1¼ hours or 117km north of
Brisbane. Map 9.

Facilities
Apartments and sub-penthouses:
one to three bedrooms, living (TV,
DVD, CD), dining, kitchen, laundry.
Pool, BBQ, day spa.

AAA Star Rating
★★★★☆

Other
Suitable for children

Resident Manager details
Geoff and Tamara Hussin
▪ stay@elementon
coolumbeach.com.au
▪ www.elementon
coolumbeach.com.au

Relaxed high-contemporary style

It's okay to feel smugly self-satisfied as you stroll back from a morning on superb Coolum Beach to your apartment in Element On Coolum. You're heading into one of the most elegant, best-designed holiday retreats anywhere along the coast from Brisbane to Cairns. As you head upstairs, grab a latte from one of the cafes on the ground floor and relax in true style.

The living is open-plan and all too easy at Element, which offers a complete range of stay options from sub-penthouses to apartments with one to three bedrooms. The design has a cool, coastal sophistication that is at once relaxing and unrepentedly modern.

All the mod-cons families want are here, from big plasma TVs connected to cable, to full laundry facilities, a huge heated in-ground pool and lift access to all apartments from secure undercover parking. You can even get apartments with their own private media rooms. Plus, there is also a day spa for those seeking some further indulgence (see page 274).

You hardly need to move to get a good feed. The acclaimed Harvest restaurant, which draws hungry gourmets from up and down the coast, is on your doorstep. Surfers in particular will love the range of waves nearby, including the world-renowned break at Yaroomba.

Malibu Luxury Beach House
Coolum Beach

13 Malibu Avenue, Coolum Beach ▪ 0404 044 866
www.beautifulaccommodation.com/malibu

Pet-friendly paradise

It is little wonder that most guests at Malibu Luxury Beach House hardly bother to leave the precinct of this marvellous property. Why would you? Nothing has been overlooked to make this a private haven of luxurious design and absolute comfort.

Malibu has a fabulously liveable design that combines contemporary style with indigenous arts. We were simply awe-struck by the immense carved wooden totem poles that were crafted in a Papuan village especially for this house.

Granite and marble are also superbly used throughout the property, which reflects its owners' world journeys.

The entertainment deck not only features a wraparound pool and spa, but everything you could possibly need for the perfect barbecue. You can even pipe your music mix from the iPod dock to anywhere in the house, including the deck, using the fully integrated sound system.

And the real surprise at this amazing house? This is one of those rare rental properties that welcome pets as much as their owners in five-star style. Families with beloved dogs will love this place.

Rates
Whole house per night from $306-$900 (up to 8 guests)
Accommodation only
Direct deposit, no credit cards

Location
1¼ hours or 117km north of Brisbane. Map 9.

Minimum stay
Seven nights (Sat to Sat only)

Facilities
Three bedrooms (king, king/twin singles, two twin singles with trundles, all with TV/DVD), dining, kitchen, lounge (TV, Austar, entertainment systems, iPod dock), two bathrooms, outdoor entertaining (BBQ, kitchenette), laundry, study, WiFi. Pool.

Other
Suitable for children
Pets welcome

Owner details
Maureen and Richard West
▪ maureen@pethols.com.au
▪ www.pethols.com.au

Noosa Holiday House

Castaways Beach (near Noosa)

16 Tropicana Rise, Castaways Beach ▪ 0418 588 631
www.beautifulaccommodation.com/noosaholidayhouse

Rates
Whole house per night from
$430-$800 (up to 6 guests)
Accommodation only
Visa, MC, DD

Location
90 minutes or 137km north of
Brisbane. Map 9.

Minimum stay
Five to seven nights (seasonal)

Facilities
One house: three bedrooms
(one king with ensuite, two with
king or twin singles), open-plan
kitchen/dining/living (TV,
DVD, CD, Austar, iPod dock,
movie library), sheltered outdoor
entertainment area (BBQ), three
bathrooms, laundry, pool.

Other
Dogs welcome

Owner details
Judith and Mario Taverniti
▪ holidays@tavco.com.au
▪ www.tavco.com.au

Modern Mediterranean beachsider

You feel glamorous just walking
into this sparkling white ocean-view
beach house. Yes, you really are
staying here in one of the smartest
properties at Castaways Beach.
Noosa Holiday House – the name
says it all, really – is a pristine
architectural statement about
the contemporary beach holiday.

Inside, modern and indigenous art
adorns the walls and every room
looks over Castaways Beach (a real
find in the Noosa area) to the blue
sea beyond. Nothing has been
forgotten from big plasma TVs to the
cosily sheltered entertainment deck
and solar-heated pool.

The master bedroom has a
commanding view with its own
private balcony; slip up there for a
sundowner or to spot the whales
passing by in season. You can even
bring the family pooch along, which
is a rare treat in such an impeccably
presented beach home.

Despite the evocative name,
Castaways Beach is only a few
minutes' drive from the best
restaurants and shopping in exclusive
Noosa and Sunshine Beach. This is
a perfect choice for a sedate and
luxurious beachside encounter for
up to six.

The Retreat Beach Houses

Peregian Beach (near Noosa)

390 David Low Way, Peregian Beach ▪ 07 5448 1922
www.beautifulaccommodation.com/retreatbeachhouses

Beachside resort bliss

Strolling back to The Retreat Beach Houses along the sand from nearby Peregian Beach village is what the perfect seaside holiday is all about. With scrumptious morning treats and coffees from the fabulous Baked Poets bakery and newspapers in-hand, a day of sun, fun and luxurious relaxation stretches ahead of you. Eat, swim, read, nap, enjoy.

The Retreat Beach Houses are right on a pristine beach with no road to cross. There is a huge stretch of golden sand, lapping waves and no crowds. Nearby Peregian has lifesavers to keep an eye on those in the water.

Each beach house design is flexible, accommodating couples or up to six family members and friends. Naturally, every beach house has a gloriously tropical Queensland ambience, with wooden louvers and lovely decks overlooking the immaculately maintained gardens.

Everything you need for simple holiday pleasures is here including a tennis court, heated lagoon pool and barbecues for evening get-togethers. We love how the local village has blossomed with some great restaurants and boutiques for retail therapy.

Rates
Beach house per night from
$165-$465 (up to 6 guests)
Accommodation only
Visa, MC, DD, Eftpos

Location
1½ hours or 127km north of
Brisbane. Map 9.

Minimum stay
Two nights

Facilities
One-, two-, and three-bedroom, two-storey beach houses, all with living (TV, Austar, DVD, CD), dining, kitchen, two bathrooms, laundry, two decks. Pool. Tennis court, BBQs, parking, tour desk.

AAA Star Rating
★★★★☆

Other
Suitable for children

Resident manager details
Maria Albiez
▪ info@theretreat.com.au
▪ www.theretreat.com.au

Lake Weyba Cottages Noosa

Peregian Beach (near Noosa)

79 Clarendon Road, Peregian Beach ▪ 07 5448 2285
www.beautifulaccommodation.com/lakeweybacottages

Rates
Whole cottage/pavilion per night
from $280-$415
Full breakfast provisions included,
dinner and catering available
Visa, MC, AMEX, Eftpos, Chq

Location
1½ hours or 133km north of
Brisbane. Map 9.

Minimum stay
Two nights at weekends

Facilities
Seven spa cottages (kitchen,
lounge, wood fire, king or queen
bed, DVD and surround sound
theatre, AC); one luxury pavilion
with two bedrooms.

AAA Star Rating
★★★★☆ and ★★★★★

Host details
Philip Bown
▪ info@lakeweybacottages.com
▪ www.lakeweybacottages.com

Lakeside retreat for adults

Lake Weyba Cottages Noosa is a
thoroughly charming escape for those
who need time away from kids and
the 'big smoke'. It has made a name
for itself as a venue for intimate
weddings and as a bonding spot for
groups of friends and couples. And
why not? The Lake Weyba location
is stunning with 20 acres of lakefront
grounds, swimming lagoons and
the odd wallaby grazing contentedly.

The luxurious centrepiece here is
the five-star Pavilion, a scrupulously
indulgent, two-bedroom beauty that
fronts its own private lily pond.
Inside is an enchanting interior with
canopied king beds, a vast open-plan
lounge, which leads to the all-weather

verandah, as well as a gourmet
kitchen and home theatre. Don't be
surprised to find a guest bag with
hand-rolled chocolates and other
goodies awaiting you.

The other seven guest cottages are
cosy little enclaves of privacy
surrounded by their own bush
havens. We love the corner spas and
the toasty fireplaces to warm lovers'
hearts in the evening.

Take time to explore the local area.
Lovely Peregian beach is a five-
minute drive and you are only 10
minutes away from the temptations
of Noosa.

Eumarella Shores Noosa Lake Retreat

Weyba Downs (near Noosa)

251 Eumarella Road, Weyba Downs ▪ 07 5449 1738
www.beautifulaccommodation.com/eumarellashores

Contemporary lakeside swish

The absolute lakefront Eumarella Shores Noosa Lake Retreat has long been a favourite of ours. Its lakehouses are coolly contemporary in their colouring, fabrics and architectural unity with the surrounding Nature Reserve and the cottages simply ooze country charm.

Since we last visited, the property has gained the astonishing new Lake Pavilion 'Gooloowaa' ('moonlight' in the local Indigenous language). Gooloowaa brings a new level of sophistication to the Retreat, whether you take it as the ultimate pad for up to six people, or envisage its space

as somewhere to cater for a stellar function, including boutique weddings or other celebrations.

It has absolute waterfrontage to Lake Weyba, which provides a perfect backdrop to the huge and intelligently integrated lounge, dining and deck areas.

There is plenty to do at Eumarella including free use of watercraft, barbecues by the lake or fishing trips and bike rides, with bikes available for hire here. It's a great stay for kids, couples and celebratory groups alike.

Rates
Cottage per night from $180-$579 (2 guests, extra from $65 per night) Full breakfast provisions included (first two days), dinner available
Visa, MC, DC, DD, Eftpos, Chq

Location
1¾ hours or 130km north of Brisbane. Map 9.

Minimum stay
Two nights

Facilities
Six Lakehouses, three Lakefront Cottages (two bedrooms, some with spa), one Lake Pavilion (three bedrooms, two with double spa). Lounge (sofa bed, fire, TV, DVD, CD), dining, kitchen. BBQ, laundry.

Member
BBFAA

Other
Suitable for children
Disabled facilities

Host details
Christine and Bill Tainsh
▪ stay@eumarellashores.com.au
▪ www.eumarellashores.com.au

Castaway Cove Resort Noosa

Marcus Beach (near Noosa)

528 David Low Way, Marcus Beach ▪ 07 5474 8890
www.beautifulaccommodation.com/castawaycove

Rates
Whole apartment, penthouse,
villa or beach house per couple
from $155-$470 (extra guests
$25 per night)
Accommodation only
Visa, MC, DD, Eftpos

Location
90 minutes or 127km north of
Brisbane. Map 9.

Minimum stay
Two to seven nights (seasonal)

Facilities
Apartments, penthouses, villas
and beach houses: kitchen,
lounge/dining (Austar TV, DVD/
CD/VCR), laundry; most with RC
AC, spa. BBQ, pool, tennis, BBQ.

AAA Star Rating
★★★★☆

Other
Suitable for children

Resident Manager details
Glen and Annamarie Toyer
▪ relax@castawaycove.com.au
▪ www.castawaycove.com.

Absolute beachfront beauty

We love the accommodation options
available at Castaway Cove Resort.
Everyone will find a place to suit their
individual needs, from families and
groups of friends looking for a relaxed
beachside holiday to honeymooners
in need of some quiet privacy. You
can choose from the secluded
heights of the penthouses and
apartments to villas or beach houses.

But one thing that every guest at
Castaway loves is the absolute
beachfront – there is no passing
parade of cars between the resort
and golden sands. Just immerse
yourself in the peace, quiet and
gentle sounds of the waves below.

The beachhouses really deserve their
own review here: they are big (up to
four bedrooms), spacious and filled
with everything you need, from air
conditioning and dishwashers to
private barbecue facilities.

Elements such as polished timber
flooring highlight contemporary styling
combined with seaside holiday
practicality.

Noosa is just minutes away,
which makes an easy escape for
a dining experience or retail therapy.
And then you get to retreat back to
the delights of Castaway Cove Resort
with its pool and tennis court.

Maison Noosa
Noosa Heads

5 Hastings Street, Noosa Heads ▪ 1800 604 054, 07 5447 4400
www.beautifulaccommodation.com/maisonnoosa

High-style beach apartments

The complete Noosa experience is right at your doorstep at the fabulously sited Maison Noosa. On one side is the iconic Australian beachside parade of Hastings Street; on the other is the Laguna Bay main beach with waves lapping just metres from Maison's stylish gardens. Swim or coffee? Shop or tan? Just turn left or right and you are there.

It is easy to see why Maison Noosa has become such a favourite among bridal parties: it exudes glamour from every corner, the photo opportunities are endless and there are plenty of room options for guests to unwind in after the celebrations.

The interior finishes are superb, with blonde timberwork, a beautiful use of glass, fabric and leather, plus lovely artworks, beach-friendly floors, gourmet kitchens and chic bathrooms. Lifts service all levels and the grounds are filled with resort-style amenities such as a pool, gym, spa and barbecues.

Noosa, of course, speaks for itself as a tourist magnet. On Hastings Street, you are at the epicentre of the town's relaxed culture, with all the best boutiques, cafes, restaurants and night spots.

Rates
Whole apartment per night from $320-$825, (2-6 guests, extra guests $30 per night)
Accommodation only
Visa, MC, AMEX, DD, Eftpos

Location
1¾ hours or 137km north of Brisbane. Map 9.

Minimum stay
Three to five nights

Facilities
One-, two- and three-bedroom apartments each with lounge/dining (flat-screen TV, Austar, DVD, CD), kitchen, balconies (most with bay views), AC, fans, WiFi. Pool (heated in winter), spa, BBQ, gym, laundry, parking, lift.

Other
Suitable for children

Manager details
Simone Wetherell
▪ info@maisonnoosa.com.au
▪ www.maisonnoosa.com.au

Noosa Springs Golf and Spa Resort

Noosa Heads

Links Drive, Noosa Heads ▪ **07 5440 3333**
www.beautifulaccommodation.com/noosasprings

Rates
Room per couple from $250-$459
(extra guests $45 per night)
Full breakfast included, dinner
available Wednesday-Saturday
Visa, MC, AMEX, DC

Location
1¾ hours or 137km north of
Brisbane. Map 9.

Minimum stay
Two nights at weekends

Facilities
Two- and three-bedroom
apartments, each with lounge
(LCD TV, Austar, DVD, CD), dining
and kitchen, AC, internet.
Restaurant, cafe, day spa, gym,
tennis, golf course and pro shop.

AAA Star Rating
★★★★☆

Manager details
Mark Brady
▪ resort@noosasprings.com.au
▪ www.noosasprings.com.au

Championship golf resort and spa

There is something about a
championship 18-hole golf course
that has a near-spiritual dimension,
with its immaculate grounds, soothing
swish of sprinklers and serenity. And
that's what we love about Noosa
Springs Golf and Spa Resort: the
stunningly manicured landscape of
Noosa's only championship course
hosts one of the most inspiring
resorts we have seen. Golfers and
non-golfers alike will find their own
bliss here.

The resort amenities are designed
to nourish body and soul, reflecting
its role as the activity hub of a
thriving, upmarket community of
pleasure seekers.

The Springs' day spa deserves its
own review (see page 275) and the
fitness centre is sure to inspire an
invigorating holiday workout.

The Pro Shop is more a stylish
boutique than a ball and club display.
Like everything else about the
Springs, its restaurant is a multi-
award winner with spectacular views.

All the dining and retail delights of
Noosa and groovy Hastings Street
are a short trip away, with a courtesy
bus to take you there and bring you
home to the peace and manicured
tranquillity of this cosseted enclave.

Picture Point Terraces
Noosa Heads

47 Picture Point Crescent, Noosa Heads ▪ 07 5449 2433
www.beautifulaccommodation.com/picturepoint

Luxury Noosa hillside apartments

The name Picture Point Terraces captures one reason why Noosa devotees love to stay up above town. You just can't beat the phenomenal views or the cooling sea breezes that moderate the afternoon warmth to a perfect temperature. But 'up the hill' does not mean far from the Hastings Street action – it's a three-minute stroll there and to the beach.

Many people, especially families, will pick and choose their times to leave Picture Point and enter the fray of town. And all will eagerly return to the marvellous facilities at the Terraces once their shopping spree or dip in the sea is over.

Why? Because every apartment has everything you need for a great time. Each has its own entertainer deck, complete with a spa and your own private barbecue, so there's no need to queue for grill time. But there is also a heated pool if you feel like socialising. The apartments enjoy subdued decorative tones and gourmet kitchens.

Noosa regulars already know this elevated secret: from these stunning terrace apartments the panoramic splendour of Laguna Bay is spread out before you in all its glory.

Rates
Whole apartment per night
from $380-$930
Accommodation only
Visa, MC, AMEX, Eftpos, Chq

Location
1¾ hours or 137km north of
Brisbane. Map 9.

Minimum stay
Three to seven nights (seasonal)

Facilities
Two penthouses and 10 apartments, each with two or three bedrooms, lounge/dining (TVs, DVD, CD), kitchen, two or three bathrooms, balcony (all with spa and BBQ), AC, wireless internet, laundry. Heated pool, gym. Inclinator.

AAA Star Rating
★★★★☆

Other
Suitable for children

Manager details
Carol and David Green
▪ info@picturepointterraces.com.au
▪ www.picturepointterraces.com.au

The Lookout Resort

Noosa Heads

1 Picture Point Crescent, Noosa Heads ▪ **07 5448 0733**
www.beautifulaccommodation.com/lookoutresort

170

Rates
Apartment from $180-$460
Accommodation only
Visa, MC, AMEX, DC, Eftpos

Location
1¾ hours or 137km north of
Brisbane. Map 9.

Minimum stay
Three nights preferred

Facilities
19 one-, two- or three-bedroom
apartments, with kitchen, lounge
(plasma or LCD TV, DVD, CD) and
laundry. AC, fans. Heated pool,
spa, gym, BBQ, undercover
parking, lifts. Massage and tour
bookings available.

AAA Star Rating
★★★★☆

Other
Suitable for children

Host details
Rick and Donna Espiner
▪ reception@lookoutnoosa.com.au
▪ www.lookoutnoosa.com.au

Chic tropical resort

All beach holiday apartments should
be like those at The Lookout Resort:
grandly spacious, set up to properly
entertain a bunch of family members
and friends, and with everything you
need in the resort to be completely
comfortable if you decide to have
a 'home' day. The fantastic Laguna
Bay or Noosa River views from
many of the higher apartments
are a wonderful bonus.

The Lookout has clearly been
custom-designed and built from the
ground up for holidaymakers with kids
or little ones in tow. Every one of the
19 apartments has spacious
bedrooms, bathrooms, and lounge
and dining areas large enough
to handle a clan get-together.

We loved the dining tables that can
seat 10 comfortably, with extra chairs
and table space on the deck if
needed. And the endless run of
bench space in the very chic kitchens
is always useful. Lifts to the upper
floors are also very welcome when
you arrive with heavy bags or a
haul from shopping excursions.

All the pleasures of Noosa are easily
reached from this base, making a
morning trip out for coffee and the
papers, or some time on the sand a
no-fuss proposition.

The Rise Noosa
Noosa Heads

37 Noosa Drive, Noosa Heads ▪ 07 5473 6500
www.beautifulaccommodation.com/rise

Designer beach apartments

The Rise Noosa apartments make their own thrilling statement about the evolution of the Australian beach house. How far we have come from hot little fibro cottages to these stunning examples of the architectural craft. They combine and unify the best of many cultural streams from a little bit of Bali to a touch of Bauhaus.

There are 39 apartments with enough room combinations to handle everyone from honeymooners to families or groups on vacation (with plenty of parking if you have extra cars). The style is practical yet alluring with, for example, a bold use of fabric on the bedcovers and lounges to offset the muted creams and pale timber.

Feeding your friends or family is easy with the big gourmet kitchens, replete with stainless steel appliances and crisp white crockery. Louvered windows suit the Queensland beach vibe.

As a Noosa location, this can hardly be beaten. It is just 400 metres from all the culinary and retail therapy seductions of Hastings Street, but far enough away not to hear any of the party zone noise. It's too easy to slide down to the beach or just float about in the heated pool.

Rates
Whole apartment per night from $330-$760 (from 1 to 6 guests)
Accommodation only
Visa, MC, AMEX, DD, Eftpos

Location
1¾ hours or 137km north of Brisbane, 30 minutes from Sunshine Coast airport. Map 9.

Minimum stay
Two to five nights (seasonal)

Facilities
39 one-, two- and three-bedroom apartments, each with kitchen, lounge (TV, DVD, CD), laundry, AC, WiFi. Heated pool, spa, parking.

AAA Star Rating
★★★★☆

Other
Suitable for children

Manager details
Hilda Morrison
▪ stay@therisenoosa.com.au
▪ www.therisenoosa.com.au

Kingfishers Manor

Doonan (near Noosa)

24 Kimberley Court, Doonan ▪ 07 5449 1600, 0407 212 260
www.beautifulaccommodation.com/kingfishers

Rates
Room per couple from $195-$265
Exclusive use rates available
(up to 6 guests)
Full breakfast included, dinner
by prior arrangement
Visa, MC, DD, Eftpos

Location
1½ hours or 131km north of
Brisbane. Map 9.

Facilities
Three ensuite rooms (one king
with spa and two queen), each
with plasma TV, DVD, CD, Austar,
RC AC. Guest lounge, WiFi.
Lagoon pool and spa. Airport
transfers available.

Other
Pets welcome

Host details
Ged Blackman
▪ kingfishersmanor@bigpond.com
▪ www.kingfishersmanor.com.au

English hunting lodge

If you and your paramour need to invest some time in resizzling the relationship in a setting of absolute opulence, skip to the address details here and book now. Kingfishers Manor is a dedicated B&B with just three suites, including the magnificent, 50 square metre Azure. It feels like a grand country house dedicated only to guests' pleasure and comfort.

A real spirit of generosity pervades Kingfishers. It shines through from the little but important things, like the free bottle of chilled wine in your fridge on arrival and the decanter of complimentary port at night to the harmonious interior tone and style.

It feels impressive when you are seated at the grand dining table but cosily intimate when you are secreted away in the absolute privacy of your room – the perfect blend of the highlife with genuine hospitality.

Kingfishers makes a perfect base for exploring the surrounding Noosa district. There are markets at Eumundi, day trips to Fraser Island, gorgeous boutiques and plenty of activities such as paragliding, beachcombing and more. But, if you're anything like us, we reckon you'll find it hard to leave your poolside position at Kingfishers.

Musavale Lodge Luxury B&B

Eerwah Vale (near Eumundi)

55 Musavale Road, Eerwah Vale ▪ 07 5442 8678, 0419 608 382
www.beautifulaccommodation.com/musavale

Country house hospitality

As the evening light dims and the yellow beacons break out across Musavale Lodge, it doesn't take too much imagination to see it as a grand galleon that has been moored against its final hillside home. It's quite appropriate, given that hosts Joe and Chris spent 30 years in the luxury yacht-charter trade before anchoring here at Eerwah Vale.

The three guest rooms are each gorgeously simple with timber plank flooring, the crispest white linens on the beds and feature pieces of furniture. You can be private in your own space or socialise in the majestic guest lounge with its roaring log fire, vaulted ceiling and big, comfy

lounges. Outside, there are decks for sunning by the pool or taking an outdoors breakfast. All this makes Musavale a great option for a gathering of friends.

There is an old-world sense of style and intimacy of service here. Joe makes his own multi-award-winning beer and there are Mediterranean themed dinners. Snoopy, the house Jack Russell, loves to meet other visitors' pets, who are also welcome at Musavale Lodge.

The location near Eumundi provides plenty of options for daytrips to markets, cafes and superb walks.

Rates
Room per couple from $220-$260
Four-plus night specials available
Full breakfast included, dinner
by prior arrangement
Visa, MC, AMEX, JCB , DD, Eftpos

Location
1½ hours or 119km north of
Brisbane. Map 9.

Minimum stay
Two nights at weekends preferred

Facilities
Guesthouse: three suites (one king, two queen), ensuite (one with spa), TV, DVD, fridge; one suite also with small lounge. Guest lounge (log fire, satellite TV), dining room. Pool, spa.

AAA Star Rating
★★★★☆

Member
BBFAA

Other
Pets welcome

Host details
Joe and Chris Russell
▪ info@musavalelodge.com.au
▪ www.musavalelodge.com.au

Melawondi Spring Retreat

Imbil (near Kenilworth, Cooroy and Gympie)

149 Melawondi Road, Imbil ▪ 0408 736 223
www.beautifulaccommodation.com/melawondi

Rates
Whole studio per couple
from $250-$295
Full breakfast provisions included,
dinner by prior arrangement
Direct deposit, no credit cards

Location
1¾ hours or 153km north of
Brisbane. Map 9.

Minimum stay
Two nights at weekends

Facilities
One studio: king bed, lounge
(eco-fireplace, TV, DVD, CD, iPod
dock), dining, kitchen, spa,
bathroom, balcony (BBQ), RC AC.

Host details
Tanya and Tony Fisher
▪ info@melawondi
springretreat.com.au
▪ www.melawondi
springretreat.com.au

Secluded bushland studio

Some properties deliver a complete guest experience of profound rural privacy, luxurious style, gourmet meals and hosts who really are experts about their local area. Melawondi Spring Retreat ticks all these boxes, making it a magnificent place for couples who want to get away for a special celebration or some memorable pampering.

Melawondi is set on 30 acres of bushland that slopes down to a creek-fed lake – look out for turtles or platypus cruising the waters for fresh yabby. The studio is architect-designed and positioned to maximise guests' enjoyment of the wonderful bush vista.

Its open-plan structure creates a feeling of space while preserving a sense of intimacy. The interior fit-out has been expertly planned and elegantly furnished.

A real treat here is the hosts' cooking. Picture yourselves under the stars eating lamb shanks that have been slow-cooked for three hours on a campfire. Breakfast provisions include thick butcher's bacon, local free-range eggs and crusty homemade bread.

The hosts have also mapped some superb walking routes through the neighbouring Imbil State Forest.

Rainbow Sea Resort

Rainbow Beach (near Fraser Island)

3-5 Ocean View Parade, Rainbow Beach ▪ 07 5486 3555
www.beautifulaccommodation.com/rainbowsea

Idyllic wilderness retreat

If the Rainbow Beach township didn't already exist, the land would have long since been set apart as a national park open only to hardy campers.

The remote peninsula setting, across the sparkling straits from world-heritage listed Fraser Island, is one of breathtaking natural beauty and pristine serenity. But forget the tent because you can stay in plush comfort at the Rainbow Sea Resort.

The Resort seems to have been beamed down into this exquisite wilderness straight from the classier end of Noosa. Its Di Henshall-designed interiors are spacious and filled with everything to make a long stay pleasurable.

Features include European kitchenware, huge comfy beds, cable TV, spa baths, wireless internet and more.

There are all the resort facilities you expect, ranging from a beautiful infinity pool to a tour desk and nearby nine-hole golf course. And from every window, spa, balcony and deck chair, those gorgeous views shine in. The apartments will suit couples on the run from urban sprawl or families who need room to spread out and enjoy some very special faraway time.

The quiet township has shops, boutiques and a range of fine and relaxed dining choices, all a short stroll away.

Rates
Whole apartment per night
from $250-$530(2 to 6 guests)
Accommodation only
Visa, MC, DD, Eftpos

Location
3 hours or 238km north of
Brisbane. Map 10.

Minimum stay
Two nights

Facilities
Apartments: one to three
bedrooms (king/twin singles),
open-plan dining/kitchen/lounge
(LCD TV, DVD, CD), laundry, RC
AC. Heated pool.

Other
Suitable for children

Resident manager details
Nigel and Fiona Worthington
▪ holiday@rainbowsea.com.au
▪ www.rainbowsea.com.au

Strandhaus

Rainbow Beach (near Fraser Island)

7 Naiad Court, Rainbow Beach ▪ 07 3102 0853
www.beautifulaccommodation.com/strandhaus

Rates
Whole house per night from
$170-$399 (up to 6 guests)
Accommodation only
Visa, MC, DD

Location
3 hours or 238km north of
Brisbane. Map 10.

Minimum stay
Three to seven nights (seasonal)

Facilities
Three bedrooms (two queen, one
twin singles; master with ensuite),
lounge (TV, DVD, CD, DVD and
book library), dining, kitchen,
bathroom, laundry. Pool.

Other
Suitable for children

Owner details
Aleks Velde and Angi Christ
▪ relax@strandhaus.com.au
▪ www.strandhaus.com.au

Euro-Aussie beach house

It is easy to see why Strandhaus has previously been named as one of the 100 Great Australian Holiday Homes by *Australian Traveller*. It combines a classic rainforest and beachfront location with magnificent architect-designed proportions. The result is a truly sympathetic and smart integration of a building with its surrounding coastal bushland.

The house has a wonderfully light European design sensibility that fits perfectly with the practical functionality of the best Aussie beach houses. Indeed, *Strandhaus* means "beach house" in German, which reflects its owners' heritage.

The use of rich, red timbers outdoors works so well with the light, airy interiors, and the whole house is anchored by a stunning pool and bushland setting. The decks and lounges flow smoothly into each other, making the Strandhaus a great entertainer for families or friends on the run from city stress.

We love the bush path that leads straight to fabulous Rainbow Beach. Don't be surprised to see a speckled goanna race up a tree or to hear kookaburras laughing in the distance.

Strandhaus can't be beaten as a base to experience the many local attractions including Fraser Island and feeding the dolphins at Tin Can Bay.

Rainbow Ocean Palms

Rainbow Beach (near Fraser Island)

105 Cooloola Drive, Rainbow Beach ▪ 07 5486 3211
www.beautifulaccommodation.com/rainbowbeach

Luxury sea-view resort

If you ever wanted to explain why Australia is a focal point for world leisure travellers, it would be enough to show a few snaps of Rainbow Ocean Palms and its gorgeous surrounds.

This very smart property has a national park on one side and a spellbinding vista of the great curving arc of Rainbow Beach on the other. Iconic Fraser Island floats mirage-like in the distance. What more could you want?

Every apartment here shares in the magnificent coastal panorama, with designs that bring in the sky and the sea to every room, which also enjoy complete privacy.

The interiors capture the essence of contemporary style with a bold (but not brash) use of strong decorative fabrics to offset the coolly subdued floor and wall hues. The new owners have made this a much-loved place to marry: the stunning views form a brilliant backdrop to the restaurant and frame gorgeous photos. Plus there is plenty of room for any combination of guests to stay.

The options for outdoors activity are endless: whale watching, sunset drinks at the famous 'sand blow' in the national park, a year-round patrolled beach and lots of places for bushwalking, scuba diving, surfing and more.

Rates
Whole apartment per night
from $225-$525
Accommodation only, full breakfast provisions available, lunch and dinner available in restaurant
Visa, MC, AMEX, DD, Eftpos

Location
3 hours or 240km north of Brisbane. Map 10.

Minimum stay
Two to five nights (seasonal)

Facilities
A range of one-, two- and three-bedroom apartments and penthouses, each with lounge (flat-screen TV, DVD), dining, kitchen, spa bath, BBQ, AC, fans. Lift. Pool, restaurant.

Other
Restaurant open: lunch/dinner Wed-Sat, breakfast/lunch, Sunday

Manager details
Mark and Tanya Beech
▪ info@rainbowocean
palms.com.au
▪ www.rainbowocean
palms.com.au

Gold Coast
& Hinterland

When it comes to the Gold Coast and its gorgeous green hinterland, you may come for the glitz but you'll stay for the sublime beauty of the highlands, with its waterfalls, walks and majestic plateaus. Many of Australia's iconic theme parks, including Dreamworld and the waterslide paradise of Wet 'n' Wild, are down by the sea, casting a magnetic spell on kids. But if you look beyond the coastal razzle-dazzle, the extraordinary Gold Coast highlands provide a rejuvenating natural antidote to the frenetic buzz below.

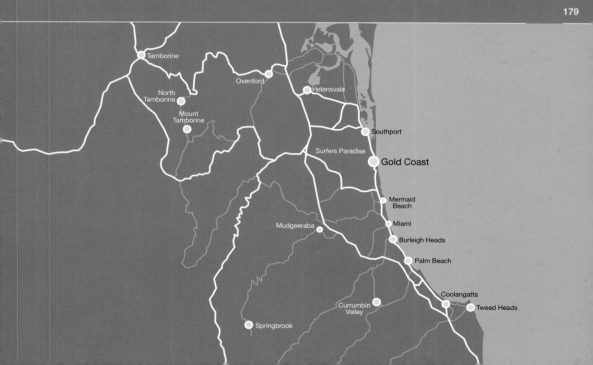

The Gold Coast easily lays claim to being the Fun Central of Queensland due to its many tourist magnets. And why not? All the big theme parks that your kids – and maybe you – have been dreaming about for years are here: Dreamworld, Wet 'n' Wild, Sea World, Movie World, Australian Outback Spectacular and many smaller ones too. Oxenford, about a 15-minute drive north of the Gold Coast's hub, is the centre point of these attractions. You can also pick your choice of beaches, which seem to roll on forever with soft golden sands lapped by warm, inviting waters. If you need sun, fun, sand and neon lights, the Gold Coast will keep you busy.

But there is another side to the Gold Coast that is equally compelling in its own exquisitely natural way: the rainforested mountains that begin just a 30-minute drive from the crush on the coast. Up in the Gold Coast hinterland where the air is clear, there are more than 100,000 hectares of national parks and eco-reserves, spliced by walking tracks and studded with an array of waterfalls, galleries, boutique accommodation, day spas, vineyards and places to eat. A better way to do the Gold Coast is to base yourself in the hills and drive down to the action before retreating pack to quiet, cool beauty of the uplands.

A short drive inland from Oxenford is Tamborine Mountain, which has three charming little communities that straddle the McPherson Range. This district has become a wedding planner's dream location with plenty of places to feast and accommodate a bridal party, with sensational photo opportunities looking back down to the high rises and seascape of the Gold Coast.

At night, all true romantics at heart will need to pause and gaze at the distant lights of the Coast, which seems to float like a shimmering fairyland against the dark backdrop of the sea. There is plenty to do by day, including hike through the rainforest to splashing waterfalls, and indulge in some retail therapy on creative arts and antiques along the Gallery Walk.

A beautiful way to do the Gold Coast is to base yourself in the hills and drive down to the action before retreating back to the quiet, cool beauty of the uplands.

Accredited Visitor Information Centres

North Tamborine
2 Main Western Road, Doughty Park
07 5545 3200
www.tamborinemtncc.org.au

Canungra
12-14 Kidston Street
07 5543 5156
www.visitscenicrim.com.au

Beaudesert
2-14 Enterprise Drive
07 5541 4495
www.visitscenicrim.com.au

Surfers Paradise
2 Cavill Avenue
07 5538 4419
www.verygoldcoast.com

Coolangatta
Shop 22, Griffith Street
07 5569 3380
www.verygoldcoast.com

The valleys beyond Tamborine Mountain are set against some of Queensland's prettiest little hill towns including Beechmont, Wonglepong and Springbrook. The Gold Coast may as well be another planet compared to these stunning valleys filled with farms, artist retreats and forested mountain walls. Nearby is Lamington National Park, which holds the striking Antarctic Beech, a tree species that dates from Gondwana times. At 900 metres above sea level, the Springbrook National Park also has Antarctic Beech and also features dramatic escarpments that have been cut by waterfalls. Highlights include the Goomoolahra Falls, Purlingbrook Falls and Canyon Lookout. Be sure to bring a picnic and allow enough time to breathe in the atmosphere.

The old saw-milling town of Canungra has morphed into a haven for artists, healers, galleries and places to relax over coffee and cake. The region's rich loamy soil is washed by fresh rain and well drained, spawning a local wine industry now producing excellent shiraz and the sub-tropical chambourcin varietal at O'Reilly's Canungra Valley Vineyards.

Pick out a few accommodation bases in the various valleys of the highlands and see the local sights. And if you can bear to leave the peaceful beauty of the hills, the raucous delights of the Gold Coast are not far away.

Peppers Ruffles Lodge and Spa
Willow Vale (near Surfers Paradise)

423 Ruffles Road, Willow Vale ▪ 07 5546 7411
www.beautifulaccommodation.com/ruffleslodge

Enticingly upmarket lodge

The night vistas of the Gold Coast hinterland from your table high up at Ruffles Lodge are outrageously romantic, seductive and inspiring.

The stunning outlook is complemented by the splendid gourmet cuisine prepared by executive head chef, Steve Houghton, who famously ran Zinc at Port Douglas in Far North Queensland. The accommodation completes an irresistible picture.

Since our last review, Ruffles Lodge has joined the Peppers Group, which is famed for its superlative dining experiences and welcoming ambience it provides.

Ruffles Lodge achieves a perfectly pitched balance between style and supreme comfort. The Executive Suite is wonderfully spacious and styled like a luxury apartment. The new Treehouse pool villas are lovely architectural follies that will appeal to your inner child and connoisseur of comfort.

All the facilities for exercise and pampering are on-site. The day spa (see our review, page 278) has a well-deserved reputation for revitalising care and you can also swim or practice your golf swing between naps and meals at the 85-metre practice area.

Rates
Room per couple from $370–$620
Full breakfast included
Visa, MC, AMEX, DC, DD, Eftpos

Location
55 minutes or 53km south of Brisbane. Map 8.

Minimum stay
Two nights over Saturday night

Facilities
Nine villas (king/twin singles, lounge, TV, DVD, stereo, internet, balcony, ensuite; some with fires, spa); three Treehouse Villas with plunge pool. Executive Suite (lounge, TV, ensuite). Lounge, dining, golf, pool, bar. Day spa.

AAA Star Rating
★★★★★

Member
HMAA

Other
Disabled facilities

Host details
Jan and John Nicholls
▪ jj@ruffleslodge.com.au
▪ www.peppers.com.au/ruffleslodge

Mountain Edge Studios

Tamborine Mountain

387 Henri Robert Drive, Tamborine Mountain ▪ 07 5545 3437
www.beautifulaccommodation.com/mountainedgelodges

Rates
Lodge per night from $270-$390,
Studio from $170-$295
Full breakfast included, weekends,
continental breakfast provisions
included, weekdays
Packages and tours available.
Visa, MC, DD, Eftpos

Location
80 minutes or 86km south of
Brisbane. Map 8.

Minimum stay
Two nights at weekends preferred

Facilities
Three studios for couples (with
spa or giant bath) and one
two-bedroom lodge (with two
bathrooms, one with spa) all with
queen bed, log fire, ensuite, TV,
CD, DVD, VCR (libraries), AC.

Other
Disabled facilities

Host details
Jean Cameron
▪ jean@mountainedge.com.au
▪ www.mountainedge.com.au

Stylish mountain-top escape

If your relationship needs rejuvenation
or perhaps just celebration, strap on
your wings and head for Mountain
Edge Studios. As you arrive and face
the full dramatic panorama of the
Gold Coast below, you can't help but
feel a transcendent sense of having
arrived somewhere special. And as
evening turns to night, the curtain of
distant lights are magically laid before
you to brighten your romantic dinner.

No wonder couples and friends love
to get away to Mountain Edge, with
its three studios and two-bedroom
lodge. There is a sacramental aura
beneath their cathedral-like roofs and
big picture windows.

The rooms have a quiet simplicity
about them, with a four-poster
bed, either a spa or huge bath,
and lounges for meditating on the
scene before you.

On Fridays and Saturdays, host
Jean Cameron and her crew fire up
the kitchen and open up the cellar,
combining the best of local produce
and wines.

There is also plenty to explore on
Tamborine Mountain, if you can
manage to leave your studio. This
includes everything from galleries and
shops to tours of local wineries and
the local distillery.

Songbirds in the Forest
North Tamborine

Lot 10 Tamborine Mountain Road, North Tamborine ▪ 07 5545 2563
www.beautifulaccommodation.com/songbirds

Rainforest chic for gourmands

There was a very good reason for using a picture of Songbirds in the Forest as the cover photo for the previous edition of this guide – it exemplifies all we are passionate about. Songbirds combines a sublimely beautiful setting with exceptional standards of style and guest care to create an unforgettable travel experience.

This multi-award-winning property has been recognised for its exquisite Asian-influenced accommodation and the extraordinary restaurant, which opens its curved back to a curtain of majestic rainforest. It was named Restaurant of the Year on the Gold Coast for two consecutive years.

The six villas are nothing short of splendid: soaked in a rich colouring of red and chocolate, framed in timber, and adorned with stunning original art. Big windows and decks embrace the tropical rainforest setting, which provides an astonishing and appealing soundscape, courtesy of many of Australia's brightest songbirds.

If you can bear to leave the yoga and massages at Songbirds behind, the local area is full of interest. There are rainforest walks, wineries, golf, ballooning, cheese making and more.

Rates
One night package per couple from $398-$625
Three-course meal included, continental breakfast provisions available
Visa, MC, AMEX, DC, JCB, Eftpos

Location
1 hour or 66km south of Brisbane.
Map 8.

Minimum stay
Two nights

Facilities
Six villas, each with king bed, lounge (gas log fire, TV, Austar, DVD, CD), bathroom (double spa with rainforest views), one with separate lounge and kitchen. Deck.

Other
Massage, yoga available
Lunch, Wednesday to Sunday
Dinner, Wednesday to Saturday

Owner details
Bonnie Rodwell
▪ info@songbirds.com.au
▪ www.songbirds.com.au

The Polish Place Chalets and Restaurant

Tamborine Mountain

333 Main Western Road, Tamborine Mountain ▪ 07 5545 1603
www.beautifulaccommodation.com/thepolishplace

Rates
Whole cottage per night from
$190-$259 (up to 2 people, extra
guest $60 per night)
Full breakfast provisions included
Visa, MC, AMEX, DD, Eftpos, Chq

Location
60 minutes or 67 km south of
Brisbane. Map 8.

Minimum stay
Two nights at weekends

Facilities
Five chalets: loft bedroom (queen),
lounge (fire, spa, LCD TV, DVD,
CD), dining, kitchen, laundry, RC
AC. Restaurant, gallery.

AAA Star Rating
★★★★☆

Other
Restaurant: morning tea, lunch,
afternoon tea seven days; dinner,
Friday, Saturday nights.
Functions for up to 40 people
Gallery open seven days

Host details
Phil and Ania Sowter
▪ info@polishplace.com.au
▪ www.polishplace.com.au

Poland in the heavens

We love showcasing funky, inspiring
or unusual stays that provide a
wonderful guest experience – and
The Polish Place has all these. It sits
high up on Tamborine Mountain with
views over the Scenic Rim and a
restaurant that regularly beats the
big-name eateries down on the
Gold Coast. The owners' passion
and pride in their Polish heritage (they
even have a gallery of Polish folk art)
make this an exceptional alternative
to the bland look-a-like tourist towers
by the sea.

The views from this mountain eyrie
are incomparable. Maybe the world
looks this way from heaven. The
landscape of rainforested ridges
and ranges rolls off into the distance,
providing a 180-degree perspective
of the sensational scenery and
fabulous sunsets. A dreamy chorus
of bird calls rise up from below,
creating a unique soundscape.

The five self-contained chalets are
timber-lined, warmed by crackling
fires and cosily comfortable. And the
multi-award-winning restaurant – with
blue ribbons for both its food and its
wine – provides an authentic
experience of hearty Polish fare.

There are loads of activities and
places to see in the neighbourhood
including Witches Falls in Tamborine
National Park, a local heritage centre
and botanic gardens. Surfers
Paradise is 40 minutes' drive away.

Clouds on Beechmont, and Old Saint John's Church
Beechmont

1805 Beechmont Road, Beechmont ▪ 07 5533 3593
www.beautifulaccommodation.com/cloudsonbeechmont

Heavenly hinterland escape

A few heavenly days spent perched on the stunning Scenic Rim of the Gold Coast hinterland at Clouds on Beechmont is pure tonic for the soul. There are three eclectic options: a timbered chalet, a swank apartment or a superbly renovated 1930s church.

The spacious cedar chalet has tasteful country-style interior finishes and a wraparound balcony to take in the incredible views over eight national parks. The ultra-chic Clouds Silver Lining apartment blends a bold interior with wonderful artworks. Its breathtaking views are best appreciated from the heated outdoor spa – with some jazz playing and a glass of sparkling wine.

We love how the open, airy feel of the sensationally restored Old Saint John's Church has been maintained by creating mezzanine bedrooms with flawless interior detailing.

The generous hosts provide full breakfast provisions, loads of local fruits and vegetables, and a homemade puttanesca pasta sauce, whcih is waiting on the stovetop on arrival. Local pubs and wineries are easily reached nearby. Heavenly.

Rates
Whole church/apartment/chalet per couple from $150-$300 (extra guests $75 per night)
Accommodation only
Direct deposit, no credit cards

Location
70 minutes or 94km south of Brisbane. Map 8.

Minimum stay
Two nights

Facilities
Chalet (two bedrooms, lounge, dining, kitchen, deck); Apartment (two bedrooms, daybed, lounge, dining, kitchen, media room, sauna, spa); Church (two bedrooms, lounge, fire, dining, kitchen, TV room). RC AC.

Other
Suitable for children
Pets welcome
Disabled facilities (chalet)

Owner details
Christine Langford and Wilson Gaythwaite
▪ info@cloudsonbeechmont.com.au
▪ www.cloudsonbeechmont.com.au

Springbrook Lyrebird Retreat
Springbrook

418 Lyrebird Ridge Road, Springbrook ▪ 07 5533 5555
www.beautifulaccommodation.com/lyrebirdretreat

188

Rates
Whole cottage per night
from $220-$290
Continental breakfast provisions
included (first morning)
Visa, MC, AMEX, DD, Eftpos

Location
1¾ hours or 107km south of
Brisbane. Map 8.

Minimum stay
Two nights at weekends

Facilities
Two cabins and two cottages,
each with queen bed, bathroom
with therapeutic spa, lounge
(fireplace, LCD TV, DVD/VCR, CD),
kitchen, BBQ, RC AC. Cottages
also have loft with double bed.
Laundry facilities.

Other
Fay and Bob Stone
▪ info@lyrebirdspringbrook.com
▪ www.lyrebirdspringbrook.com

Cosy rainforest reverie

Do yourself a favour when you arrive
at the gorgeous Springbrook Lyrebird
Retreat and turn off the mobile phone,
power down the iPad and allow
yourself to just *be* here.

You are deep in your own private
world of rainforest with a complete
symphony of sounds and scents to
experience. This retreat is all about
reconnecting with a more primal
world while cosseted in total comfort.

There are just two cabins and
two cottages here and we love their
honey-toned walls of timber and
craftily arrayed windows that frame
painterly pictures of the sun-dappled
greens outside.

The upstairs lofts in the cottages are
worlds unto themselves that will lure
couples to hide away and dream.
Each cottage is fully self-contained
with complete kitchens, specially
designed therapy spas and cosy
fires for the evenings.

The Retreat's new owners have only
improved on the property since our
last review and are fully committed to
preserving the local ecology.

The region has wonderful walks
and waterfalls to explore, and some
excellent cafes and restaurants can
be found dotted around the ranges.

Wallaby Ridge Retreat
Wonglepong (near Canungra)

88 Bambling Road, Wonglepong ▪ 07 5543 4340
www.beautifulaccommodation.com/wallabyridge

Romantic hinterland escape

Wallaby Ridge Retreat is set in the secluded foothills of Tamborine Mountain. Here you can bask in the gorgeous valley views or toddle off to the region's popular vineyards. It makes a perfect escape for short breaks or longer stays.

The three comfortable retreats here embrace the stunning panorama. Each is fully self-contained but you can order up a romantic candlelit dinner or enjoy a fun night of making wood-fired pizzas in the brilliant alfresco dining area.

The hosts believe in using fresh local produce and keeping food miles low. The result? Breakfast baskets and meals brimming with home-grown vegetables, hand-gathered eggs and regional products.

Your days can be as busy as you like. We suggest playing explorer: head off for wine tasting, bushwalking or mountain hopping between the stunning Tamborine, Binna Burra and Lamington National Parks.

Wallaby Ridge's blissful setting makes it ideal for couples and it is popular with special interest groups such as artists, birdwatchers and wine buffs, as well as wedding parties from the local wineries.

Rates
Room per couple from $145-$185 (extra guests $25 per night)
Full breakfast provisions included, dinner by prior arrangement
Visa, MC, AMEX, DD

Location
55 minutes or 67km south of Brisbane. Map 8.

Minimum stay
Two nights at weekends

Facilities
Three suites: each with one bedroom (two with queen, one with king/twin singles), lounge, sofa bed, dining, kitchen, ensuite, RC AC, fans. Al fresco dining (pizza oven, BBQ), pool, spa, laundry.

AAA Star Rating
★★★★

Other
Disabled facilities
Eco-Friendly Star Accredited
Accredited Tourism Business Australia

Host details
Robyn and John Fortescue
▪ relax@wallabyridge.com.au
▪ www.wallabyridge.com.au

BRISBANE

Toowoomba, the Golden West
& Southern Downs

Toowoomba
the Golden West & Southern Downs

The Great Dividing Range provides a stunning backdrop to Toowoomba and the welcoming townships of the Golden West and Southern Downs. Dotted with picturesque vineyards and delightful historic villages, come here to slow down and enjoy the crisp, clean air. Take some time to explore Toowoomba's notable gardens, the beautiful Bunya Mountains and the dramatic Granite Belt wine region. The whole area is packed with history and overloaded with natural beauty, making it a superb travel choice.

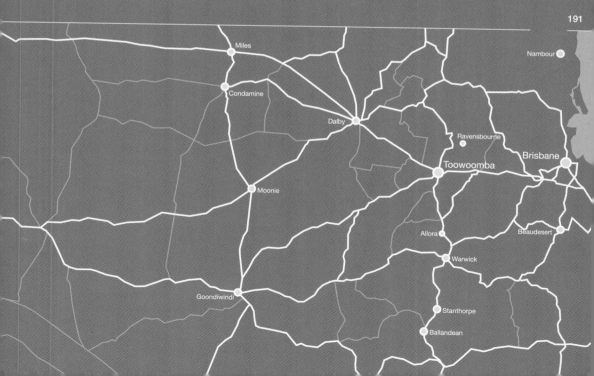

Toowoomba's beautifully preserved heritage buildings and pretty tree-lined streets provide a charming backdrop for your morning coffee.

Looking for excuses to visit Toowoomba? Clear blue skies, crisp mountain air and miles of stunning natural scenery are usually enough to draw people to the breathtaking Golden West and Southern Downs. The historic city of Toowoomba is the region's heart and home to heritage architecture, wide open spaces and gorgeous views over Lockyer Valley.

Toowoomba is a 90-minute drive from Brisbane, making it perfect for overnight stops or longer getaways. It is perched 800 metres above sea level on the edge of the Great Dividing Range. This elevation gives Toowoomba a distinctive and refreshing microclimate, with four distinct seasons and cooler nights

that make an appealing escape from sultry summers on the state's coast.

Australians love their food and wine, and Toowoomba is a favourite among connoisseurs of regional cuisine. The town's bustling dining scene celebrates the diverse local produce, ranging from richly marbled steaks to luscious cheeses and olive oils. Its beautifully preserved heritage buildings and pretty tree-lined streets provide a charming backdrop for your morning coffee. Shoppers can get their fix at the local boutiques or country stores.

In September, Toowoomba hums with all the vibrant colour and promise of spring when it hosts the Carnival of Flowers.

But with more than 240 parks and gardens, this urban landscape offers a year-round celebration of all things horticultural.

The Great Bunya Drive winds through rich, fertile farmlands, charming country villages and the extraordinary Bunya Mountains National Park. The park has scenic walking tracks, cool waterfalls and the largest remaining Bunya Pine rainforest in the world.

Travel south of Toowoomba and you soon reach the sandstone buildings and fragrant rose gardens of Warwick. The town is 160km from Brisbane and strategically located astride highways from Brisbane, Sydney and Melbourne. The Warwick Rodeo, held each October, is a must-see event

that attracts Australia's finest bull riders and horse wranglers.

Wine lovers should detour through Queensland's Granite Belt and spend some time in Stanthorpe. The rich soil and elevated position – 1000 metres above sea level – make it perfect for growing grapes and fruit. There are more than 45 tasting opportunities at vineyards, wineries and cellar doors.

Further south in the wine region is Ballandean, a peaceful respite from the big city. Classic homesteads, winding country lanes and views across flourishing vineyards provide photo opportunities at every turn.

Bushwalkers love venturing to the Southern Downs to explore the granite rock landscapes and spring wildflowers at Girraween National Park. The nearby Boonoo Boonoo, Bald Rock and Sundown National Parks also offer spectacular walks and dramatic views of the region.

Tenterfield is officially in New South Wales but close enough to the border for any southern Queensland itinerary. The legendary town was immortalised in Peter Allen's ballad *Tenterfield Saddler*, about his childhood growing up in the town with his grandfather.

With its appealing climate, charming towns and lengthy list of things to do, this region will suit many types of holiday makers. Drink in the scenery, browse the antique stores and finish your day with a dinner of delicious local food and wine.

Toowoomba
86 James Street
07 4639 3797
www.toowoombaholidays.info

Stanthorpe
28 Leslie Parade
07 4681 2057
www.granitebelt
winecountry.com.au

Warwick
49 Albion Street
07 4661 3122
www.southerndowns
holidays.com.au

Banksia Cottage
Toowoomba

5 Norwood Street, Toowoomba ▪ 07 5594 5113, 0402 806 609
www.beautifulaccommodation.com/banksia

194

Rates
Whole cottage per night $150
(up to 5 guests)
Continental breakfast provisions
included (first day)
Visa, MC, Eftpos

Location
1¾ hours or 126km west of
Brisbane. Map 7.

Facilities
One cottage: two bedrooms
(one queen and one twin single
bedroom), lounge (wood fire, TV,
DVD), kitchen, bathroom, laundry,
gas heating.

Minimum stay
Two nights at weekends preferred

Other
Suitable for children
Pets welcome

Owner details
Tanya and Terry Dicker
▪ banksia-cottage@optusnet.com.au
▪ www.banksiacottage.com

Country town Australiana

There is something so blatantly
charming about Banksia Cottage
that it is hard to pin down exactly
what gives it this appeal. From the
moment you walk in the front door
you are taken back in time.

This 1890s Toowoomba worker's
cottage has been nipped and tucked
to perfection and accommodates up
to five guests. The garden is a delight
and the lounge glows a rosy red from
the open fire at night. Match this with
a newly renovated bathroom and you
have history with comfort.

Banksia is pitched squarely at
families in what is one of Australia's
prettiest and highest inland regional
capitals, Toowoomba.

There is plenty of room for everyone
to sprawl out – including the family
pet – between the bedrooms and the
lounge full of comfy armchairs. The
timber fretwork is dramatic and we
love the big country kitchen. Don't
feel like cooking? Banksia Cottage's
Thai caretaker lives over the road and
will happily whip you up an authentic
Thai feast.

With Banksia as your base, a few
days of exploring Toowoomba is truly
rewarding. It has one of the finest Art
Deco cinema-art centres in Australia
(The Empire was built in 1933) and
glorious parks, which host the famous
Carnival of Flowers in September.

Twylalee Cottage
Toowoomba

60 Mort Street, Toowoomba ▪ 07 4632 1156, 0417 755 841
www.beautifulaccommodation.com/twylaleecottage

1920s cottage charmer

Twylalee Cottage was built for Downs Co-operative workers in the 1920s but they might not recognise this adorable cottage now.

The amiable original character lends an intriguing air of history to the structure, yet all of the necessary modern features have been quietly blended into the vintage charm. Here is all the warm simplicity of a country town cottage.

The renovations were recently completed, so it all feels fresh. Timber-panelled walls and polished floors are complemented by different soothing tones – blue, apricot and a subtle pale green – in each bedroom. The soft furnishings have been carefully chosen to add colourful highlights.

The large kitchen is capable of catering for all the family, plus there is a selection of games and DVDs to keep everyone amused. And this is the beauty of Twylalee – it caters to a couple or a family with equal measures of style and practicality. Ample off-street parking is a bonus.

Twylalee's comforts are within an easy walk of central Toowoomba, making it easy to get to the annual flower festival attractions, shopping, entertainment or dining. But you can also choose to self-cater in the cottage's fully appointed kitchen or on the barbecue.

Rates
Whole cottage per couple $170 (extra guests add $20; up to 6)
Accommodation only
Weekly rates available
Visa, MC, Eftpos

Location
1¾ hours or 126km west of Brisbane. Map 7.

Minimum stay
Two nights

Facilities
One cottage: three bedrooms (queen, double, twin singles; all with heating), lounge (flat-screen TV, DVD, CD/ DVD library, AC), kitchen, bathroom, laundry, BBQ.

AAA Star Rating
★★★★

Other
Suitable for children
Accredited Tourism Business Australia

Owner details
Des and Lou Beavis
▪ twylaleecottage@gmail.com
▪ www.twylalee.com

Goomburra Forest Retreat

Goomburra

268 Forestry Reserve Road, Goomburra ▪ 07 4666 6058
www.beautifulaccommodation.com/goomburra

Rates
Whole cottage per night from
$155-$195 (up to 2 guests)
Full breakfast provisions included
Visa, MC

Location
Under 2 hours or 142km southwest
of Brisbane. Map 7.

Minimum stay
Two nights at weekends preferred

Facilities
Three cottages: two studio and
one with separate bedroom. All
with queen bed, lounge/dining
(wood fire, DVD for movies),
kitchen, bathroom, fans, BBQ,
undercover parking.

AAA Star Rating
★★★★

Other
Disabled facilities

Owner details
Margaret Cairns
▪ relax@goomburraforest
retreat.com.au
▪ www.goomburraforest
retreat.com.au

Natural forest retreat

When you feel the need to shrug
off the business suit and slip on the
walking shoes you will find no finer
place than Goomburra Forest
Retreat, which is set in one of
southern Queensland's most idyllic
natural spots. The property is a
registered nature refuge: it has
resident wallabies and such an array
of bird life that it is mentioned in the
birdwatchers' bible *Birding Australia*.

There are three cottages at
Goomburra Forest Retreat, each one
comfortably fitted out for a cosy stay
(wool quilts, wood fires, spacious
bathrooms). Everything has been
thought of on your behalf; all you

need to do is grab something to
throw onto your barbecue and be
sure to bring a bottle of wine to enjoy
on the private balcony.

The Retreat is on the doorstep of the
exquisite Main Range National Park
(Goomburra Section) with its beautiful
walking trails, spectacular lookouts
(Mount Castle, Sylvester) and the
delightful Araucaria Falls. There are
inspirational walks to suit all levels,
from the easy one-kilometre
Dalrymple Circuit (a chance to
spot a family of native Australian
pademelons) to the more challenging
12-kilometre Winder track.

Coachman's Inn Warwick
Warwick

91 Wood Street, Warwick ▪ 07 4660 2100
www.beautifulaccommodation.com/coachmansinn

Modern regional inn

Travelling in regional Australia can be fraught with hard choices as the sun sets, the eyes droop and hunger rumbles the belly. That age-old question kicks in – where to stop for a warm bed, a quiet room and good cuisine? In Warwick, the easy answer is the Coachman's Inn.

The family-run Coachman's is the newest and most contemporary accommodation in Warwick. It has luxury motel units, king spa suites and self-catering, two-level townhouse apartments for families or longer stays. The rooms have been acoustically designed with double-glazed windows to ensure a great night's sleep for weary travellers.

The on-site restaurant, Rupert's Bar & Grill, is open seven nights and it serves up an array of flame-grilled favourites and house specialties that celebrate the fine fresh produce of the region.

Special occasions, private functions and meetings are all catered for here, and corporate packages can be tailored to suit. You could even consider a staff getaway here to coincide with the Warwick Rodeo, which is held each October.

The Coachman's team is passionate about providing quality service in regional Australia – and it shows.

Rates
Apartment per night from $220-$280 (up to 6)
Room per couple from $120-$180
Accommodation only
Visa, MC, AMEX, DC, DD, Eftpos

Location
2 hours or 155km southwest of Brisbane. Map 7.

Minimum stay
Two nights (apartments)

Facilities
Rooms (queen, ensuite, three with spa; some with singles/trundle). Apartments (queen, twin singles, sofa bed, kitchen, lounge/dining) TV, DVD, RC AC. Pool, broadband, room service. Restaurant.

AAA Star Rating
★★★★

Member
Accommodation Association of Australia

Other
Suitable for children
Disabled facilities

Owner details
Karen Bradshaw and Paul Spiteri
▪ reservations@coachmans.com.au
▪ www.coachmans.com.au

Hope Cottage Country Retreat

Leslie (near Warwick)

24 Serisier Road, Leslie via Warwick ▪ 07 4661 3393, 0407 613 323
www.beautifulaccommodation.com/hopecottage

Rates
Whole cottage per night from
$125-$150 (up to 5 guests)
Accommodation only, full breakfast
provisions/dinner by arrangement
Visa, MC, DD, online booking only

Location
2 hours or 180km southwest of
Brisbane. Map 7.

Minimum stay
Two nights at weekends preferred

Facilities
One cottage: two bedrooms
(queen and twin single) and
sunroom (single), lounge/dining
(TV, DVD), kitchen, bathroom,
laundry (second toilet). Central
heating, fans.

Other
Suitable for children
Disabled facilities

Host details
Susan and Bill Goddard
▪ retreat@assmanshausen
winery.com.au
▪ www.assmanshausen
winery.com.au

Peaceful rural escape

Sit back on the shady verandah, soak up the sweeping rural views and listen to nothing but the native birds as you allow yourself to totally unwind at Hope Cottage on Assmanshausen Winery – Queensland's first winery. In this totally unpretentious setting, peace and quiet reign over an idyllic farm landscape.

Hope Cottage is a fully self-contained two-bedroom weatherboard cottage with a big, comfortable lounge and sunroom. Hosts Susan and Bill live on the property and they can help out with sightseeing tips. A tour of the heritage-listed sandstone winery with Bill is a must.

Alternatively, if you choose to be completely independent in your own private country retreat, the smell of a roast wafting out of the well-appointed country kitchen will have mouths watering.

Leslie Dam is great for a spot of fishing and, for those needing a fix of town life, nearby Warwick offers historic buildings and comprehensive shopping options.

The adorable farm dog Topsy is a major attraction, and also a minor star after playing an extra in the film *Shadows of the Past*, which was shot on the property.

There is abundant bird life and exquisite butterflies, providing loads of stunning photo opportunities.

Fergies Hill Cottage at Granite Ridge Wines

Ballandean (near Stanthorpe)

157 Sundown Road, Ballandean ▪ 07 4684 1263, 0428 841 263
www.beautifulaccommodation.com/fergies

Country winery experience

We often write about all the cellar doors to visit during your forays from our beautiful accommodations. But why bother leaving at all? At Fergies Hill Cottage you are just steps away from the vines and winery of Granite Ridge Wines.

Granite Ridge has made a real name for itself in recent years: its Goldies Unwooded Chardonnay was the first Queensland wine to be named an official selection of that state's Parliament House. Other major achievements have been made with its Cabernet Sauvignon, Tempranillo and Sauvignon Blanc.

From the broad verandah of Fergies Hill Cottage you look out across the rustling rows of vines to the valley vista beyond. Inside are two comfortable queen bedrooms and two bathrooms (one with a spa), making Fergies a great place for a couple or a group of wine aficionados to get away together. A complimentary bottle of wine on arrival and a breakfast basket filled with provisions including homemade bread and jams awaits each guest.

Here you have the opportunity to explore the whole winemaking process with the knowledgeable hosts and vintners Dennis and Juliane. Guests are offered great discounts on the marvellous wines.

Rates
Whole cottage per couple from $160-$200 (extra couple $100 per night)
Continental breakfast provisions included
Three-plus night specials available
Visa, MC, Eftpos

Location
3 hours or 238km southwest of Brisbane. Map 7.

Facilities
One cottage: two queen bedrooms (one with ensuite and spa), lounge (sofa bed, wood fire, TV, DVD/VCR, CD with libraries), second bathroom, kitchen. Large deck with views. Cellar door.

Other
Suitable for children
Cellar door discount

Host details
Dennis and Juliane Ferguson
▪ info@graniteridgewines.com.au
▪ www.graniteridgewines.com.au

Fraser Coast, the South Burnett,
the Whitsundays & Central Queensland

This dazzling and diverse region manages to cover every aspect of the ultimate Queensland holiday checklist. Want lush rainforests, fertile farmlands and world-famous beaches? Here you can have all that and much more. The amazing birdlife, visiting whales and dolphins, and idyllic islands just waiting to be explored will keep romantic adventurers and eco-travellers happy during the warm, sunny days. Pack your sunscreen and expect stunning sunsets, clear night skies and views to make your heart sing.

Never heard of Pumpkin Island? That's because it is the Whitsundays' best-kept secret.

Looking for a rural retreat, a secluded beach or an island-hopping jaunt? Then relax, this region ticks all the boxes. Stretching from the Fraser Coast all the way up to the Whitsunday Islands – and taking in the rich inland agricultural towns of South Burnett – this expansive region encapsulates the quintessential Queensland holiday.

South Burnett is dotted with friendly country farming towns and vineyards. Blackbutt, named after the towering Eucalypts that surround the town, is a true timber town. The native forests provide plenty of pretty spots for creek-side picnics and nature walks.

The farming township of Kingaroy mixes wide, shady streets with giant peanut silos and provides lots of shopping opportunities with craft and antique stores. Those who enjoy discovering the gastronomic delights of a region will find plenty of places to pack their baskets with local wines, olives and cheese before heading off to explore the glorious countryside.

The nearby Bunya Mountains are a precious home to an amazing selection of native wildlife, birds and flora. Walks through the cool mountain rainforest will give keen twitchers the chance to see striking regent bower birds, crimson rosellas and the colourful king parrots.

Maryborough, on the banks of the Mary River, was once a thriving port town. These days it is a pleasure-seeker's paradise with riverside dining, cruises and excellent fishing.

Whale watchers the world over know to head to Hervey Bay between July and November for the chance to see pods of giant humpback whales on their annual migration to the southern seas. The 40km of white sand beaches is an added bonus.

Pristine beaches, freshwater lakes and cool clear streams keep Fraser Island atop many travellers' wish lists. The World Heritage-listed sand island is the only place in the world with rainforest growing on sand. Agnes Water and its sister township of 1770 are serene seaside villages offering surf, still-water beaches and heart-melting scenery in every direction.

Accredited Visitor Information Centres

Agnes Waters
3 Captain Cook Drive
07 4902 1533
www.gladstoneregion.info

Blackbutt
Les Muller Park, Hart Street
07 4163 0633
www.southburnett.qld.gov.au

Tiaro
Mayne Street
07 4129 2599
www.frasercoast.qld.gov.au

Kingaroy
124-128 Haly Street
07 4162 6272
www.southburnett.qld.gov.au

Maryborough
City Hall, 388 Kent Street
07 4190 5742
www.visitmaryborough.info

Rockhampton
Gladstone Road
07 4921 2311
www.capricorntourism.com.au

Proserpine
Bruce Highway
07 4945 3711
www.tourismwhitsundays.com.au

Bowen
South Bruce Highway,
Mount Gordon
07 4786 4222
www.tourismbowen.com.au

Never heard of Pumpkin Island? That's because it is the Whitsundays' best-kept secret. Catch the Pumpkin Xpress from Yeppoon to this secluded island, which has resident turtles and passing dolphins and whales. Just north of Yeppoon, you will find the lush rainforest hideaway of Byfield.

Airlie Beach is the perfect base if you want to experience the best Whitsundays options. This base on the mainland has great snorkelling, swimming and water sports and is the gateway for island exploration. Reef cruises and day trips – including the stunning Whitehaven Beach that Oprah Winfrey visited on her recent trip – immerse you in this exquisite landscape.

With 74 islands, the Whitsundays can cater for every holiday party. Warm tropical waters, abundant marine life and clear night skies will satisfy the adventurer and the romantic. Long Island is a wonderfully cloistered habitat, with a coconut palm-fringed beach and gentle walking tracks.

It is said that with an average of eight hours of sunshine every day, Bowen may just have the best climate in Australia. This makes it all the more enjoyable to take advantage of the area's reef swimming, snorkelling and eight stunning beaches.

Lush rainforests, fertile farmlands and some of the best beaches on the planet make this region a truly life-enhancing destination.

Wiikirri Retreat

Blackbutt

15 Bowman Road, Blackbutt ▪ 07 4170 0395, 0409 479 023
www.beautifulaccommodation.com/wiikirri

Rates
Room per couple from $175-$215
Single rates available
Breakfast provisions included,
dinner by prior arrangement
Visa, MC, DD, Eftpos

Location
1¾ hours or 150km northwest of
Brisbane. Map 7.

Facilities
Two rooms with separate
entrances (one queen with ensuite
and one king/twin singles with
bathroom) both with fans and
ducted heating. 'The Snug' lounge
(TV, DVD, library). Garden day bed,
BBQ.

AAA Star Rating
★★★★

Host details
Julie Taylor-Dixon and Terry Dixon
▪ julie_terry@wiikirriretreat.com.au
▪ www.wiikirriretreat.com.au

Australian rural haven

As you lie serenely in your hammock
in Wiikirri's gorgeous garden, only the
wafting aroma of tonight's Sicilian
chicken or Moroccan lamb cutlets
need remind you of the time of day.
You are here to relax or, as *wiikirri*
means in the Ngiyampaa language,
to "sit, stay and live". This site seems
to have radiated a profound solace
since time immemorial.

There are two spaces for guests.
Each has its own entrance but they
are connected by The Snug, which
is a cosy communal lounge where
guests can sip complimentary port
while browsing the library, selecting
a DVD or chatting with other guests.

This set-up makes Wiikirri ideal
for couples or small parties.

The rooms are brilliantly finished,
complete with Raffles chairs and
wrought-iron bedsteads. Meals and
professional rejuvenation massages
are available. A self-contained cabin
is also planned for those seeking a
self-catering experience.

Nearby is the renowned Brisbane
Valley Rail Trail, which is superb for
cycling or walking – be sure to keep
an eye out for for the 70-metre tall
Blackbutt eucalypts. Cellar doors
and farmers' markets complete the
local colour.

Taabinga Homestead

Haly Creek (near Kingaroy and the Bunya Mountains National Park)

7 Old Taabinga Road, Haly Creek ▪ 07 4164 5531
www.beautifulaccommodation.com/taabingahomestead

Colonial country grandeur

On visiting Taabinga Homestead, you may wonder why the verandah disappeared from Australian houses. Like an Akubra brim, it makes things easy on the eyes when surveying the scene across the mature gardens. This magnificent property was built in 1846 as part of a pastoral station and it is tempting to imagine cattle folk relaxing here in the shade after a day mustering.

Outbuildings and workers' dwellings – The Single Men's Cottage and The Store – have been carefully maintained, and their modern appointments, such as air-conditioning and fully equipped kitchens, would have been much appreciated in the pioneer days.

Ideal for couples or families, the cottages are self-contained. Breakfast baskets, evening meals or fully catered stays can be arranged.

Taabinga guests can join in farm activities, stroll the historic grounds and enjoy the occasional music performance that is held through the year in the concert barn or homestead sitting room.

Nearby is the town of Kingaroy and the Bunya Mountains National Park is also within easy reach to explore. It has a huge forest of bunya pines, superb views, native mammals and about 120 bird species.

Rates
Whole cottage per couple from $100-$130 (extra guests $20)
Accommodation only, meals by prior arrangement
Visa, MC, DD, Eftpos, Chq

Location
3¼ hours or 235km north of Brisbane. Map 7.

Facilities
Two cottages: each with two or three bedrooms (various bed configurations), lounge, fireplace, bathroom, kitchen, RC AC. Grand sitting and dining rooms.

Other
Suitable for children
Pets by arrangement
Disabled facilities

Host details
Colin Marshall and Libby Leu
▪ taabhome@hotmail.com
▪ www.taabingahomestead.com

Flora Alba Cottage and Jacaranda On Pallas

Maryborough

306 Pallas Street, Maryborough ▪ 07 4122 3361
www.beautifulaccommodation.com/floraalba

Rates
Whole cottage/house per night
from $110-$130 (up to 2 guests,
extra guests $20 per night)
Full breakfast provisions included
No credit cards

Location
3¼ hours or 255km north of
Brisbane. Map 10.

Facilities
One cottage: separate bedroom
(double bed, ensuite), lounge (LCD
TV, DVD, CD), kitchen. One
Queenslander-style house: three
bedrooms, lounge (LCD TV, DVD,
CD), dining and kitchen. Pool.

Other
Suitable for children
Pets by arrangement

Host details
Maureen McAdam
▪ mamca@bigpond.com
▪ www.floraalba.com.au

Charming Queenslander and cottage

The Fraser Coast is a magnet for
visitors to the delights of coastal
Queensland: leaping whales, Fraser
Island and the architectural gems of
Maryborough (some of the best
Queenslander homes are found
there). That's why Flora Alba Cottage
and Jacaranda On Pallas keep
earning a place in *Beautiful
Accommodation* – they exemplify the
laid-back charm of this historic town.

The two properties are linked by
a private garden with its own pool.
Jacaranda On Pallas is the real
Queenslander experience: it's a
generous three-bedroom residence
with casement windows and ceiling
fans that whisper a soothing back

note to the bird calls from the
shady Jacaranda outside. Maureen
McAdam has refurbished it in a fresh
shabby-chic style that accentuates
the beautiful furniture used throughout
Jacaranda On Pallas.

Flora Alba is a one-bedroom charmer
with stained glass and silky oak
highlights that frame the verdant
garden views.

These two are a great choice for
those who want some space to
spread out and a real sense of
historic Maryborough. Bridal parties
love the option of having family in the
house and the couple in the cottage.

Akama Resort
Hervey Bay

625 Charlton Esplanade, Urangan ▪ 07 4197 0777
www.beautifulaccommodation.com/akama

Marina-side luxe apartments

Sometimes you really should just give into the temptation to bliss out at a luxury resort. You know what we mean: sumptuous, marble-covered bathrooms, plasma and LCD TVs, granite-topped kitchens, huge soft towels, a heated pool... you get the picture. If you're ready for some of that by the warm waters of Hervey Bay, we have exactly the right place for you: the five-star Akama Resort.

This is Hervey Bay's newest and finest apartment-style property. The architecturally designed main tower is a spellbinding ornament to the marina district and it is close to all the best food, coffee and tours in the region. In season, you can spot whales from your balcony or take a whale-watching tour.

You can choose from one-, two-, or three-bedroom layouts or a penthouse, making Akama a good choice for families, couples or travelling groups. The kitchens, dining and living areas combine a well-modulated contemporary style with beachside practicality.

Hervey Bay has rightfully earned its place as one of Queensland's great holiday spots. Akama puts you centre stage.

Rates
Whole apartment/penthouse per night from $145-$550 (up to 6)
Accommodation only
Visa, MC, AMEX, DD, Eftpos, Chq

Location
4 hours or 290km north of Brisbane. Map 10.

Minimum stay
Three nights at peak periods

Facilities
One-, two-, three-bedroom apartments and penthouse. Each with king/twin single and double beds (LCD TV in master), lounge/dining (plasma TV), kitchen, lift, laundry, balconies. Broadband (fee), AC, Austar, pool, spa, BBQ.

AAA Star Rating
★★★★★

Other
Suitable for children

Host details
Matt and Pia Bysher
▪ book@akamaresort.com.au
▪ www.akamaresort.com.au

Fraser Island Beach Houses

Fraser Island

Eliza Street, Fraser Island ▪ 07 4127 9205
www.beautifulaccommodation.com/fraserisland

Rates
Whole house per night
from $240-$450 (up to 6 guests)
Accommodation only
Visa, MC, DD, Eftpos

Location
4 hours or 290km north of
Brisbane. Map 10.

Minimum stay
Two to five nights (seasonal)

Facilities
A range of studio, two- and
three-bedroom beach houses, each
with lounge (flat-screen TV, DVD,
CD), dining, kitchen, laundry. Pool,
heated spa, wading pool,
playground.

AAA Star Rating
★★★★

Other
Suitable for children

Host details
Fiona and Nigel Worthington
▪ fibh@bigpond.com
▪ www.fraserisland
beachhouses.com.au

Luxurious holiday houses

Breathtaking Fraser Island is the
world's largest sand island, making
it a holiday destination that draws
visitors from around the world. The
more-than 100km of pristine
beaches, native bushland,
spectacular rainforests and freshwater
lakes are just some of the reasons
that keep guests coming back.

Fraser Island Beach Houses
are set in a stunning beachfront
location and offer accommodation
options – from luxury studios to
three-bedroom family houses – to
suit every travelling party. Each house
is individually designed but all feature
spacious bedrooms and generously
proportioned living spaces with
comfy couches. The views from the
balconies over the deep blue seas
and surrounding bush will help even
the most stressed-out traveller to
switch off. The resort complex also
features a pool, water slide and
barbecue for guests to enjoy.

Local attractions include the
irresistible aquamarine waters and
white sand of Lake McKenzie, and
the deliciously named Champagne
Pools, perfect for picnics and rock
pool swims. The hosts also operate
the Rainbow Sea Resort at Rainbow
Beach (see page 175 for our review),
the perfect stopover to Fraser Island.

Sunbird Gardens

Agnes Water (near Town of 1770)

27 Joseph Banks Boulevard, Agnes Water ▪ 07 4974 7245
www.beautifulaccommodation.com/sunbirdgardens

Tropical garden villas

No wonder Captain Cook stopped near here in 1770: the fringe of tropical vegetation and sandy beaches of Agnes Water and Town of 1770 (hence the name) were as alluring then as they are now.

This hidden pocket of Queensland's long coast is a gem that visitors who are seeking quiet and warmth find it hard to leave. Sunbird Gardens is our choice for a stay here.

Sunbird has three secluded villas set in a neatly trimmed bushland garden of palms. And, yes, you will hear sunbirds calling from the trees above. Couples travelling together love this place as an oasis away from the tourist towers.

The villas are self-contained and very private but it is easy to gather for a stroll to the beach or to the new surf club for a meal. We suggest tossing together a salad in the kitchen and throwing a few steaks on the barbecue outside as you sip a crisp white wine and watch the glow of the setting sun. Follow that with a soothing spa in your gazebo and life's good.

Owners Angie and Phil Draheim are a real asset to visitors. During our visit, Phil directed us to some hidden coves and beaches we would never have discovered on our own. The local area includes some wonderful national parks and tour options.

Rates
Whole villa per couple
from $130-$150
Accommodation only
Visa, MC, DD

Location
6½ hours or 490km north of
Brisbane. Map 10.

Minimum stay
Two nights at weekends preferred

Facilities
Three villas: each with one queen
bedroom, ensuite, lounge (TV,
DVD), dining, kitchenette, spa
pavilion, BBQ, laundry, fans.

AAA Star Rating
★★★★

Owner details
Angie and Phil Draheim
▪ info@sunbirdgardens.com
▪ www.sunbirdgardens.com

Rainforest Ranch

Byfield (near Rockhampton and Yeppoon)

76 Yaxleys Road, Byfield ▪ 07 4935 1555, 0437 216 619
www.beautifulaccommodation.com/rainforestranch

210

Rates
Whole cottage per couple
from $135-$250
Accommodation only, breakfast
and dinner provisions available
Visa, MC, DD

Location
8½ hours or 710km north of
Brisbane; near Rockhampton.
Map 10.

Minimum stay
Two nights preferred

Facilities
Six cottages: each with king bed,
lounge (wood fire, TV, Austar,
DVD), dining, kitchenette,
claw-foot bath, ensuite, RC AC.
Pool, heated spa, BBQ. Lagoon
pavilion for functions.

Other
Pets by arrangement

Host details
Warren and Jean O'Leary
▪ mail@rainforestranch.com.au
▪ www.rainforestranch.com.au

Secluded rainforest cottages

As you enjoy the scenic drive to Byfield and Rainforest Ranch, you feel that sense of leaving the world behind and returning to nature. On arrival at this beautifully manicured property, time seems to stop and the bliss begins. It's no wonder this is a favourite escape for couples seeking private time together.

The six open-plan cottages are discreetly placed around the park-like grounds of Rainforest Ranch. Each is ideal for rest and relaxation, perhaps in the deep claw-foot baths or king-size beds, and the interiors are accented by timber panelling, slate floors and arched roofs.

Screened verandahs make a perfect setting for a private candlelit dinner for two or a sunny tropical breakfast. You can bring your own food or hosts Jean and Warren can provide for you. The property also includes a reception pavilion beside its gorgeous lagoon, which is perfect for intimate weddings or ceremonies.

If you like exploring, there are some excellent rainforest, river and coastal locations to seek out including the famed and pristine Five Rocks and Nine Mile Beach. There is even a great little restaurant nearby.

Pumpkin Island

(near Rockhampton and Yeppoon)

Pumpkin Island, near Yeppoon ▪ 07 4939 4413
www.beautifulaccommodation.com/pumpkinisland

Tropical island retreat

This is one of Australia's hidden gems, a truly exceptional experience that only allows a select few at a time to partake in its pristine environment. Off the Capricorn Coast near Yeppoon, Pumpkin Island is a sparkling jewel nestled within the Great Barrier Reef Marine Park.

Here you will find five very stylish, eco-friendly, self-catering cottages powered by wind and sun, overlooking a crystalline beach. Each accommodates between four and eight guests, with a maximum of 30 on the island at any one time. They are fully self-contained, with contemporary flair and they have also been thoughtfully separated from one another.

There is so much to do on this island treasure: harvest oysters off the rocks, fish the rich waters, snorkel or view the coral reefs from a glass bottom kayak.

And, of course, there are secluded beaches to wander or you can enjoy the sublime pleasure of gazing out to the horizon while whale spotting.

Pumpkin Island is wonderful for families, utterly romantic for honeymooners and a hoot for a group of friends. For overseas guests, this will be an unspoilt paradise that will define their trip Down Under.

Rates
Whole cottage per night from $330-$650 (up to 4 guests, extra guests $50 per night) Accommodation only, catering or provisions by prior arrangement Visa, MC, DD

Location
16km off Yeppoon, near Rockhampton. Boat transfer from Keppel Bay Marina on Pumpkin Xpress. Map 10.

Minimum stay
Two nights

Facilities
Five cottages with double, single and bunk beds. kitchen, lounge/dining. BBQ. Entertainment deck, beach hut, unpowered watercraft.

Other
Suitable for children
Certified Advanced Ecotourism

Host details
Wayne and Laureth Rumble
▪ bookings@pumpkinisland.com.au
▪ www.pumpkinisland.com.au

at Water's Edge Resort Whitsundays and at Marina Shores

Airlie Beach, the Whitsundays

at Water's Edge, 4 Golden Orchid Dr ▪ 07 4948 4300 ▪ at Marina Shores, 159 Shingley Dr, Airlie Beach ▪ 07 4964 1500
www.beautifulaccommodation.com/atwatersedge

Rates
Apartment per couple from $210-$450 (extra guests $30 per night)
Accommodation only
Visa, MC, AMEX, DD, JCB, Eftpos

Minimum stay
Two nights at weekends preferred

Location
30 minutes or 35km north of
Proserpine airport. Map 11.

Facilities
Two resorts, each with a range of one-, two- and three-bedroom apartments, pool, spa, internet and gym. Water's Edge also with bar and restaurant.

AAA Star Rating
★★★★☆ and ★★★★★

Member
at Hotel Group

Other
Disabled facilities
Eco-Friendly Star Accredited

Resident manager details
Marie Golding
▪ stay@marinashores.com.au
▪ www.athotelgroup.com

Water view resort apartments

The same management runs 'at Marina Shores' and 'at Water's Edge Resort Whitsundays' to the same exceptionally high standards. Whether you are seeking a perfect honeymoon spot or looking to take a big party away for a wedding or a corporate rewards event in the Whitsundays, there are plenty of accommodation options here.

The quality of the fit-out and attention to detail at these properties is sensational. Marina Shores has a contemporary, cool vibe, featuring chocolate and cream lounges, groovy stainless steel kitchen gear and highlights. The splendid bedrooms have spa ensuites.

Waters Edge Resort has three cascading pools and a spa, places to eat and drink, barbecues and a gym. Its interiors are wonderfully restful with woven cane furnishings and a gorgeous use of colour.

The Marina Shores is right on the waterfront and just around the corner from Abel Point Marina. A delightful boardwalk leads to the Airlie Beach retail-therapy and dining precinct, making for a most romantic stroll at sunset. The Water's Edge Resort is just 100 metres from the main street in an elevated position that breathes in fantastic views of the Coral Sea and its islands.

at Waterfront Whitsunday Retreat
Airlie Beach, the Whitsundays

438 Shute Harbour Road, Airlie Beach ▪ 07 4948 6500
www.beautifulaccommodation.com/atwaterfront

Indulgent seaside luxury

There are times when you owe yourself a stay at somewhere like these luxurious boutique apartments in the Whitsundays. But what really surprised us about at Waterfront Whitsunday Retreat is the extraordinary value it represents. This is very upmarket accommodation at a very affordable tariff. No wonder it has been a Tourism Whitsunday Accommodation Award winner.

As always, we look to the bathroom first to quickly gauge how hard a property is trying. Result: 'A' grade. The pebbled ensuites are generously provisioned with indulgent Kudos spa lotions and beauty products, and all suites have spas on their balconies.

There is also a six-person Jacuzzi on the deck of the penthouse.

The marbled kitchens have wine fridges, the lounges have home theatres with 50-inch plasma TVs, and the bedrooms are suave and simple in their grace and beauty. Guests love the indulgences to be found in the well-stocked mini-bar. There is even a four-poster bed draped in silk in the divine penthouse.

The location and view are unbeatable. It is just 200 metres from Airlie Beach village and the iconic islands of the Whitsundays are easily admired from the refreshing depths of the infinity pool.

Rates
Whole apartment per couple from $275-$450 (extra guests $30 per night)
Accommodation only
Visa, MC, AMEX, DD, JCB, Eftpos

Location
30 minutes or 35km north of Proserpine airport. Map 11.

Minimum stay
Two nights at weekends preferred

Facilities
Five suites and one penthouse: each with one to three bedrooms, lounge (plasma/cable TV, home theatre, DVD, CD, iPod dock, Playstation, mini bar), dining, kitchen, balcony (spa; Jacuzzi in penthouse), WiFi. Serviced daily.

Member
at Hotel Group

Other
Disabled facilities

Resident manager details
Scott Hamilton
▪ stay@waterfront whitsunday.com.au
▪ www.athotelgroup.com

Whitsunday Moorings Bed and Breakfast

Airlie Beach, the Whitsundays

37 Airlie Crescent, Airlie Beach ▪ 07 4946 4692
www.beautifulaccommodation.com/whitsundaymoorings

214

Rates
Room per couple from $135-$195
Seven night specials available
Full breakfast included
Visa, MC, AMEX, DC, Eftpos

Location
30 minutes or 35km north of
Proserpine airport. Map 11.

Facilities
Two studios (queen, double sofa
bed, kitchenette, ensuite) and one
double suite. All with patio, AC,
TV (two with Austar), daily
serviced. Pool, laundry, WiFi.

Other
Suitable for children

Host details
Peter Brooks and Glen Wrigley
▪ info@whitsunday
mooringsbb.com.au
▪ www.whitsunday
mooringsbb.com.au

Panoramic harbour-view B&B

The list of repeat visitors to
Whitsunday Moorings Bed and
Breakfast is long enough to form
its own club. Their shared interests
would include a love of unrivalled
Coral Sea panoramas and an
addictive desire to gaze at that view
while breakfasting on one of the best
tropical meals we have seen. Add to
that some great coffee and morning
papers, and it's a club we are more
than happy to join.

The two Moorings apartments look
out over a gorgeous garden terrace
and colonnaded pool to the Abel
Point Marina. There is nothing
pretentious about these eminently
comfortable, well-appointed units.

They have an authentic North
Queensland ambience with cane
furniture and fittings, tiled floors and
a real indoors-outdoors lifestyle.

Hosts Peter and Glenn are renowned
for their generosity, which extends
from a computer for guests to big
cakes of bath soap, and those
silver-service breakfasts of
homemade jams, free-range eggs,
slathers of bacon and plenty of
seasonal fruits.

Airlie Beach is a focal point for tourists
to the fabled Whitsundays. All the
main tours run from here, and there
are plenty of places for shopping,
pampering and eating.

Hamilton Island Private Apartments

Hamilton Island, the Whitsundays

Hamilton Island ▪ 1300 679 559
www.beautifulaccommodation.com/hamiltonislandapartments

Apartments in Paradise

When Oprah Winfrey was making her must-see list for Australia, Hamilton Island was up there with Uluru and the Sydney Opera House. Why? Because this gorgeous island provides the quintessential Whitsundays experience: limpid tropical waters, glorious beaches, restaurants, bars, golf, sailing and 20km of wilderness walking trails. The place is a paradise for holidaymakers but where should you stay?

There are accommodation and budget options to suit everyone, from honeymooning couples to families with kids and, well, Oprah. That's why we include Hamilton Private Apartments here: it has the only range of AAA-rated apartments on the island.

You could lash out and stay at one of the sumptuous four-bedroom, three-level Yacht Villas, which have private terraced gardens looking over the Dent Passage – these are great fun for friends or couples seeking time out in seventh heaven.

If you're a couple needing just one bedroom, the Anchorage apartments are beautifully finished with big sea-view balconies and barbecues. There are also family-friendly places that include toys and high chairs.

Wherever you stay, all the pleasures of Hamilton are nearby. You can have fish and chips on the beach, a slap-up gourmet feast, hit the boutiques or golf buggy over to the 18-hole course.

Rates
Whole apartment per night
from $275-$750
Accommodation only, full breakfast
provisions available
Visa, MC, DD, AMEX, Eftpos

Location
Hamilton Island (flights daily to
the island and Proserpine).
Map 11.

Minimum stay
Three nights

Facilities
A range of one- to four-bedroom
apartments and penthouses with
various living configurations, all
with kitchen. Most with pool.

AAA Star Rating
From ★★★☆ to ★★★★★

Other
Suitable for children

Manager details
Richard Knuppe
▪ info@hamiltonisland.biz
▪ www.hamiltonisland.biz

Paradise Bay Eco Escape
South Long Island, the Whitsundays

South Long Island, Whitsundays ▪ 07 4946 9777
www.beautifulaccommodation.com/paradisebay

Rates
Per person per night (twin share)
from $498-$698 (up to 2; $200
single supplement applies)
All meals and private sailing
excursions included
Visa, MC, AMEX, DD

Location
South Long Island. Helicopter
transfer from Hamilton Island or
Airlie Beach ($290 per person).
Map 11.

Minimum stay
Three nights

Facilities
Waterfront bungalows with king
bed, ensuite, balcony, fans. Guest
lounge/dining. Catamaran trips,
use of kayaks and other facilities.

Other
Suitable for children over 15 years

Manager details
Steve and Rosie George
▪ info@paradisebay.com.au
▪ www.paradisebay.com.au

Island eco-paradise

Can a completely eco-conscious
resort also provide a totally luxurious
stay? The answer is an emphatic
'yes' at Paradise Bay Eco Escape.
This divinely situated boutique resort
has garnered rave reviews and ratings
from *Frommer's* and *Trip Advisor*.
The winning formula here is a mixture
of idyllic seclusion (it's fly-in, fly-out
by helicopter), gourmet food,
gorgeous bungalows and staff with a
gift for pampering. There are no
day-trippers on the beach, no kids
running rampant and no mobile
phones to cause distraction.

The resort reflects owner Peter
Spann's desire to recreate the simple
pleasures of his childhood in the
Whitsundays: running barefoot on
beaches, snorkelling pristine waters,

boating, kayaking and plenty of fresh,
gourmet meals. The bungalows are
ravishing and feature carved
Australian hardwoods, ultra-premium
king beds and Jurlique goodies in the
recently renovated bathrooms.
The rainwater showers pour soft
solar-heated bliss all over your body.

Peter's idea of a great day is a
fabulous breakfast when you wake,
a morning adventure of boating and
exploring, sunset cocktails with
canapés, and a scrumptious meal
shared with new friends. It's a recipe
that works every time, inspiring
pleasure, reflection and a sense
of awe at the majestic beauty of
the Whitsundays.

Coral Cove Apartments
Bowen

2B Horseshoe Bay Road, Bowen ▪ 07 4791 2000
www.beautifulaccommodation.com/coralcove

Cinematic beachside luxury

It's all too easy to feel that Coral Cove Apartments could be the setting for a movie about how the other half live. Its curving architecture echoes the white-beach coves just a few steps away across verdant lawns. You can't get beachfront more "absolute" than this. It's little wonder that people travel all the way from the southern states to spend a month or longer basking in the sun here.

Coral Cove offers the complete luxury package. All apartments have outdoor furniture on private balconies that overlook the marvellous beach. Main bedrooms have king-size beds, walk-in robes and ensuites.

Air-conditioning, laundries and kitchens equipped with European appliances make life easy. When you need to kick back and relax, there are home theatres, cable television, radio, stereo and broadband access. There's also a ground-floor restaurant, a resort-style pool and secure undercover parking.

Nearby Bowen is the friendly town where much of the movie *Australia* was filmed. Mullers Lagoon in the centre is made up of parkland, botanical gardens and wetlands that host more than 170 bird species.

Rates
Room per couple from $210-$500
(up to 6 guests)
Accommodation only, continental
breakfast provisions available
Visa, MC, AMEX, DC, JCB, Eftpos

Location
2¼ hours or 200km or south
of Townsville. Map 11.

Minimum stay
Two nights (three-bedroom and
penthouse apartments)

Facilities
One-, two-, and three-bedroom
apartments and penthouse. All
with lounge (home theatre, LCD TV,
Austar, DVD, CD), dining, kitchen,
internet. Pool, spa, lifts, undercover
parking. Restaurant.

AAA Star Rating
★★★★☆

Other
Suitable for children

Manager details
Dianne and Bruce Dalton
▪ stay@coralcoveapartments.com.au
▪ www.coralcoveapartments.com.au

Cairns & Cairns Highlands,
Mission Beach & Magnetic Island

BRISBANE

Cairns & Cairns Highlands,
Mission Beach & Magnetic Island

The coastline from Cairns to Townsville contains some of Australia's best tropical beaches and island hideaways. Many of the region's names – Magnetic Island, Palm Cove and Mission Beach – have become synonymous with pristine Coral Sea beaches and an utterly laid-back lifestyle. Away from the coast at Cairns are the magnificent Cairns Highlands, which rise 700 metres above the sea. They are dotted with mysterious crater lakes, exotic flora and fauna, and quaint hill-country towns.

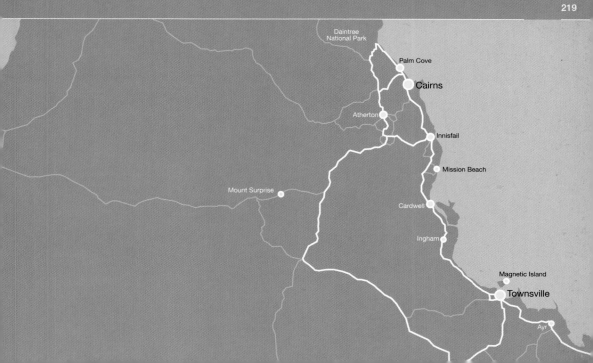

A great Cairns option is to base yourself in one of the quiet, palm-fringed beach villages out of town and slip into Cairns for some occasional retail therapy.

The Cairns waterfront

buzzes with Great Barrier Reef tour operators, shopping strips and restaurants full of fresh seafood. Backpackers mix with Japanese honeymooners, European nomads and Aussies in search of balmy warmth. The groovy atmosphere is offset by tropical architectural gems such as the 1936 Cairns Regional Gallery, which features local artists' work and wonderful exhibitions.

A great Cairns option is to base yourself in one of the quiet, palm-fringed beach villages out of town and slip into Cairns for some occasional retail therapy. Nearby Holloways Beach has a classic North Queensland coastal vibe of swaying coconut palms and limpid

waters lapping soft, warm sand. Forget cooking, grab yourself some grilled red emperor, hot chips and some icy, cold beers, and enjoy a sunset dinner on the grassy esplanade overlooking the Coral Sea. Local markets add colour and shopping opportunities.

Kewarra Beach is a virtual marine park. Its sheltered bay welcomes seagrass-grazing dugongs and bottlenose dolphins. Families love Kewarra for its waterside parkland and child-friendly waters, netted against stingers in summer. Parents can keep a lazy eye on the kids as they burn off energy. The rainforested hills behind Kewarra echo to the sing-song calls of myriad birds including the glorious wompoo fruit dove.

Stroll north along Kewarra Beach and you soon reach one of Australia's great resort towns – Palm Cove. As the sun sets, amble up to Palm Cove for a frozen daiquiri and feast at one of the local restaurants. Palm Cove is a favourite hideaway for upmarket travellers who seek pampering at superb day spas and want luxurious digs. It is all blended with a chilled-out vibe, making it all too easy to relax.

Inland from Cairns are the Cairns Highlands (also called the Atherton Tableland). The spectacular 7.5km Skyrail cable car to Kuranda soars over the rainforest canopy. At up to 1200 metres above sea level, the Tableland has a distinctive microclimate, flora and fauna,

Accredited Visitor Information Centres

Cairns
51 Esplanade
07 4051 3588
www.cairnsgreatbarrierreef.org.au

Kuranda
Therwine Street
07 4093 9311
www.kuranda.org

Atherton
Cnr Silo Road & Main Street
07 4091 4222
www.atherton
informationcentre.com.au

Mission Beach
Porter Promenade
07 4068 7099
www.missionbeachtourism.com

Townsville
Flinders Street Mall
07 4721 3660
www.townsvilleholidays.info

including the strange curtain tree fig, a strangler species that finds and overwhelms a host tree. Atherton was the first town settled on the Tableland and retains some stunning Queenslander architecture. It also provides easy access to many walks, swimming holes and parks. Look for the little village of Tarzali, nestled among rainforest.

Yet more ravishing beaches are south of Cairns. Favourites include Bramston Beach, first discovered by 1960s TV stars and fishing fanatics, Bob and Dolly Dyer. Mission Beach is set in a theatrically beautiful landscape. Here, the Barrier Reef is at its closest to the mainland (40km offshore) and World Heritage-listed

rainforest runs to the shoreline. The result? An idyllic environment for everything from total relaxation to white water rafting, skydiving with a beach landing or reef diving. The mood is exceptionally casual – thongs and sarongs and you are almost over-dressed – with a selection of places to stop for snacks, coffee or a full meal of local seafood.

Magnetic Island, a 15-minute boat ride from Townsville, has become a favourite among those needing to recharge the batteries and escape traffic, stress and the mainland. Three-quarters of the island is national park and there are 23 bays and beaches for swimming, including the stunning Picnic Bay and Alma Bay.

Jungara

Cairns (Redlynch)

20–22 Robb Road, Redlynch ▪ 07 4039 1892, 0429 391 892
www.beautifulaccommodation.com/jungara

222

Rates
Room per couple from $120-$140
(extra guests $30 per night)
Continental breakfast included
Visa, MC, DD

Location
About 10 minutes or 12km from
Cairns CBD. Map 12 and 13.

Minimum stay
Three nights preferred

Facilities
Three rooms: each with queen bed
(one also with single), ensuite, TV,
bar fridge, AC, fans. Shared full
kitchen, BBQ. Saltwater pool with
spa jets.

Host details
Kim and Marilyn McCarroll
▪ info@jungara.net.au
▪ www.jungara.net.au

Sparkling homestead retreat

On a large parcel of land with
sweeping lawns and surrounding
rainforests, Jungara sparkles like
a stunning jewel on the tropical
landscape.

Hosts Kim and Marilyn McCarroll
offer guest accommodation in a
completely separate wing of their
magnificent homestead-style house.

The three queen-size ensuite rooms
feature polished timber floors and
crisp linens, and they are perfect
for couples, families or friends.

This is no traditional bed and
breakfast. Guests have their own
private entrance and the magnificent
dedicated guest kitchen provides
the convenience of self-catering.

The hosts are available if you
seek advice on local touring, and
you can enjoy a delicious self-service
continental breakfast at your leisure.
The resort-style pool takes full
advantage of the hinterland views.

Just 12km from central Cairns,
Jungara offers peaceful respite from
the holiday throng while being close
enough to town for further
adventures. Reef tours, island cruises
and the Kuranda Railway are all easy
day trips from Jungara. This is also
ideal when flying in or departing from
Cairns airport. Free airport pickup
is available for stays of three or
more nights.

67 Casuarina
Cairns (Holloways Beach)

67 Casuarina Street, Holloways Beach ▪ 07 4053 4181, 0409 765 305
www.beautifulaccommodation.com/67casuarina

Contemporary beachside haven

There is something Taj Mahal-like about the pristine white structure of 67 Casuarina. Its cool floors and soaring architect-designed lines command the surrounding grounds with a quiet authority. This, it announces grandly, is the place for a big group to settle in for a bonding beach holiday.

The interior is flawless and perfectly designed for sandy feet returning from fabulous Holloways beach – it is a vast tiled expanse that is cool to the touch.

The property can be rented as two separate spaces but most parties take the lot, making use of the two lounges and two kitchens and five bedrooms to feed, entertain and sleep the whole clan.

We love the spacious interiors and the unadorned simplicity of the bedrooms, which are calm, restful havens. Both decks are perfect locations to enjoy the evening breeze and have views across a silhouetted skyline of palms to the gentle waves.

Holloways beach is a gorgeous stretch of sea and sand just to the north of Cairns but well away from the milling crowds. However, all the Cairns tourist attractions and dining options are easily reached from your shimmering white palace at 67 Casuarina.

Rates
Whole house per night from $320-$420 (up to 10 guests)
Apartment per night from $180-$280
Accommodation only
Direct deposit, no credit cards

Location
12 minutes or 12km north of Cairns. Map 12 and 13.

Minimum stay
Four nights

Facilities
One house or two self-contained apartments. Upstairs with three bedrooms; downstairs with two. Each with lounge (TV, DVD), dining, kitchen, laundry, AC, BBQ. Pool (shared).

Other
Suitable for children

Owner details
Dulcie Bird and Henry Bird
▪ info@67casuarina.com.au
▪ www.67casuarina.com.au

Bedrock
Palm Cove

30 Savannah Street, Palm Cove ▪ 0438 198 967
www.beautifulaccommodation.com/bedrock

Rates
Whole house per night $250-$350
(up to 8; $25 per extra person)
Accommodation only
Direct Deposit, PayPal

Location
30 minutes or 26km north of
Cairns. Map 12 and 13.

Minimum stay
Three nights

Facilities
One house: four bedrooms
(master with queen and ensuite;
one queen; one double; and one
'retreat' with king/twin singles,
ensuite, lounge (TV, DVD), main
lounge (TV, DVD, CD), dining and
kitchen, third bathroom, laundry.
Pool, BBQ, double garage.

Other
Suitable for children
Pets welcome

Owner details
Alexis and Alexander Winslow
▪ bedrockpalmcove@me.com
▪ www.beautifulaccommodation.
com/bedrock

Gliding high above Palm Cove

This is the Coral Sea panorama that
postcards try to capture: a sheet of
aquamarine water stretching to the
horizon and dotted with mysterious
islands. And that's the bird's eye vista
from Bedrock at Palm Cove. This
beautiful contemporary house is
perched on a hillside that takes full
advantage of its position, drawing in
light, views and cooling sea breezes.

Bedrock has been purpose-built for
holidaymakers who want the absolute
best in appointments, fittings and
design. There are four wonderful
bedrooms and three bathrooms
(including two ensuites), enough to
house a party of up to eight friends or
family members, or even a small
wedding party.

Feeding your crew will be a
communal pleasure with a kitchen
blessed with Miele appliances. We
were besotted with the incredible
views from the whole kitchen-dining-
lounge area, which is glazed with
tall windows that bring the tropical
world to you.

The downstairs retreat will thrill teens
who want a separate space. Out the
back is a pool with sea views and a
barbecue deck for your seafood
catch or steak.

Palm Cove's beach, restaurants, bars
and tours are all a three-minute drive
down the hill but we doubt you'll
leave your hilltop perch for long.
This is definitely a place to linger.

Sanctuary Palm Cove
Palm Cove

6 Cedar Road, Palm Cove ▪ 1800 684 684, 07 4059 2200
www.beautifulaccommodation.com/sanctuarypalmcove

Leafy resort luxury

Palm Cove is all that its name evokes: a warm, sandy curve of beach, fringed by swaying tropical palms. This is the archetypal romantic movie setting, with you happily placed in the director's chair, calling all the shots at Sanctuary Palm Cove.

Sanctuary has brought a new level of style to the Palm Cove district, with a gorgeous open ambience and distinctive decorative aesthetic.

Designed by architect John Mainwaring, the apartments are in a spacious parkland setting complete with lakes and water lilies. The open feeling continues indoors, with interiors that are distinguished by an ingenious use of space and light.

Each apartment is subtly positioned to take in panoramic views of the gardens from private balconies with fully opening window walls. In contrast to much beachside accommodation, this is the epitome of privacy, tranquillity and style.

If you need to leave, it's all just a short saunter to the beach or the laid-back streetlife of boutiques, cafes and award-winning restaurants. Cairns is just down the road for reef tours and shopping indulgence.

Rates
Whole apartment per night
from $175-$500 (up to 6 guests)
Accommodation only
Visa, MC, AMEX, DC, DD, Eftpos

Location
30 minutes or 26km north of Cairns.
Map 12 and 13.

Minimum stay
Three nights

Facilities
One-, two- and three-bedroom apartments, each with king and twin beds in a range of configurations; lounge (TV, Austar, DVD, CD), dining, kitchen, private balcony and laundry. Fans, AC, WiFi. Pool (heated in winter).

AAA Star Rating
★★★★★

Other
Suitable for children
Disabled facilities

Manager details
Scott and Jane Gallagher
▪ info@sanctuarypalmcove.com.au
▪ www.sanctuarypalmcove.com.au

Bramston Beach House

Bramston Beach

46 Evans Road, Bramston Beach ▪ 02 9008 1330
www.beautifulaccommodation.com/bramstonbeachhouse

Rates
Whole beach house per night
from $410-$610 (up to 8 guests)
Accommodation only,
catering by prior arrangement
Visa, MC, AMEX, DD, Chq

Location
1 hour or 81km south of Cairns.
Map 12.

Minimum stay
Two nights

Facilities
Four bedrooms (king with ensuite,
TV; queen; and two with twin
singles), lounge (TV, Austar, DVD,
Bose system, iPod dock), dining,
kitchen (Nespresso machine),
office, laundry. Deck (BBQ,
kitchenette) pool. AC, WiFi.

Other
Suitable for children

Owner details
Benjamin Chong and
Dugald Mackenzie
▪ info@bramstonbeach
house.com.au
▪ www.bramstonbeach
house.com.au

Absolute beachfront beauty

This beach was 'discovered' in the
1960s by the TV legends Bob and
Dolly Dyer (of *Pick-A-Box* fame). Bob
loved the superb fishing and Dolly
liked the peace and solitude away
from big city celebrity life.

Amazingly, Bramston Beach is still as
secluded now as it was then – one
government study even nominates it
as the cleanest beach in the
Australian tropics.

Bramston Beach House is decades
removed from the fibro beach shacks
of the 1960s. This is a state-of-the-
art beachfront home, complete with
a wrap-around pool and an
entertainer's floor plan.

The design flows from the comfy
lounges in front of the big flat-screen
TV and Bose speakers to the
eight-seat dining setting and deck.

It offers sublime bedrooms, including
a master with its own ensuite and
Austar TV feed. Just bring your food
and drink, and settle in for some
chilled-out time away from the world.

Nearby is the classic Queensland
cane town of Babinda. You can take
a boat trip to the Frankland Islands,
visit a crocodile farm or walk the
rainforests. Bliss.

The Summit Rainforest Retreat and The Summit B&B

Atherton

22 Twelfth Avenue, Atherton ▪ 07 4091 7300
www.beautifulaccommodation.com/thesummit

227

Versatile rainforest retreat

On the lip of a long-extinct volcano and overlooking the township of Atherton, The Summit Rainforest Retreat and The Summit B&B command brilliant views.

This versatile retreat is actually two properties and offers a secluded luxury getaway for business, pleasure or a combination of the two.

There really is something for everyone here: a five-bedroom house and one-bedroom apartment that can be configured to accommodate any travelling party. There is even a boutique conference centre, which can handle meetings of up to 35 delegates.

Next door there is a separate self-contained Queenslander that can be booked by the room on a B&B basis or as an entire house. Light, bright interiors with rich natural timbers and contemporary rustic-toned furnishings blend perfectly with the panoramic views from this fabulous setting.

The area is surrounded by ancient rainforests and fertile tablelands. You can expect frequent visits from some very special guests including pademelons, bandicoots and Lumholtz tree kangaroos. It all makes this a quintessentially Australian holiday destination.

Rates
House per night from $250-$880
Room per couple from $180-$250
Single/corporate rates available
Accommodation only, breakfast provisions available
Visa, MC, AMEX, DC, DD, Eftpos

Location
1¼ hours or 77km northwest of Cairns. Map 12.

Minimum stay
Two nights

Facilities
Five-bedroom house and/or one-bedroom apartment let to one group at a time. Lounges (TV, DVD, CD), kitchen (kitchenette in apartment). Pool, BBQ. Conference facilities. B&B has four bedrooms (ensuite, TV), lounge (TV), kitchen, pool, spa, BBQ.

Other
Suitable for children

Host details
John and Helen Donovan
▪ info@summitrainforestretreat.com
▪ www.summitrainforestretreat.com

The Canopy Rainforest Treehouses

Tarzali

247 Hogan Road, Tarzali ▪ 07 4096 5364
www.beautifulaccommodation.com/thecanopy

228

Rates
Whole tree house per couple
from $227-$399 (extra guests
$40 per night)
Specials for three-plus nights
Accommodation only,
hampers by arrangement
Visa, MC, AMEX, DC, DD, Eftpos

Location
1¼ hours or 75km southwest of
Cairns. Map 12.

Minimum stay
Two nights

Facilities
Six tree houses: five with two
bedrooms; one with three
bedrooms. Each with lounge
(fireplace, TV, DVD, CD, WiFi), spa
bathroom, kitchen, BBQ, laundry.

Member
Ecotourism Australia

Other
Suitable for children

Host details
David and Sharon Gibson
▪ stay@canopytreehouses.com.au
▪ www.canopytreehouses.com.au

Luxury rainforest tree houses

This incredible location, set among
100 acres of private rainforest, is
strictly for guests' enjoyment and
a plethora of local critters who love
sharing this space.

Resident assowaries, rare tree-
kangaroos and pademelon wallabies
are just some of the locals to be seen
at this luxury rainforest retreat. Even
the timid platypus can often be
spotted splashing in the waters
of the magical Ithaca River.

Choose from six delightful tree
houses that sit elegantly nestled
among the treetops of this gorgeous
rainforest reserve. Each hideaway
features cathedral ceilings that
complement the soaring old-
growth forest.

Local timbers and handcrafted
furniture echo the natural beauty
of the region.

Enjoy the leafy views from the deep
corner spa or curl up by the cosy fire
on cooler evenings. And you need
only step onto your balcony to enjoy
a meet-and-greet with coppery
brushtail possums and a stunning
array of rainforest bird life.

Walk the lush trails, feed the wildlife,
explore the river or book in for a spa
treatment on your own elevated
balcony. Bursting with exotic wildlife
and surrounded by majestic forest,
this is the ultimate rainforest getaway.

Bella Coola
Mission Beach

Location on enquiry, Mission Beach ▪ 07 4088 6699
www.beautifulaccommodation.com/bellacoola

Seaside beach cottages

Bella Coola was the accommodation of choice for the cast and crew of the television drama *Sea Patrol*, and the reasons are obvious. It has an absolute beachfront location, stunning views of Dunk Island and the flexibility to book just one or all three of these gorgeous one-bedroom cottages.

Tofino is the original beach shack with front deck views over the Coral Sea. The warm rustic finishes and Calypso-coloured furnishings give this cottage a feeling of relaxed seaside holiday fun.

Chilko and Lillooet, the two new cottages perched behind Tofino, have been elevated to ensure guests experience the soft sea breezes.

Its warm natural timbers and wicker furniture create the perfect tropical hideaways atmosphere.

The lovingly maintained gardens provide lots of nooks for quiet contemplation or you can just dip your feet in the pool and soak up the sunshine.

A short stroll through the swaying palm trees leads to Mission Beach village, which has all the holiday essentials and a relaxed cafe scene.

Just a little further along, cruises depart for Great Barrier Reef adventures and visits to the breathtaking Dunk Island.

Rates
Whole cottage per couple
from $200-$230
Accommodation only
Visa, MC, AMEX, DC, DD, Eftpos

Location
90 minutes or 140km south of Cairns. Map 12.

Facilities
Three cottages: Lillooet and Chilko are elevated, overlooking pool and garden. Tofino overlooks reserve and beach. All with one bedroom (queen), lounge (TV, DVD, CD), dining, kitchen, fans, AC. Pool, undercover parking.

Agent details
Mission Beach Holidays
8 Porter Promenade,
Mission Beach
▪ stay@bellacoola.com.au
▪ www.bellacoola.com.au

Alani

Mission Beach

20 Donkin Lane, Mission Beach ▪ 0418 325 055
www.beautifulaccommodation.com/alani

230

Rates

Whole house, including annexe,
per couple from $395-$520
(extra guests $20, maximum 8)
Accommodation only
Visa, MC, DD

Location

90 minutes or 140km south of
Cairns. Map 12.

Minimum stay

Five nights (seven in high season)

Facilities

One beachfront house with
apartment: four bedrooms (one
king, two queen, two king/twin
singles, three with ensuite and a
fourth bathroom). Two kitchens,
two lounge/dining rooms (both
with TV, DVD, CD). AC, fans. Pool,
BBQ, laundry.

Other

Suitable for children

Owner details

Judy and Peter Lawrence
▪ twin1@netspace.net.au
▪ www.alanimissionbeach.com.au

Private beachfront residence

The paradoxical theme for this prized
beachfront setting could be 'together
but separate'. Extended families,
gatherings of friends and groups will
love the flexibility offered here against
a perfect backdrop of sea, sun and
sand. Yet those who need rest can
have that too. Your car can also take
a break because Alani is just a
short stroll from shops, boutiques
and eateries.

Alani is notable for its two distinct
residences, but it is only ever let
out to one lucky bunch of people.
The main house has an expansive
feel with bi-fold doors opening to
the vibrant green lawns and the
beach beyond.

Alani's creamy walls form a backdrop
to the subtly toned furnishings and
cool, tiled floors complete the picture
of comfort and relaxation.

The stylish poolside apartment
sleeps two and is perfect for
energetic teens, grandparents
or even an eccentric uncle.

Owners Judy and Peter Lawrence
have created a peaceful enclave.
The more adventurous members of
your group will love using this spot
as a base for activities such as
skydiving, water sports and
bushwalking. Those who prefer
more placid activities can indulge
in bird watching or simply exploring
the nearby islands.

Seasons
South Mission Beach

25 Mitchell Street, South Mission Beach ▪ 0418 325 055
www.beautifulaccommodation.com/seasons

Poetic beachside retreat

Seasons is a favourite with *Beautiful Accommodation* readers and it's easy to see why. The idyllic setting has breezy views out to both Dunk and Bedarra islands, which hover enticingly on the horizon. Inside, delicate fabric wafts over the bed, ruffled by the soothing tropical zephyrs that blow in from the sea. It's the perfect setting for a couple or three in need of a transforming break away.

This charming cottage evokes a certain nostalgia for the past but manages to incorporate all the up-to-date amenities that make for a revitalising stay. Concertina windows bring the tropical ambience into the main areas, which combine understated soft furnishings with gorgeous timber tables and floorboards. The seductive bedrooms can also be opened up, and graceful nets envelop guests as they recline in beds of crisp linen.

A 13-metre lap pool offers the chance to keep up a fitness program while you're away or just float lazily and watch fluffy clouds do the same. You can almost touch the beach sand from the terrace.

The Dunk and Bedarra island silhouettes are pure poetry, and there must be a rhyming couplet waiting to be created from all the reasons for Seasons.

Rates
Whole house per night
from $395-$520
Accommodation only
Visa, MC, DD

Location
90 minutes or 140km south of
Cairns. Map 12.

Minimum stay
Five nights

Facilities
Three ensuite bedrooms (one king, one queen or king/twin singles), kitchen, lounge/dining (TV, DVD, CD), beachfront deck. 13-metre lap pool, BBQ. Laundry.

Owner details
Judy and Peter Lawrence
▪ twin1@netspace.net.au
▪ www.seasonsmission
beach.com.au

Lillypads
Mission Beach

Mission Beach, exact location on enquiry ▪ 07 4088 6133
www.beautifulaccommodation.com/lillypads

232

Rates
Whole cottage per couple $250
(extra guests $25 per night)
Accommodation only
Visa, MC, AMEX, DC, Eftpos

Location
90 minutes or 140km south of
Cairns. Map 12.

Facilities
Two pads, each with screened
verandah (lounge, dining), two
bedrooms (queen and king/twin
single), lounge (plasma TV, DVD,
CD, surround sound), kitchen,
bathroom, internet, AC. Screened
spa deck. Pool, badminton court,
rainforest massage pavilion.

Member
Mission Beach Holidays

Other
Suitable for children
Disabled facilities

Owner details
Vicki and Steve Wiltshire
▪ info@lillypads.com.au
▪ www.lillypads.com.au

Tropical lagoon chalets

This patch of paradise is hidden
among six acres of spectacular
gardens, joyous with birdsong and
fringed with banana palms. Lillypads'
two imaginative cottages are in
a dramatic rainforest setting with
sparkling streams and tropical flowers.

Lagoon views, timber floors and
spacious indoor-outdoor living provide
the quintessential tropical holiday
vibe. The cottages each have two
bedrooms and bathrooms, making
Lilypads an ideal spot for families or
couples travelling together.

You can expect to be pampered
when you cross the bridge to the
Body Temple, a truly magical riverside
massage pavilion.

Take advantage of the gardens,
which are bursting with tropical fruit
– pick your own for a fruit salad or
even to dress up your pre-dinner
cocktail on the all-weather spa deck.

Stunning Mission Beach, with its
seemingly endless stretch of white
sand, is a gentle 15-minute walk or
three-minute drive from your door.

And if you feel like going seaside,
the owners also offer Lillypads By The
Beach where Moorish style soars to
tropical heights (read our review,
right).

Lillypads By The Beach
Mission Beach

2 Conch Street, Mission Beach ▪ 07 4088 6133
www.beautifulaccommodation.com/lillypadsbeach

Luxurious Moroccan house

The moment you step through the front door of this luxurious property you will feel transported to another time and place. With their love for the tropical lifestyle and a passion for colourful Moorish style, the owners have created a Mission Beach house without equal.

The melding of indoor and outdoor living spaces with a marvellous mix of cultural influences is enchanting. The open-plan kitchen and living area has a soaring five-metre ceiling. There are three bedrooms – one with a sensational spa bathroom, ideal for star-gazing – at the heart of the house.

A distinctive screened wrap-around verandah creates another dining and living space. The courtyard, with its Moroccan-style font and manicured garden, offers an exceptional setting for alfresco dining. Couples will love sneaking up to the elevated plunge pool and rooftop turret with its two hammocks for romantic starlit trysts.

There is plenty to do beyond your beachside sanctuary such as exploring the Barrier Reef or indulging in some eco-touring and, of course, enjoying 14km of unspoilt beaches.

Rates
Whole house per night from $300-$500 (up to 6 guests)
Accommodation only
Visa, MC, AMEX, DC, DD, Eftpos

Location
90 minutes or 140km south of Cairns. Map 12.

Minimum stay
Two nights

Facilities
Three bedrooms (two queen with ensuites, one with spa; one king/twin single; all with LCD TV, AC), lounge, third bathroom, kitchen, media nook (TV, Austar, DVD, CD, iPod dock), dining, lounge, fans, courtyard. Laundry, internet, pool.

Member
Mission Beach Holidays

Other
Suitable for children
Disabled facilities

Owner details
Vicki and Steve Wiltshire
▪ info@lillypads.com.au
▪ www.lillypads.com.au

Sejala Beach House

Mission Beach

Pacific Parade, Mission Beach ▪ 07 4088 6699
www.beautifulaccommodation.com/sejalabeachhouse

Rates
Whole house per night $660
(1-2 people, extra guests $50)
Accommodation only
Visa, MC, AMEX, DC, Eftpos, Chq

Location
90 minutes or 140km or south of
Cairns. Map 12.

Minimum stay
Two nights

Facilities
Three bedrooms (king/twin
singles, AC), upstairs lounge
(wide-screen TV with Austar,
DVD, VCR, CD), beachfront and
pool terraces, kitchen. Pool. Fans,
laundry, BBQ. Housekeeping every
three days.

Member
Mission Beach Holidays

Other
Suitable for children

Agent details
Mission Beach Holidays
▪ info@sejala.com
▪ www.sejala.com.au

Impeccable tropical indulgence

As Oscar Wilde had it, fashion is so unbearable we are compelled to change it every six months. The acerbic Wilde would have no such problems with Sejala Beach House. Nestled among coconut palms on absolute beachfront, Sejala is timeless style rather than passing fashion.

Its elegance stems from attention to detail, fine appointments and myriad delights such as monogrammed bed linen and bath towels, French linen blankets, sarongs and L'Occitane toiletries. Sejala has so many thoughtful touches: chilled and filtered drinking water, a teppanyaki plate in the five-star kitchen,

beach chairs and towels, and a beach shower room.

The lovely timber house is tropical in all senses. Rooms are light and airy, shielded by shuttered doors and windows if need be, with nearby frangipani adding their fragrance to the setting. The sitting room flows through to a terrace and the beachfront tropical garden beyond, and a glass-tiled pool offers total privacy.

Sejala is a casual stroll away from morning coffee and papers or a relaxed evening meal at the charming township of Mission Beach.

Sejala Beach Huts
Mission Beach

Pacific Parade, Mission Beach ▪ 07 4088 6699
www.beautifulaccommodation.com/sejalabeachhuts

Beachcomber chill pads

These delightful hideaways may be huts in a dictionary sense, but they are also huts in the same way the palace of Versailles was the Sun King's 'country cottage'. But here, Sejala Beach Huts are much more fun and affordable.

What you get is a tropical garden setting with a funky self-contained pad that opens to unite inside with the garden and beach beyond. The colourful interiors have taken inspiration from the lush tropical landscape, while the waves washing onto the shore provide calming sounds in the background. In addition to the shutters and overhead fans, air-conditioning is available to aid an afternoon nap.

Among Sejala's stylish inclusions are Egyptian cotton bed linen, L'Occitane toiletries and beach towels, which all add to the indulgent setting.

Each hut opens onto a verandah offering a barbecue, dining setting and the alluring temptation of deck chairs or a hammock. You can choose to self-cater, perhaps with the barbecue or with a pre-arranged seafood platter.

All this is just seconds from a glorious beach, a few minutes by bike or on foot from shops and cafes, and hardly any time at all from as much outdoor adventure as you desire.

Rates
Whole hut per couple
from $239-$260 (extra guests $20; maximum 4)
Accommodation only
Visa, MC, AMEX, DC, Eftpos, Chq

Location
90 minutes or 140km south of Cairns. Map 12.

Facilities
Three huts (two facing the beach), each with queen bed, sofa bed, ensuite, lounge (TV), kitchenette (microwave), BBQ, AC and screens. Pool.

Member
Mission Beach Holidays

Other
Suitable for children

Agent details
Mission Beach Holidays
▪ info@sejala.com
▪ www.sejala.com.au

Coco Loco

Mission Beach (Bingil Bay)

Location on enquiry, Bingil Bay, ▪ 07 4068 7637
www.beautifulaccommodation.com/cocoloco

Rates
Whole shack per night
from $170-$180
Accommodation only
Direct deposit, no credit cards

Location
90 minutes or 140km south of
Cairns, 5 minutes north of Mission
Beach village. Map 12.

Minimum stay
Three nights

Facilities
Coco Loco comprises two shacks:
one with queen bed (ensuite); the
other with lounge (TV, DVD, iPod
dock), kitchen, bathroom, BBQ.

Owner details
Steve and Mem Russell
▪ cocoloco@top.net.au
▪ www.cocolocomissionbeach.com

Exceptional secluded escape

Overlooking the beautiful Brooks
Beach is Coco Loco, a property as
eclectic and enchanting as its name
suggests. This private retreat takes a
maximum of just two guests making
it an ideal lovers' getaway or perhaps
a place to escape from the everyday
and indulge in a soul-searching
journey.

Enjoying an absolute beachfront
position, this amazing property
dazzles with its warm citrus tones
and rich red exterior. Both the
king-size bedroom and the living
room feature tropical-style French
doors that allow the cooling Coral
Sea breezes to flow through the
entire cottage.

Soft furnishings are a mix of colourful
stripes and solids, creating a sense
of vibrant holiday fun.

Coco Loco is fully self-contained so
just pack your essentials and come
prepared to disappear for as long as
you need.

Swimming, snorkelling and fishing
opportunities abound. And rainforest
walks are a great way to meet the
locals: the cute green tree frog or
the brilliantly hued and endangered
flightless cassowary. For restocking
the pantry and a cafe latte and
croissant fix, Mission Beach village
is just a five-minute drive away.

Pandanus Beachfront Apartments

Mission Beach (Wongaling Beach)

Cnr Reid Road and Whiting Street, Wongaling Beach ▪ 07 4068 8989, 0418 688 930
www.beautifulaccommodation.com/pandanus

Flexible tropical freedom

A sandy colour scheme enlivened by floral hues gives the impression that Pandanus Apartments have grown organically out of this superb beachside setting ringed with lush tropical vegetation.

Families love the two-bedroom layouts, and couples can enjoy complete privacy in the studio penthouse, which has its own verandah and balcony Jacuzzi.

The happy blend of colours and textures extends indoors, with tempting sofas, elegant dining settings and peaceful sleeping zones. The apartment near the pool is protected by a large shade sail and especially popular with parents of smaller children.

It's easy to keep an eye on things while relaxing on the terrace or preparing meals in the fully equipped kitchen. Adults love the pool waterfall, which melts away any residual stress from real life.

If the mood takes you, nature's own waterfalls are waiting to be seen in the rainforest nearby. Those who want more vigorous pursuits can paddle a kayak to Dunk Island or go on a guided jet ski expedition.

And if the magnetic pull of the Great Barrier Reef finally tears you away from magnificent Mission Beach, tours are easily arranged.

Rates
Whole apartment per couple from $120-$320 (up to 6 guests, extra guests $20)
Weekly rates available
Accommodation only
Visa, MC, AMEX, Eftpos, Chq

Location
2 hours or 140km south of Cairns. Map 12.

Minimum stay
Two nights at weekends preferred

Facilities
Three two-bedroom apartments and one studio penthouse, each with lounge (TV, Austar, DVD, CD), dining, kitchen, bathroom, laundry, BBQ. Penthouse with balcony Jacuzzi. AC. Pool.

Other
Suitable for children

Host details
Sharalyn and Mark Dennis
▪ info@pandanusmissionbeach.com
▪ www.pandanusmissionbeach.com

The Wongalinga

Mission Beach (Wongaling Beach)

64 Reid Road, Wongaling Beach ▪ 07 4068 8221
www.beautifulaccommodation.com/thewongalinga

238

Rates
Whole apartment per night
from $190-$320
Accommodation only
Visa, MC, AMEX, Eftpos

Location
90 minutes or 140km south of
Cairns. Map 12.

Facilities
A range of one-, two- and
three-bedroom apartments, each
with lounge (TV, DVD, CD),
dining, kitchen, patio or balcony,
laundry. Pool, BBQ, tour desk.

AAA Star Rating
★★★★☆

Other
Suitable for children

Manager details
Wendy and Rob Anderson
▪ info@wongalinga.com.au
▪ www.wongalinga.com.au

Graceful beachfront resort

In the movie industry, a slate is held in front of the camera to mark the limits of a scene. But that cool, attractive stone has the opposite function at The Wongalinga apartments.

At this slate-floored haven on Mission Beach, the scene has no beginning and no end, offering cinemascope vistas of Dunk and Bedarra islands in the azure Coral Sea. And just like those who make the movies, you can call for as much or as little action as you like.

The self-contained apartments are designed along tropical plantation house lines, with full-length glass doors that seem to draw the lawn and trees inwards with a mysterious magnetism. Forget crossing roads with arms full of swimming gear – the golden beach is the main feature in close-up, ready and waiting as you relax over a meal prepared on the barbecue. When it's time to cool down, the soothing decor, cane furniture, air-conditioning and ceiling fans are handy. Or an interval by the pool could be what the script requires.

If an action adventure is on the cards, try kayaking, sailing, skydiving or many other 'missions possible', then follow up with a siesta on the green grass in the shade of coconut palms.

Hinchinbrook Marine Cove Resort

Lucinda

47 Dungeness Road, Lucinda ▪ 1800 002 338, 07 4777 8377
www.beautifulaccommodation.com/hinchinbrookresort

Versatile fishing resort

Pristine waterways, stunning reefs and untouched islands provide the backdrop to Hinchinbrook Marine Cove Resort. Sitting at the entrance to the Hinchinbrook Channel, this is the spot for an encounter with nature and a dose of tropical adventure.

There is an accommodation choice for everyone: island-view studio rooms and apartments, poolside water-view one-bedroom bungalows, two-bedroom poolside townhouses and four-bedroom fully self-contained luxury riverfront houses.

Tropical gardens surround the two resort-style pools and children's playground, and there is a restaurant and cafe for dining.

For lovers of nature, the varied bird life around the resort will enchant. Many guests also include on their itineraries a visit to the local national parks, where breathtaking waterfalls including Jourama and Wallaman are not to be missed.

Numerous Australian Sportfishing records have been claimed in these waters and this is a popular location for filming television fishing specials.

At the end of a day full of adventure, what could be more relaxing than a sundowner followed by seafood on the barbecue or a meal in the restaurant at this resort?

Rates
Whole unit, bungalow, townhouse or house per night from $115-$400 (1-8 guests)
Accommodation only
Visa, MC, AMEX, DD, Eftpos

Location
1¾ hours or 135km north of Townsville. Map 11 and 12.

Minimum stay
Four nights (houses only)

Facilities
A range of accommodation, sleeping up to 8; all with TV, AC; most with kitchen, lounge, dining. Two pools, BBQs, laundry, boat ramp. Licensed restaurant, cafe, general store.

Other
Suitable for children
Disabled facilities

Owner details
Mark and Lisa Blyth
▪ reservations@hinchinbrook marinecove.com.au
▪ www.hinchinbrook marinecove.com.au

Best at Bright Point

Magnetic Island (Nelly Bay)

146 Sooning Street, Nelly Bay, Magnetic Island ▪ 0412 326 506, 0433 322 300
www.beautifulaccommodation.com/bestatbrightpoint

240

Rates
Whole apartment per night
from $200-$400 (up to 7 guests)
Accommodation only
Visa, MC, DC, DD, Eftpos,
Chq, PayPal

Location
20 minutes by ferry from
Townsville. Map 11.

Minimum stay
Two nights

Facilities
Two apartments (two- and
three-bedrooms with king, queen
and single beds), with lounge
(large LCD TV, DVD, CD), dining,
kitchen, laundry, BBQ, ducted AC.
Four pools, spa, gym.

Other
Suitable for children
Disabled facilities

Owner details
Penny and Phil Coleman
▪ bestonmi@gmail.com
▪ www.beautifulaccommodation.
com/bestatbrightpoint

Nouveau seaside chic

That magic phrase – "absolute
waterfrontage" – means what it says
at this modern island resort. There
is no passing traffic between your
apartment at One Bright Point and
the languid waters that lap Magnetic
Island. You can watch the dolphins
leaping as you sip a morning brew
of coffee in the comfort of your
king-size bed.

No expense has been spared to
make the two privately owned and
operated 'Best At Bright Point'
apartments world-class additions
to the increasingly upmarket pool
of Magnetic Island accommodation
options. The interiors have a timeless
modernism, with clean, white walls

and fittings soothingly offset by
blonde timber doors and luscious
leather sofas in nouveau tones.

The beds combine rich timber bases
with heavenly mattresses and crisp,
cool contemporary linens. And we
appreciated the thought that has
clearly gone into selecting the original
artworks that adorn the walls.

The resort facilities are excellent, with
four pools (including an infinity one
that seems to blend straight into the
sea beyond), a spa, gym, barbecues
and undercover parking.

Shops, restaurants and beaches are
just a short stroll away.

Mandalay House
Magnetic Island (Nelly Bay)

26 Mandalay Avenue, Magnetic Island ▪ 07 4778 5435, 0416 015 247
www.beautifulaccommodation.com/mandalayhouse

Timber tropical romance

Magnetic Island has evolved into a sophisticated island stay for discerning travellers who want the pleasure and privacy of a secluded north Queensland scene. But kids and pets are welcome too, particularly when you stay at the stately Mandalay House.

The very name Mandalay conjures up a tropical aesthetic and romantic style. And this Mandalay has the complete Rudyard Kipling package of wooden floors, French doors opening to deep, shady verandahs and the soft, sweet aroma of tropical vegetation wafting in from the garden.

There are four big bedrooms, including a queen bedroom with ensuite, plus there's another bedroom, which is its own pavilion off the verandah.

The property is fully self-contained, which means feeding the tribe doesn't need to cost a fortune every time the hunger pangs call. Just throw some marinated chicken on the barbecue and sit back on the verandah with a gin and tonic tinkling in your hand.

Exotic birds call from the trees in the trim garden and your kids will soon be in the pool or off to nearby Nelly Bay beach to build a sandcastle.

Magnetic Island is a World Heritage-listed national park and it makes a great base for trips to the outer Barrier Reef and Townsville.

Rates
Whole house per night from $270-$550 (up to 10 guests)
Accommodation only
Direct Deposit, no credit cards

Location
30 minutes by ferry from Townsville. Map 11.

Minimum stay
Two nights

Facilities
One house: four bedrooms (accommodating up to 10), lounge (flat-screen TV, Austar, DVD), dining, kitchen, laundry, AC. Pool, BBQ.

Other
Suitable for children
Pets welcome

Owner details
Judi Ross
▪ jpross3@bigpond.com
▪ www.beautifulaccommodation.com/mandalayhouse

Lotus House

Magnetic Island (Horseshoe Bay)

Pacific Drive, Horseshoe Bay, Magnetic Island ▪ 07 4778 5955
www.beautifulaccommodation.com/lotushouse

242

Rates
Whole house per night from
$800-$1150 (up to 6 guests)
Accommodation only
Visa, MC, AMEX

Location
20 minutes by ferry from
Townsville. Map 11.

Minimum stay
Three nights

Facilities
Three bedrooms (two king, one
queen; all with satellite TV and
AC), four bathrooms, lounge
(plasma TV, satellite, DVD, CD),
dining, kitchen, undercover decks.
Saltwater temperature-controlled
pool. Internet, security, laundry,
undercover parking.

Member
Best of Magnetic

Owner details
Kelvin and Fiona Dyson
▪ lotus@bestofmagnetic.com
▪ www.lotusonmagnetic.com

Premium Australasian beach house

The usual superlatives are not
enough for this dream beach
house on Magnetic Island's
exquisite Horseshoe Bay. Lotus
House is a stunning fusion of
contemporary Australian beach style
with a meticulous, Asian-inspired
attention to every detail of luxury and
comfort. No expense has been
spared in making this one the very
best beach pads we have seen.

Where to start? The gorgeous
ambience of the place captures
your heart first: the minutely tended
gardens, the soaring cathedral roofs
and detailed woodwork, and then
there's all of the stylish furniture and

quality fittings that grace every corner
of this house.

There is plenty of entertainment room
for up to six people, with the perfect
mix of shared space and private
corners for solitude, both indoors and
out. And we found the three master
bedrooms to be little pleasure
palaces in their own right.

The 40-metre frontage on Horseshoe
Bay is fringed by the immaculate
gardens. There are fine places to eat
on Magnetic Island and booking a trip
to the outer Barrier Reef is easy. But,
really, why would you want to leave
Lotus House?

Pure Magnetic
Magnetic Island (Nelly Bay)

9 The Esplanade, Nelly Bay, Magnetic Island ▪ 07 4778 5955
www.beautifulaccommodation.com/puremagnetic

Bali-influenced garden villas

Somebody has waved the magic resort wand here, taking the very best of Balinese-inspired villa architecture and embedding it on the site with the best beachfront proximity on Magnetic Island. That's how it feels when you enter the privileged grounds of Pure Magnetic. Style and graceful harmony reign everywhere.

There are 10 fully self-contained villas, each with everything a family or group needs for some well-earned rest and relaxation. You can chill in the quiet privacy of your villa, take a dip in the pool, or settle back with a glass of shiraz and the tongs before the courtyard barbecue.

The facilities and furnishings of each villa are faultless, from plasma satellite TVs and WiFi to wonderful cane furniture, timber floors and louvered tropical windows.

The front villas look across a superb maritime vista and the internal villas will suit those who enjoy either pool or garden perspectives.

All the Townsville attractions and Barrier Reef tourism facilities are a short ferry ride away. But why cross the waters when you can enjoy the pleasures of Magnetic Island?

Rates
Whole house per night from $195-$325 (up to 4 guests)
Accommodation only
Visa, MC, AMEX

Location
20 minutes by ferry from Townsville. Map 11.

Minimum stay
Two nights

Facilities
10 villas: each with two bedrooms (king/twin single and queen, plasma TV), two bathrooms (one with spa), kitchen, lounge (plasma satellite TV, DVD), dining, private courtyard (BBQ) and verandah. Pool, WiFi.

Member
Best of Magnetic

Owner details
Kelvin and Fiona Dyson
▪ pure@bestofmagnetic.com
▪ www.puremagnetic.com

Port Douglas
the Daintree & the Far North

As you travel north from Cairns to Port Douglas and beyond, there is the excitement of heading into an ancient, mysterious landscape. The road leads to the Daintree, Australia's greatest rainforest wilderness, and to some of the country's best boutique accommodation. Here you will find an irresistible combination of exotic vistas, extraordinary wildlife and pampering for all the senses. At least once in your life, we think you should treat yourself and visit this World Heritage-listed treasure.

As you travel north of Port Douglas, the rainforest draws closer and the ancient landscape begins to reveal its secrets.

The Far North of Queensland really begins at the tropical harbour town of Port Douglas, a marvellously preserved relic of the days when sea travel was the only way in or out. It retains the quiet aura of a relaxed bush town while providing all the pleasures holidaymakers want. Attractions range from day spas and resorts to ice cream vendors and bling retailers along famous Macrossan Street.

The Sunday market at the waterfront park has exotic tropical fruits, books, old tools, hats, great food and more. As you wander back towards town, a gourmet compendium of restaurants and cafes presents itself including the historic Court House Hotel, which has

been serving cold beer since 1878. In Port Douglas, choose between cafes with chai and toasties, and five-star restaurants offering fresh seafood. Celebrity spotters: keep your eyes open.

Flagstaff Hill rises up behind town, offering a stunning vista over Four Mile Beach. The beach is an iconic rainforest-by-the-sea setting, ideal for freewheeling bike rides on the sand.

As you travel north of Port Douglas, the rainforest draws closer and the ancient landscape begins to reveal its secrets. The Whyanbeel Valley is a verdant paradise of vines, trees and fluttering blue Ulysses butterflies. Its sheer beauty attracts many artists.

The actor and former wife of Sean Connery, Diane Cilento, has built her Karnack Playhouse in the valley (set in a great natural amphitheatre). As you explore the area, expect to find glassblowers, galleries and some great eateries for grazing on local treats.

The traditional owners of the Daintree area, the Kuku Yalanji people, have long loved what is now known as Mossman Gorge, just on the outskirts of Mossman. The Gorge's granite boulders are spliced by glassy waters and surrounded by lush rainforest with walking tracks to meander along.

The wild country of the Daintree deepens as you drive further north.

Cairns
51 Esplanade
07 4051 3588
www.cairnsgreatbarrierreef.org.au

At the Daintree River crossing, a vehicle punt chugs trucks and cars over the crocodile-infested river. Beyond the river, phone coverage begins to falter and the electricity grid ends. Before disappearing into the jungle ahead, take a crocodile viewing cruise and learn about the local estuarine environment and history.

The Daintree Forest is studded with creek crossings, beaches, bays and unexpected vistas of the Coral Sea. The small community of Cow Bay is a unique and historic outpost nestled in the Daintree. The bay itself is about 10 minutes' drive and is a marvellously deserted stretch of beach. The last petrol station is at Diwan on the road to Cape Tribulation.

Despite its ominous sounding name given by Captain James Cook in 1770, Cape Tribulation is a thrilling rainforest eco destination. You can take night tours of the rainforest (and spot tropical pythons coiled in the trees), ride horses on the beach, swim in season at the many beaches, or relax and soak up the atmosphere wherever you choose to stay.

Cooktown is a few hours north of Cape Tribulation and one of Australia's most isolated townships. The ultimate northern wilderness adventure, Bloomfield, and the renowned Bloomfield Lodge will cosset you in the heart of this pristine rainforest setting where you can enjoy some serious pampering.

Coral Sea Retreat

Oak Beach (near Port Douglas)

7-11 Bruce Avenue, Oak Beach, Port Douglas ▪ 07 4099 3617
www.beautifulaccommodation.com/coralsearetreat

Rates
Tree House per couple
from $129-$149
Accommodation only,
full breakfast available
B&B room per couple from
$119-$139, full breakfast included
Visa, MC, DD

Location
50 minutes or 58km north of
Cairns, 10 minutes south of Port
Douglas. Map 13.

Minimum stay
Four nights (Tree House)

Facilities
One tree house (two bedrooms,
open living, kitchenette, bathroom,
AC) and two studio rooms (queen
or king/twin single bed, ensuite,
AC, TV for DVDs, bar fridge). Pool,
spa and treetops pavilion.

Other
Suitable for children

Host details
Marie and Denise, and
Michael and Michelle
▪ info@coralsearetreat.com
▪ www.coralsearetreat.com

Gourmet tree house experience

What child has never dreamed of
having a tree house? Well, for anyone
who wasn't so lucky to enjoy one as
a child, it's a dream come true for
guests who come to Coral Sea
Retreat – an experience that has
been endorsed by an enthusiastic
review in the respected *The Wall
Street Journal*.

To get an idea of the funky Tree
House apartment design, imagine
a cube with two smaller cubes within
it – these serve as the bedrooms.
The rest is a generous space that
incorporates a lounge, dining and
kitchen, complete with a large
screened wall that opens to Coral
Sea views.

On top of that, guests can share the
Treetops pavilion – an open-air lounge
above the Tree House with a
television to watch DVDs, and comfy
lounges for relaxing and taking in the
rainforest and ocean. Bed and
breakfast rooms are also available.

Dinners are lovingly created, from
light meals to full celebratory dining
in Thai and other styles. Divine
breakfasts can include glorious
tropical fruits such as black sapote,
often called chocolate pudding fruit.

Everything is at your doorstep, from
trendy Port Douglas to the Daintree,
the spectacular Skyrail to Kuranda
and even the Atherton Tablelands.

Dreamcatcher Apartments
Port Douglas

26-28 Reef Street, Port Douglas ▪ 07 4099 1800
www.beautifulaccommodation.com/dreamcatcher

Relaxed tropical resort

Dream catchers are protective charms designed to block bad dreams and allow sweet ones to filter through for a night of peaceful sleep. With its quiet leafy location – barefoot strolling distance from Four Mile Beach – DreamCatcher is the perfect place to switch off from the buzz of city life and unwind in truly special surroundings.

The passion and energy of the owners is evident in all aspects of this refreshingly relaxed property: lovingly maintained tropical gardens, dazzling exteriors bursting with colour and sunny interiors that radiate comfort.

Each one-bedroom or studio apartment has luxury fittings,

a spacious bathroom and a modern entertainment system – they even have WiiFit and Playstation available for your stay, as well as office facilities. But for those seeking a quieter time, squeeze some limes for your afternoon cocktail and relax on your private balcony or patio, or slip down to the saltwater pool for a pre-dinner swim.

A special inclusion is the Suzuki 4WD that's available for guests to use – just pay for petrol – and local guides will pick you up from the front door. It makes trips to the nearby golf courses, restaurants, diving and fishing haunts so easy.

Rates
Apartment per night $145-$220
Accommodation only
Visa, MC, AMEX, Eftpos

Location
1 hour or 67km north of Cairns.
Map 13.

Minimum stay
Two nights

Facilities
Six one-bedroom apartments (king/twin single, kitchen; four connect to form two bedrooms), six studios (queen) with lounge (TV, DVD, CD), dining, patio/balcony. Pool, courtesy car.

AAA Star Rating
★★★★☆

Other
Suitable for children
Pets by arrangement

Manager details
John Wladysiuk and
Annie Schoenberger
▪ info@dreamcatcher
apartments.com
▪ www.dreamcatcher
apartments.com

Driftwood Apartment

Port Douglas

65-67 Macrossan Street, Port Douglas ▪ 0428 841 445
www.beautifulaccommodation.com/driftwoodportdouglas

Rates
Whole apartment per night from
$200-$250 (up to 4 guests)
Accommodation only
Direct deposit, PayPal,
no credit cards

Location
1 hour or 67km north of Cairns.
Map 13.

Minimum stay
Five nights

Facilities
One apartment: two bedrooms
(one king with ensuite; one with
king/twin singles), lounge (TV,
DVD), dining, kitchen, second
bathroom (spa). Pool, spa, BBQ,
laundry.

Owner details
Peter and Heather Wells
▪ peterheatherwells@hotmail.com
▪ www.beautifulaccommodation.
com/driftwoodportdouglas

Sunlit resort apartment

This privately owned apartment is
located in the Driftwood-Mantaray
tropical resort complex, which is
surrounded by landscaped gardens
and towering palms. Plus it's at the
pleasantly quiet seaside end of Port
Douglas village.

Each of the two bedrooms – the main
with an ensuite, the second with a
spa – is quite separate from one
another, providing plenty of privacy
for couples travelling together.

A full kitchen allows for self-catering
and the spacious north-facing
balcony is perfect for evening drinks,
overlooking one of the resort's two
enticing saltwater swimming pools.

Decorated in earthy tones with
contemporary modern wicker lounges
and elegant plantation-style decorator
touches, the apartment is styled for
a luxury adult holiday. Its coveted
corner position allows the natural
sunlight to flood the apartment and
sliding doors allow the gentle lap of
the Coral Sea to lull you to sleep.

Just a short stroll away are stunning
beaches and an array of chic
boutiques and cafes. Port Douglas
has much to offer: horse riding,
historical walks, reef cruises and
rainforest exploration tours are all
available, and operators will collect
you from your apartment.

Martinique on Macrossan
Port Douglas

66 Macrossan Street, Port Douglas ▪ 07 4099 6222
www.beautifulaccommodation.com/martinique

Intimate resort for couples

Why do honeymooners and love birds flock back time and again to this French Caribbean-inspired resort? To relive the idyllic romantic times that Martinique inspires. Located near the heart of laid-back Port Douglas village and just moments from spectacular Four Mile Beach, this is the ideal spot for lazy afternoons.

Martinique hums with tropical energy: its vibrant colours and thriving gardens reflect the upbeat personality of the managers, whose passion extends to every aspect of the presentation.

Each one-bedroom apartment has a queen-size bed, kitchenette and private balcony perfect for after-dinner drinks.

The relaxed interiors feature rattan furniture and thoughtfully included freshly cut flowers, and they are flooded with natural light.

A heated saltwater pool is laid with a kaleidoscope of Moorish tiles and it is private enough for moonlight swims.

Port Douglas is the stepping off point for Great Barrier Reef cruises and rainforest discovery tours, while its local cafes are great for morning coffee and leisurely brunches.

The beautiful white sand beaches, fringed with coconut palms, are postcard-perfect for sunset strolls and inviting swims in the clear Coral Sea.

Rates
Whole apartment per couple from $150-$195
Accommodation only
Visa, MC, JCB, Eftpos

Location
1 hour or 67km or north of Cairns. Map 13.

Facilities
One-bedroom apartments (queen bed), each with ensuite, lounge (DVD, CD), kitchenette, balcony. Laundry. Heated saltwater pool, tour desk, WiFi.

AAA Star Rating
★★★★

Other
Disabled facilities

Manager details
Antonia and Fred Eggers
▪ info@martinique.com.au
▪ www.martinique.com.au

Port Douglas Cottage and Lodge
Port Douglas

4 Owen Street, Port Douglas ▪ 07 4098 5432, 0427 639 463
www.beautifulaccommodation.com/portdouglascottage

Rates
Whole Cottage per couple $375
Whole Lodge per night $475
(up to 4 guests)
Specials packages available
Accommodation only
Visa, MC, DD

Location
1 hour or 67km north of Cairns.
Map 13.

Minimum stay
Three nights

Facilities
Cottage: one queen ensuite
bedroom, kitchenette, lounge
(LCD TV, DVD, iPod dock), pool,
spa, AC, fans. Lodge: two king/twin
single ensuite bedrooms, lounge
(LCD TV, DVD, iPod dock), dining,
kitchen, pool, BBQ, AC, fans. WiFi,
laundry, parking.

Other
Suitable for children

Owner details
Sue and Graeme Lawrence
▪ portdouglascottage@bigpond.com
▪ www.portdouglascottage.com

Tropical designer retreats

Port Douglas Cottage and Lodge
are exactly how one imagines a
stylish tropical escape: white, fresh,
uncomplicated and breezy. It has
the feel of a tropical hinterland
escape and echoes the style of the
famous St Mary's By The Sea church
in Port Douglas.

There are two distinct choices here
or you may opt to take both: the
Cottage, a romantic couples escape,
and the Lodge, which is ideal for
families or two couples travelling
together. Each architect-designed
property is in the traditional
Queenslander style, intended to
capture the cool afternoon breezes

and featuring the understated
elegance of bright, clean interiors.

Both options have their own private
swimming pools and sundecks
surrounded by verdant gardens.
The thoughtful hosts provide gourmet
pantry essentials such as olive oil,
balsamic vinegar and spices for tasty
poolside barbecues.

The central location is walking
distance to beaches, cafes and the
marina, ensuring you can enjoy
a car-free holiday. Ask your hosts
for some insiders' tips on local
sightseeing and tours.

Port Douglas On Macrossan Apartments
Port Douglas

Various locations on Macrossan Street, Port Douglas • 0424 322 181
www.beautifulaccommodation.com/pdapartments

Private boutique apartments

Port Douglas has justly become one of the great tourist destinations for local and international visitors who prefer a relaxed, small-town Queensland vibe to the frenzied go-go of its big-town southern counterparts. The town is blessed with some unique accommodation options, including this boutique collection at Port Douglas On Macrossan Apartments.

The owners have put together a highly individual and diverse portfolio of apartments along the cruisy food and retail-therapy precinct of Macrossan Street. Each unit has been furnished by an interior designer with a strict focus on comfort and unfussy style.

The beds are cushion-packed and restful, the kitchens are well appointed and the lounge areas feature private balconies with lounge settings – ideal for a tropical siesta. Two apartments are within 100 metres of Four Mile beach and another overlooks the historic St Mary's By The Sea church.

Visitors who are new to Port Douglas will appreciate the personalised service that comes with a Port Douglas On Macrossan apartment. The local manager who runs the property meets every guest on arrival, and they can tell you about the best spots to eat in town, and advise on and even book your tours.

Rates
Whole apartment per couple
from $145-$285
Accommodation only
Visa, MC, DD, Chq

Location
1 hour or 67km or north of Cairns.
Map 13.

Minimum stay
Five nights

Facilities
A collection of one- and two-bedroom apartments, each with lounge (TV, DVD, CD), dining, kitchen, bathroom, balcony, pool, RC AC.

Owner details
Phil and Lisa Hopper
▪ portdouglas.apts@internode.on.net
▪ www.portdouglasapartments.net.au

Reflections of Port Douglas

Port Douglas

70 Macrossan Street, Port Douglas ▪ 07 4099 4555
www.beautifulaccommodation.com/reflections

254

Rates
Whole apartment per couple from
$230-$430 (extra guests
$20-$30 per night)
Accommodation only
Visa, MC, AMEX, DC, Eftpos, Chq

Location
1 hour or 67km north of Cairns.
Map 13.

Minimum stay
Three nights

Facilities
Eight serviced apartments: two or
three bedrooms, each with two
bathrooms (both with bath, some
with spa), lounge (TV, Austar,
DVD/VCR, CD), indoor/outdoor
terrace, kitchen, laundry, AC.
Heated pool, tour desk, parking.

AAA Star Rating
★★★★☆

Other
Suitable for children

Host details
Carmel Angelino and John Jensen
▪ carmel@reflectionsofpd.com.au
▪ www.reflectionsofpd.com.au

Gracious tropical apartments

The images of these lovely apartments only give you a glimpse of the gracious style of Reflections of Port Douglas. But they can't convey the quality of the brilliant management here, headed by Carmel Angelino. She figures frequently in the rave reviews guests leave about Reflections – and with good reason. Carmel is a life-long local who just loves to share her infectious passion for Port Douglas.

This intimate resort has eight apartments, giving it an uncrowded friendly vibe. We love the generous mix of space and amenities provided for guests. Every apartment – even the two-bedders – has two bathrooms, with either a bath or spa.

The kitchen and entertainment spaces are some of the largest in Port Douglas. They are swankily finished with individual designer touches and soft lamplight to create a relaxing tropical vibe.

Reflections is right on Macrossan Street, which means you can walk to the beaches, shops and restaurants while the car stays cool in the undercover parking. Just bring the family or a crew of friends and let the good times roll.

Shantara Resort and Spa
Port Douglas

27-31 Davidson Street, Port Douglas ▪ 1800 427 100, 07 4084 1400
www.beautifulaccommodation.com/shantara

Luxurious tropical sparkle

For a romantic tropical odyssey to Port Douglas, you want to be assured of superb facilities. Shantara Resort and Spa delivers on both counts. This sparkling resort is worth every one of its five stars. And, if you want to escape from noisy kids, you'll love Shantara even more; this is a retreat designed for adults.

The accommodation options include self-contained studio rooms with kitchenettes and one-bedroom apartments with a spacious lounge and full kitchen. You can combine one of each to create a two-bedroom haven, which would give two couples togetherness, but with privacy.

Honeymooners should note that for the ultimate indulgence, you'll want to book in advance for one of just four Shantara Apartments that feature their own private courtyard Jacuzzi. And thanks to a brilliant design, all the ground-floor studios and apartments feature pool decks so you can slide straight into one of the two resort pools.

The interior style is supremely tasteful with cool tiled floors and shoji-style screen doors that separate spaces. There is also a gym and day spa to keep the body pepped up and relaxed during your break.

Shantara is perfectly placed for access to Four Mile Beach and Macrossan Street – both a 400-metre stroll – so a car is not required.

Rates
Whole studio or apartment per couple $205-$420
Accommodation only
Visa, MC, AMEX, Eftpos

Location
One hour or 67km north of Cairns.
Map 13.

Minimum stay
Three nights

Facilities
Studio rooms (queen, kitchenette, ensuite, balcony; some with pool deck); One- and two-bedroom apartments (king bedroom with spa ensuite, lounge, dining, kitchen; some with pool deck); Four Shantara apartments also with Jacuzzi and pool deck. Two pools (one heated), gym, day spa, BBQs.

AAA Star Rating
★★★★★

Manager details
Marianna and Luigi Bonomi
▪ info@shantara.com.au
▪ www.shantara.com.au

The White House Holiday Apartments
Port Douglas

19 Garrick Street, Port Douglas ▪ 07 4099 5600
www.beautifulaccommodation.com/thewhitehouse

256

Rates
Whole apartment per night from
$190-$395 (rates are for 2-6 guests)
Accommodation only
Visa, MC, DD, Eftpos, Chq

Location
1 hour or 67km north of Cairns.
Map 13.

Minimum stay
Three nights

Facilities
Nine one-, two- and three-
bedroom apartments (a range
of bed configurations). All with
lounge (TV), dining, kitchen,
laundry, fans, AC. Pool, BBQ,
undercover entertaining area,
tour desk.

AAA Star Rating
★★★★

Other
Suitable for children

Manager details
Margaret Wilson
▪ info@whitehouse
portdouglas.com.au
▪ www.whitehouse
portdouglas.com.au

Tropical Plantation-style apartments

Port Douglas is the quintessential
north Queensland harbour town
without the fuss and hurry of bigger
places along the coast.

The White House Holiday Apartments
fit in perfectly here, with their breezy
plantation mansion style of shady
verandahs and tropical gardens.
As you laze on a banana lounge by
the landscaped pool with a cold beer
in your cooler, you soon see why
people love the climate up here.

There are nine fully self-contained
apartments in this quiet, superbly
maintained property. These are not
cookie-cutter units; there is a full
range of bedroom and layout options
including a funky two-level apartment.

The interior style continues the
tropical theme with very comfy
furniture, cooling tiles underfoot
and fans overhead.

The undercover entertainment area
and barbecue are ideal for outside
living, and even better for avoiding
mess in the kitchen.

The White House apartments are
tucked a block away from the main
Port Douglas food and shopping
precinct of Macrossan Street,
providing easy access but also
ensuring a hushed evening quiet.
Four Mile Beach is a short stroll from
the apartments, through a small park.

Villa San Michele
Port Douglas

39-41 Macrossan Street, Port Douglas ▪ 07 4099 4088
www.beautifulaccommodation.com/villasanmichele

Tropical-Mediterranean apartments

Families and couples love Villa San Michele and it is easy to see why. It makes a perfect base for exploring all that Port Douglas has to offer.

Villa San Michele is set back from Macrossan Street and provides immediate access to the township's central tour and entertainment zone but with the relaxed privacy of a walled Mediterranean compound.

There are 40 fully self-contained one- and two-bedroom apartments in the complex, which gives Villa San Michele the scale to support two saltwater pools, a spa, guest laundries and barbecue facilities. These all make it an ideal stop for families and friends who don't want to pull out the credit card to dine out for every breakfast, lunch and dinner during their holiday.

The apartments are brilliantly suited to the environment. They have cooling terracotta tiled floors, fans, air conditioning, and a breezy design that is both tranquil and comfortable.

All the best restaurants, ice-creameries and shopping boutiques of Port Douglas are on the doorstep of Villa San Michele. It is also an easy walk to the famous Four Mile Beach and Marina Mirage, where tour boats depart for the Great Barrier Reef or up the river.

Rates
Room per couple from $160-$190 (extra guests $25 per night)
Accommodation only
Visa, MC, AMEX, DC, Eftpos

Location
1 hour or 67km north of Cairns. Map 13.

Facilities
40 one- and two-bedroom apartments: each with queen and/or twin beds, lounge (TV, Austar, DVD), dining, kitchenette, balcony, WiFi, AC, fans. Two saltwater pools, spa, BBQ, undercover parking, laundry.

AAA Star Rating
★★★★

Other
Suitable for children

Manager details
Olivia and Al Spence
▪ info@villasanmichele.com.au
▪ www.villasanmichele.com.au

Boonooloo Beach House

Newell Beach (near Port Douglas)

Newell Beach, exact location on enquiry ▪ 0419 232 322
www.beautifulaccommodation.com/boonooloo

Rates
Whole house per night from
$600-$660 (up to 6 guests)
Accommodation only, catering
or chef by prior arrangement
Visa, MC, DD

Location
75 minutes or 80km north
of Cairns. Map 13.

Minimum stay
Five nights

Facilities
One house: three bedrooms (king/
twin singles, AC; two with ocean
views), two bathrooms, lounge
(TV, DVD), dining, kitchen. Pool,
BBQ, sauna.

Other
Suitable for children

Owner details
Ronni Leigh
▪ info@oceaniabeachhouses.com
▪ www.oceaniabeachhouses.com

Spectacular beachfront architecture

Boonooloo Beach House was
designed by the famed North
Queensland luxury home architect,
Chris Vandyke, and it is clear she
relishes her beachfront location. It's
right on the water's edge with views
across the bay to cosmopolitan Port
Douglas. Boonooloo means
"surrounded by water" and everything
about her design celebrates this
absolute beachfront setting.

Boonooloo's interior perfectly suits
the climate and vibe of Newell Beach:
open-plan with high ceilings and
plenty of discrete spaces to soak
up the tropical glow at different times
of the day.

In typical Vandyke style, the house
brilliantly employs timber and glass
to frame the surrounding land and
seascapes, bringing the outside
up close.

The infinity wet edge pool is just 20
paces from the water's edge so it's
your choice whether to lounge on
a deck chair or swing in a hammock
under the shade of a palm tree.
When you need to wash off the sand
and sun lotion, you'll covet the natural
marble bathrooms.

Families will love Boonooloo but
we can also picture it as the perfect
spot for a group of girlfriends or a
guys' hideaway. It is also the ultimate
venue for a honeymoon or special
occasion, with the oceanfront deck
able to seat up to 60 people.

Daintree Beach House

Wonga Beach (near Port Douglas)

44 Esplanade, Wonga Beach ▪ 0419 027 807
www.beautifulaccommodation.com/daintreebeachhouse

Wondrous Wonga Beach

If you don't remember the simple pleasures of beach holidays in the 1950s – no traffic, fires on the beach in the evening, everyone in togs and barefoot around the house – here is your opportunity to recreate that lost lifestyle.

Daintree Beach House is a funky, renovated tropical pad at Wonga Beach. It has four bedrooms (enough for a 1950s-size family) and a breezily laid-back style. From the shady pool deck you can look up from your book and gaze through the screen of coastal palms to the Coral Sea. Heaven!

The interior design is a totally unaffected blend of Australian beach house simplicity and Asian decorative features.

Bright rainbow bed spreads, comfy lounges and marble benchtops in the well-equipped kitchen all help to imbue this gem with a relaxed and inviting atmosphere.

The two bathrooms are stocked with fluffy towels and fine soaps. A cooling sea breeze wafts languidly through the breezeways but if it gets warm, there are also fans and reverse-cycle air-conditioning.

All the suppliers you need for holiday feasting – a butcher, bottle shop, fruit and veggie dealer – are nearby. And Port Douglas is a short jaunt through rainforest and cane fields for tours, fine food and boutique shopping.

Rates
Whole house per night $330
(up to 4 people, $35 per extra person aged over 3 years)
Accommodation only
Direct deposit, no credit cards

Location
1¼ hours or 95km north of Cairns.
Map 13.

Minimum stay
Four nights

Facilities
One house: four bedrooms (queen with ensuite, king/twin single, queen and king single/trundle), lounge room (TV, DVD/VCR), kitchen, second bathroom, covered patio living, laundry. Pool. BBQ.

Other
Suitable for children
Pets by arrangement

Owner details
Schell Clancy
▪ info@daintreebeachhouse.com
▪ www.daintreebeachhouse.com

Port Douglas Valley Retreat

Mowbray Valley (near Port Douglas)

49 Grays Creek Terrace, Mowbray Valley ▪ 07 4098 5252, 0409 679 935
www.beautifulaccommodation.com/portdouglasvalleyretreat

Rates
Whole house per night from
$390-$410 (up to 6 guests,
extra guests $20)
Accommodation only, breakfast
and dinner hampers available
Visa, MC, DD

Location
1 hour or 72km north of Cairns.
Map 13.

Minimum stay
Two nights

Facilities
One house: three bedrooms and
one 'sleepout' (sleeps 9), lounge
(TV, DVD, CD), dining, kitchen,
verandahs and decks (BBQ). AC,
internet, library. Pool, parking.

Other
Suitable for children
Pets welcome

Manager details
Peter and Kerry Muller
▪ info@portdouglasvalley
retreat.com.au
▪ www.portdouglasvalley
retreat.com.au

Luxurious rainforest Queenslander

Driving through the rustling cane fields and Mowbray Valley to Port Douglas Valley Retreat is the start of a colourful and sensory experience. The Retreat describes itself as a 'Queenslander' – with all the simplicity and relaxed charm that implies – but it is so much more. This traditional Queenslander has been ramped up into an utterly gorgeous, totally luxurious holiday retreat in the rainforest.

As you walk the lush grounds of the Retreat, it's hard to believe Port Douglas is just a 10-minute drive away. The main house sits in graceful harmony with the surrounding landscape of manicured gardens, rainforest and a turquoise pool.

Inside, the use of rare local timber produces a richly rustic feel. There are three big bedrooms and, our favourite, a 'sleepout' verandah with a romantic four-poster bed.

The furnishings are immaculate, the kitchen is divine and we love the bathroom with its soaking tub that overlooks the garden. A private garden shower is also connected to the house by a decked walkway.

The Daintree and Port Douglas are easily reached for reef tours, shopping and splurges on the local seafood.

The Cassowary

Shannonvale (near Port Douglas)

Lot 25 Cassowary Road, Shannonvale ▪ 07 4098 4136
www.beautifulaccommodation.com/thecassowary

Exceptional rainforest eco-palace

The Cassowary is a true testament to its creators' years of globe-trotting. They have crystallised the best of the best into one palatial architect-designed refuge, which is set in one of the world's greatest eco-travel locations – the far north of Queensland.

This design blends luxury with green self-sustaining technology. Style radiates from every timber highlight and fabric texture.

The bedrooms are calming retreats that are decked out with plasma TVs and blu-ray DVD players. We love the bathrooms, some of which include divine soaking baths.

It's little wonder that *House and Garden* rated The Cassowary one of Australia's Top 50 interiors in 2009.

It's all here, from the stunning wet-edge pool and the gym, to a multi-purpose room for meetings and even mountain bikes for exploring the local area.

The Cassowary's secluded setting masks its proximity to Port Douglas, The Daintree and the Great Barrier Reef. You can stay in or easily slip away for a tour, shopping or a gourmet restaurant treat.

Rates
House per night $750-$1000 (up to 4, extra guests $50 per night) Accommodation only, catering by prior arrangement
Visa, MC

Location
1 hour or 72km north of Cairns. Map 13.

Minimum stay
Three nights

Facilities
Five bedrooms (honeymoon suite with king and spa ensuite; two king suites with ensuites; two double/twin single suites; all with TV, DVD in kings, AC, fans). Lounge (TV, DVD), dining, kitchen, spa bathroom. Pool, BBQ, gym, WiFi, bikes, meeting room.

Other
Suitable for children
Pets welcome
Disabled facilities

Host details
Terry and Sheelagh Horseman
▪ cassowarybookings@gmail.com
▪ www.thecassowary.com

Janbal

Whyanbeel Valley (near Mossman and Port Douglas)

Kahana Road, Whyanbeel ▪ 07 4098 8334
www.beautifulaccommodation.com/janbal

Rates
Whole house per night from
$350-$400 (up to 6 guests)
Accommodation only
Direct deposit, no credit cards

Location
30 minutes or 34km north
of Port Douglas. Map 13.

Minimum stay
Three nights

Facilities
One house: three bedrooms
(master with queen and ensuite,
queen and twin singles), lounge
(cable TV, DVD), dining, kitchen,
library, extensive decks, two
bathrooms. Pool, BBQ.

Owner details
Sue Bingley
▪ info@janbal.com.au
▪ www.janbal.com.au

Magical rainforest hideaway

The drive to Janbal, past tropical
fruit farms and acres of sugar cane,
is a sublime experience. But arriving
at this property is pure magic,
passing over the rushing stream
and wandering through butterfly-filled
gardens that blend seamlessly with
the surrounding rainforest, is
pure magic.

Janbal is named after the Blue
Quandong fruit favoured by the
Wompoo pigeon and the property
is a registered nature refuge.

This luxurious pole house has
the feel of a tree house, with an
open-plan design that harnesses the
soft dappled rainforest light to gently
illuminate the glorious interiors.

Plantation-style rattan furniture
and soft curtains moved by gentle
breezes add to the ambience.
The distinctive collection of local art
and antiques is a testament to the
passion with which Janbal is
presented. With several balconies
facing the pool and gardens, Janbal
offers various spaces for quiet
contemplation, relaxation and
wildlife spotting.

Secluded seaside swims can be
enjoyed at Newell and Wonga, nearby
cafes are great for casual dining and
you can visit Diane Cilento's Karnack
Playhouse. The Daintree River, with
crocodile spotting and cruises, is just
20 minutes away.

Moo Bay Muse
The Daintree (Cow Bay)

Lot 163, Wattle Close, Cow Bay ▪ 0419 717 092
www.beautifulaccommodation.com/moobaymuse

Eco-cool hippy hideaway

The Daintree is a magical landscape that sings its song in bursts of vibrant birdcall, a chorus of frogs, tropical downpours and an array of mysterious rainforest sounds. If this is the type of setting you are seeking from an eco getaway, we have found the perfect place: Moo Bay Muse.

This hideaway is 'polished hippy' in its style, blending pretty mosaics, colourful fabrics and an eclectic music collection with meticulous presentation and attention to detail. The airy, open design embraces the enveloping forest and is self-sufficient in power and water – you won't impact on the world while you stay here.

The interior is cleverly designed with a loft bedroom and another private space downstairs, and at every turn there are vistas to the gardens and rainforest beyond. The name is apt. Moo Bay refers to nearby Cow Bay, a pristine curve of sand and lapping waves.

Undoubtedly, Muse will resonate within your jaded soul as you reconnect with nature: that desire to sketch a tree or photograph a golden frog sunning itself beside a stream or just strip off for a dip in the water hole. You can even bring your dog. Peace.

Rates
Whole cottage per couple
from $200-$250 (extra guests
$25 per night)
Accommodation only
Direct deposit, no credit cards

Location
2 hours or 121km north of Cairns.
Map 13.

Minimum stay
Three nights

Facilities
One house: one bedroom (king)
and loft (king/twin singles), lounge
(TV, DVD, CD), dining, kitchen,
outdoor undercover bathroom.
Bikes, snorkelling gear, games,
CDs, DVDs, internet. Fans.

Other
Pets by arrangement

Owner details
Sam Matthews
▪ info@moobaymuse.com.au
▪ www.moobaymuse.com.au

Wait-a-While Retreat

The Daintree (Cow Bay)

Buchanan Creek Road, Cow Bay ■ 07 4098 5252, 0409 679 935
www.beautifulaccommodation.com/waitawhiledaintree

Rates
Whole house per night from
$390-$410 (up to 6 guests,
extra guests $20 per night)
Accommodation only
Visa, MC, DD

Location
2 hours or 121km north of Cairns.
Map 13.

Minimum stay
Two nights

Facilities
Three bedrooms and one mezzanine
(sleeps 9), lounge (billiard table),
dining, kitchen, two bathrooms;
mezzanine with TV, DVD, internet.
Fans. Pool, BBQ, outdoor shower,
parking.

Other
Suitable for children
Pets welcome
Disabled facilities

Owner details
Peter and Kerry Muller
■ kerry@waitawhiledaintree.com.au
■ www.waitawhiledaintree.com.au

Magical rainforest eco-retreat

You will see more rainforest life during
one late afternoon relaxing on the
verandah at Wait-a-While Retreat
with a cooling glass of Chardonnay
in hand than in a month of harried
bus tours.

This astonishing solar-powered
eco-retreat is one of the wonders
of the Daintree and provides a true
rainforest-by-the-beach experience.

The Retreat is modelled on a New
Guinean long house, with a soaring
timber roof and decking that brings
the rainforest right to your table. We
love the use of timber in the house,
which is the largest private dwelling
north of the Daintree River.

The atmosphere is idyllically relaxed,
with airy, open communal spaces
for play or relaxation, three huge
bedrooms and a pool overlooking
the rainforest. Better still, you can
even bring your pets with you so
that all the family can enjoy the
tropical adventure.

Dog-friendly Cow Bay beach is a
short stroll through the rainforest
and there is wonderful reef snorkelling
just offshore. The owners, Kerry and
Peter, have lived in the Daintree for
many years and are expert guides to
all the local secret spots and tours.

Daintree Cascades
The Daintree (Diwan)

202 Stonewood Road, Diwan ▪ 07 4098 9239, 0437 059 908
www.beautifulaccommodation.com/daintreecascades

Natural nirvana refuge

To imagine a perfect tropical setting, you might give priority to crystal-clear streams with sparkling waterfalls sweeping over spectacular polished stone formations. Lush rainforest could also be included in this picture, with oodles of native wildlife. If that sounds just right, then nature has already done it all here at Daintree Cascades.

This amazing retreat offers two secluded options: The Cottage sleeps four and the Round House sleeps six, or they can both be reserved for larger groups. Each one is an architectural gem, making extensive use of timber and capitalising on its own private nook.

The owners have created a zen-like pebbled area around the buildings so that sun and air can enter, and the cooling forest damp can be savoured at a slight distance.

Guests in each dwelling have their own private access to the streams that flow through the property. You can take a dip in the pure waters while appreciating the soothing current is also generating enough electric current to power the entire property.

You will share this breathtaking wonderland with cassowarys, tree kangaroos, pademelons, myriad songbirds, water dragons, turtles and jungle perch.

Rates
Round House per night $300
(up to 6 guests)
Cottage per night $250
(up to 4 guests)
Accommodation only
Direct deposit, no credit cards

Location
2 hours or 121km or two hours north of Cairns. Map 13.

Facilities
Round House: two queen bedrooms, kitchen, lounge, dining, laundry, BBQ. Cottage: one queen bedroom, lounge, kitchenette. Both with sofa bed, TV, DVD, iPod dock, fans.

Other
Suitable for children

Owner details
James and Ali Kerr
▪ james@daintreecascades.com.au
▪ www.daintreecascades.com.au

Eden Escape

The Daintree (Diwan)

25 Ironbark Road, Diwan, Daintree ▪ 0448 176 004
www.beautifulaccommodation.com/edenescape

Rates
Whole cottage per night
from $225-$300 (up to 6 guests)
Accommodation only
Visa, MC, DC, Eftpos

Location
2 hours or 121km north of Cairns.
Map 13.

Minimum stay
Two nights

Facilities
One house: large attic bedroom
(two queen beds), open-plan
kitchen/dining/lounge (TV, DVD,
sofa bed), separate bathroom
pavilion. Garden deck with plunge
bath. Laundry, BBQ.

Other
Suitable for children

Owner details
Liz and Scott Young
▪ info@edenescape.com.au
▪ www.edenescape.com.au

Natural rainforest cottage

How can we enjoy sensitive environments without blighting the natural beauty that attracts us in the first place? Eden Escape shows how. It combines timber, stone and slate in a Daintree National Park refuge that seems to have sprung from the 110- million-year-old rainforest around it.

A brilliant open-plan design features views of this magical landscape from every picture window, making it appear like vivid paintings on the rendered walls. Sea breezes cool the house and the water supply is pure Daintree rain.

The solar-powered gadgetry includes a full kitchen of appliances, lighting, television and DVD player.

The inside-outside living areas will appeal to families and friends who like to slip from one activity to another, including enjoying the outdoor plunge bath tranforms into a hot tub in the cooler months.

The gardens are subtly sympathetic to the World Heritage rainforest, with butterflies and birds right at home near the house.

Cape Tribulation is nearby and you can sea kayak, "jungle surf" in the forest canopy or visit the Daintree Entomological Museum's astonishing butterfly collection. The property also has parking for a car and boat.

Bloomfield Lodge

The Daintree (Weary Bay, near Ayton)

Weary Bay, exact location on enquiry ▪ 07 4035 9166
www.beautifulaccommodation.com/bloomfieldlodge

Romantic seclusion

Eco-tourists travel across the world to reach the Daintree, but few ever experience its full pristine glory unless Bloomfield Lodge makes it on to their itinerary. This Lodge is still the most remote Queensland destination in our collection of handpicked properties and we make no apologies for including it once again. It combines an unparalleled location with a luxurious tropical design sensibility.

The 17 retreats and cabins at Bloomfield recall the romance of rooms in a Somerset Maugham short story: all louvered glass windows, beds draped in flowing nets, cane chairs and the evocative contrast of creamy paints and fabrics with dark timber fittings. The restful interiors are beautifully offset by the collage of tropical green rainforest and azure seas in the distance.

The tariff includes transfers from Cairns and the wonderful cuisine that combines fresh local ingredients with a dash of Australian flair. All you have to do is plan your next activity, whether it be snorkelling, fishing, walking or some pampering in the day spa (see page 278).

Rates
Per person from $380-$620
Meals, select activities and flight transfers from Cairns included
Visa, MC, AMEX, DC, DD, Eftpos

Location
A 35-minute flight north of Cairns, followed by a 4WD trip and a boat ride. Map 13.

Minimum stay
Four-night package recommended

Facilities
17 ensuite rooms and cabins (queen or twin beds). Restaurant, bar, library, games room, pool, spa pool, laundry, day spa. Meals, transfers to/from Cairns, river cruise and rainforest walks included. Bloomfield Falls, fishing and snorkelling tours available.

General manager details
Ben and Courtenay Morley
▪ bloomfield@tfaustralia.com
▪ www.bloomfieldlodge.com.au

Day spas and spa retreats
New South Wales
& Queensland

Nothing completes a getaway like a day spa indulgence.
The following retreats are alphabetised by destination.

Lavenderluscious Day Spa

Blackheath and Katoomba

The Lavenderluscious Spa is a treat reserved for guests of the three delightful Lavender properties in the Blue Mountains spa towns of Katoomba and Blackheath: Lavender Manor, Lavender Cottage and the new Lavender Majestic (see page 36).

Spa treatments are available at each property, including relaxing massages using essential oils, deluxe European facials, hot stone massages and luxurious body wraps. After your treatment, it is just a few steps back to your room for a snooze.

For enquiries:
02 4782 2385, 0412 884 061
www.beautifulaccommodation.com/
lavenderluscious

Location
Lavender Blue Mountains
and Lavender Majestic.
Map 3.

Spa Menu
Full range of spa treatments

Products
Biodroga and Australian-made products
Exclusively for guests at
Lavender Manor and Cottage, and
Lavender Majestic

Payment
Visa, MC, DD

Owner details
Nicky Vaux
info@lavender
bluemountains.com
www.lavenderblue
mountains.com

Bellachara Boutique Hotel

Gerringong (near Kiama)

We are great fans of the Bellachara Boutique Hotel (see our review on page 101) and its divine, top-floor day spa gives us even more reasons to visit. Arriving is a treat thanks to the stunning guest lounge, which leads to five treatment rooms that are each designed to cosset guests. There are two double rooms (ideal for spousal refurbs or girls' treats) and a special pedicure room. Get in early to enjoy a soothing tea in preparation for your treatment. The spa uses the highly respected hypo-allergenic product line – Payot Paris – for smoothing the lines and buffing the skin.

For enquiries:
02 4234 1359
www.beautifulaccommodation.com/
bellacharaspa

Location
Bellachara Boutique Hotel
1 Fern Street, Gerringong.
Map 2.

Spa menu
Full range of spa treatments

Products
Payot Paris

Payment
Visa, MC, AMEX, DD, Eftpos

Member
ASPA

Owner details
Gregg Currie
hello@bellachara.com.au
www.bellachara.com.au

Tumbling Waters Retreat Spa

Stanwell Tops

Location
Tumbling Waters Retreat
End of Stonehaven Road,
Stanwell Tops.
Map 2 and 4.

Spa menu
A range of massage styles,
body wraps and facials

Products
Biosculpture

Payment
Visa, MC

Owner details
Sonja Keller
info@twr.com.au
www.twr.com.au

Spa locations rarely come better located than that of the Tumbling Waters rejuvenation centre. It is based in one of the most spectacular boutique properties on the east coast of Australia, with serene gardens for walking meditations, superb accommodation (see our review on page 28) and wonderful food.

Plus, there is the unforgettable view out to sea, which you can enjoy from your spa treatment room. The spa offers a full range of deep tissue and relaxation massages plus the thermotherapy of hot stone treatment, which induces profound feelings of wellbeing and relaxation.

For enquiries:
02 4294 1888
www.beautifulaccommodation.com/
tumblingwatersspa

Stephanies Spa Retreat

Brisbane

Stephanies has been a real hit with our readers and you only have to peek inside to know why. It combines the steam bath aesthetic of the Turkish bathhouse masters with every modern therapeutic technology, product and massage technique.

The result is a day spa experience of unparalleled excellence and real sensual delight. The truly divine Opul Rasul Temple steam bath is a masterpiece of spa architecture. Its gorgeous mosaic craftwork is well worth savouring with a partner or friends while you baste your skin with cooling oils and therapeutic muds. A life-enhancing experience.

For enquiries:
07 3221 8800
www.beautifulaccommodation.com/
stephanies-sofitel

Location
Sofitel Brisbane Central.
Level 3, 249 Turbot Street,
Brisbane. Map 8.

Spa menu
Spa body therapies

Products
Thalgo, Payot, Glasshouse, iKOU

Payment
Visa, MC, AMEX, DC, Eftpos

Owner details
Stephanie Shepherd
info@stephaniessparetreat.com
www.stephanies.com.au

272

Beautiful Beings

Brisbane (Kangaroo Point)

We were already firm fans of Beautiful Beings – a glass of chilled bubbly on arrival really sets you and the girls up for a fine time of pampering – but we love it even more now. Why? Because success has enabled them to upgrade to a gorgeous new spa at Kangaroo Point. The dramatic use of marble flooring, rococo lights, timber and candlelight is a sensual treat in itself.

This spa has thrived because its core attribute is generosity. Apart from the welcome bubbles and nibbles, they provide expert advice and a sense of fun.

For enquiries:
07 3391 8998
www.beautifulaccommodation.com/
beautifulbeings

Location
5 minutes from Brisbane CBD.
51 Darragh Street,
Kangaroo Point.
Map 8.

Spa Menu
Personally tailored spa experiences

Products
ELEMIS

Payment
Visa, MC, AMEX, DC, Eftpos

Owner details
Carolynne Todd
dayspa@beautifulbeings.net
www.beautifulbeings.net

Stephanies Urban Spa

Brisbane (Bulimba)

Location
10 minutes from Brisbane CBD.
9/77 Oxford Street,
Bulimba. Map 8.

Spa menu
Spa body therapies

Products
Thalgo, Dermalogica, Payot,
Glasshouse, iKOU

Payment
Visa, MC, AMEX, DC, Eftpos

Owner details
Stephanie Shepherd
info@stephanies.com.au
www.stephanies.com.au

This leafy riverfront Bulimba day spa is where the Stephanies story began and a trip here soon shows why her spas flourish. At the Urban Spa, Stephanie got the formula right for providing the perfect therapeutic experience. And she has only kept improving it since then.

The secret? A true understanding of what the stressed and weary want from their day spa: relaxation, highly personalised treatment, world-class products and exquisite luxury. No wonder Stephanies has devotees everywhere. For added pleasure, arrive by ferry and lunch afterward along leafy Oxford Street.

For enquiries:
07 3899 5333
www.beautifulaccommodation.com/
stephanies-bulimba

Stephanies Mountain Spa

273

Clear Mountain

Location
Mercure Clear Mountain Lodge
Spa and Vineyard
564 Clear Mountain Road,
Clear Mountain.
Map 8 and 9.

Spa menu
A full range of spa
treatments and therapies

Products
Payot, Thalgo, Ikou

Payment
Visa, MC, AMEX, DC, Eftpos

Manager details
Stephanie Shepherd
info@stephanies
mountainspa.com.au
www.stephanies.com.au

Gather the girls, your partner or Mum and head for the gorgeous new Stephanies Mountain Spa. This sparkling spa haven offers a range of indulgences including the newest anti-aging treatment from France – Vinotherapy. This divine treatment releases the antioxidants from grapes directly into the skin, soothing away sun damage and wrinkles.

Around half an hour from Brisbane's CBD, it's an easy run for some pure bliss. As usual with Stephanies spas, the service and spa cuisine are outstanding and the views are sensational.

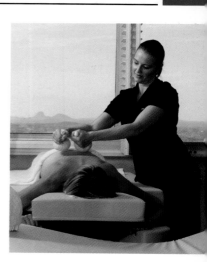

For enquiries:
07 3298 6622
www.beautifulaccommodation.com/
stephanies-mountain

Element On Coolum Day Spa

Coolum

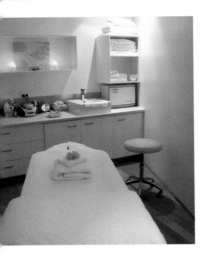

We are great fans of the stylish Element on Coolum (see review, page 160) and our love extends to its intimate day spa too. It is perfectly set up to add an extra layer of well-deserved indulgence to your holiday.

Just slip on your bath robe and wander down for one of the Sanctuary's Element Signature Treatments: a 90-minute body makeover that starts at your toes and finishes with one of the best facial rejuvenations around. Relaxed? Just glide up to your apartment, shed the slippers, and lie back in bliss.

For enquiries:
07 5455 1777
www.beautifulaccommodation.com/
elementdayspa

Location
Element On Coolum Beach.
1808 David Low Way,
Coolum Beach. Map 9.

Spa Menu
Spa, beauty therapy and skin treatments

Products
Baborganic

Payment
Visa, MC, DD, Eftpos

Manager details
Geoff and Tamara Hussin
stay@element
oncoolumbeach.com.au
www.element
oncoolumbeach.com.au

Ikatan Spa

Noosa

We think that Ikatan Spa is unique in Australia as the only authentically Balinese-inspired garden spa. The classic motifs of Balinese architecture and art have been faithfully recreated here as well as that culture's warm, nurturing approach to treating massage as a high art form.

The spa's superb performance is consistent, with Ikatan having been nominated four times as the Best Destination Spa in Australia. It features a full range of Elemis, Environ and Balinese products, as well as arrestingly beautiful gardens for the ultimate in relaxation and replenishment.

For enquiries:
07 5471 1199
www.beautifulaccommodation.com/
ikatandayspa

Location
Ten minutes from Noosa.
46 Grays Road, Doonan. Map 9.

Spa menu
A full range of spa treatments

Products
Elemis and Balinese products

Payments
Visa, MC, AMEX, Eftpos

Contact details
info@ikatanspa.com
www.ikatanspa.com

Noosa Springs Golf and Spa Resort

Noosa Heads

Location
Noosa Springs Golf
and Spa Resort
Links Drive, Noosa Heads.
Map 9.

Spa menu
A full range of spa treatments

Products
Eminence Organic Skin Care

Payment
Visa, MC, AMEX, DC

Spa details
spa@noosasprings.com.au
www.noosasprings.com.au

One of the reasons we covet the Noosa Springs Golf and Spa Resort (see page 168) is because it is home to one of the finest fully featured spa facilities in Australia. The atmosphere is decadently Romanesque, especially the stunning domed roof of the impressive hydro massage pool. This is what luxury is all about.

Whether you choose a traditional massage, or a day of pampering with your partner or friends, the spectacular setting ensures an unforgettable experience. But why visit for a few hours when you can make this resort your next holiday?

For enquiries:
07 5440 3355
www.beautifulaccommodation.com/
noosaspringsspa

Stephanies Ocean Spa

Noosa Heads

Location
Outrigger Little Hastings Street
Resort & Spa.
Level 2, Sunrise Building, Little
Hastings Street, Noosa. Map 9.

Spa menu
Spa body therapies

Products
Payot, Terrake, iKOU

Payment
Visa, MC, AMEX, DC, Eftpos

Owner details
Stephanie Shepherd
info@stephaniesoceanspa.com.au
www.stephanies.com.au

The Stephanies Day Spa name is among the most highly respected in its very competitive field. Why? Because Stephanies focuses complete attention on providing personalised service in a therapeutic realm of absolute luxury.

Walking into the Ocean Spa off Hastings Street in Noosa is like arriving at that blissful place you've been seeking for too long. The staff will take you on a personal journey of relaxation, rejuvenating treatment and ultimately education about how your particular skin type can be best nourished day in and day out. Do yourself a favour and visit.

For enquiries:
07 5473 5353
www.beautifulaccommodation.com/
stephanies-noosa

The Reef House Spa

Palm Cove

The Reef House Spa is one of tropical Queensland's crown jewels. This is a distinctively Australian spa experience that draws its inspiration from the ancient landscape and flora of this continent through the use of the LI'TYA spa care range.

The wooden Vichy beds have been carved by hand in the shape of melaleuca leaves, and these fragrant trees surround the spa. The Reef House pioneered the use of Kodo Gubbera hot stone treatments, using 1.2 billion-year-old stones only found in the mystical Kimberley. This is an award-winning spa for connoisseurs.

For enquiries:
07 4055 3633
www.beautifulaccommodation.com/
exclusivespas-reefhouse

Location
The Sebel Reef House
99 Williams Esplanade,
Palm Cove. Map 12 and 13.

Spa menu
A full range of spa treatments
and therapies

Products
LI'TYA

Payment
Visa, MC, AMEX, DC, Eftpos

Manager details
Loreen Bradley
info@espa.net.au
www.espa.net.au

Exclusive Spas at Peppers Beach Club

Port Douglas

We have always loved Exclusive Spas' offerings and their pampering sanctum at Peppers Beach Club lives up to our expectations. Here you can start your chosen treatment with a traditional smudging ceremony and then allow your skin to soak up the nutrients from Australian Dreamtime-inspired LI'TYA lotions.

As part of the spa experience, amazing handcrafted Vichy tables, which were inspired by lilypads, support and cosset your body as you indulge in water therapies. You don't have be a guest at Peppers to book this incredible experience.

For enquiries:
07 4087 1000
www.beautifulaccommodation.com/
exclusivespas-peppers

Location
Peppers Beach Club Resort
20–22 Davidson Street,
Port Douglas. Map 13.

Spa menu
A full range of spa treatments
and therapies

Products
LI'TYA

Payment
Visa, MC, AMEX, DC, Eftpos

Manager details
Clotilde La Chat
info@espa.net.au
www.espa.net.au

Port Douglas Day Spa

Port Douglas

Location
8 Macrossan Street,
Port Douglas. Map 13.

Spa menu
Tribal and traditional
in a modern context

Products
Natural handmade products

Payment
Visa, MC, DC, Eftpos

Owner details
Lisa McLeod
portdayspa@bigpond.com
www.portdouglasdayspa.com

Scores of our readers have flocked to this relaxed day spa in search of down-to-earth calming. Whether you choose to float away your cares or be caressed by a range of massage styles, this is a real holiday.

Those descending from the altitude of flight will find recovery, the sun-drenched will find relief and lovers will find precious time together. And for a gaggle of girls, this is the place to catch up. Whatever your reason, Indo-Asian themes, evocative beats and heavenly aromas will wash away your blues. You're up in the tropical north, so why not go troppo?

For enquiries:
07 4099 5009
www.beautifulaccommodation.com/
portdouglasdayspa

Q1 Spa

Surfers Paradise

Location
Q1 Resort and Spa.
Hamilton Avenue,
Surfers Paradise. Map 8.

Spa menu
Full range of
exclusive spa treatments

Products
LI'TYA and Pevonia Botanica

Payment
Visa, MC, AMEX, DC, Eftpos

Manager details
Melinda Nelsen
info@q1spa.com
www.espa.net.au

You don't need to be a guest at the Q1 Resort to indulge in its most beguiling offering: The Q1 Spa welcomes all who seek pampering in breathtaking style. Fusing ancient therapies from the Dreamtime using the uniquely Australian LI'TYA spa care range together with exquisite Pevonia Botanica products, the aim is to provide treatments that restore as well as pamper.

Weave some 'you' time into your holiday or bring a friend or two for a party. Brides and their ladies can come here before stepping up to the altar (and grooms and their best men could do the same too).

For enquiries:
07 5539 9293
www.beautifulaccommodation.com/
Q1spa

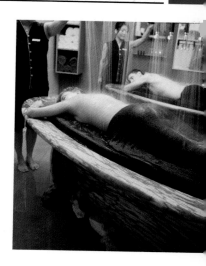

Bloomfield Lodge Sanctuary

Weary Bay, Far North Queensland

Take one of the world's finest and remotest resorts (Bloomfield Lodge, see page 267) add a day spa of unsurpassed quality, and you begin to get a sense of the Bloomfield Lodge Sanctuary experience. They don't need piped bird music, rainforest-scented fragrances or heating set to tropical warmth here – the real thing is all around.

Given the pristine rainforest setting, it is fitting that the Sanctuary uses healing natural essences and botanicals. We think the Bloomfield bride treatment should be on everyone's list, bride-to-be or not.

For enquiries:
07 4035 9166
www.beautifulaccommodation.com/
bloomfieldsanctuary

Location
Bloomfield Lodge.
Weary Bay,
North Queensland. Map 13

Spa menu
Aromatherapy and
beauty treatments

Products
Dermalogica

Payment
Visa, MC, AMEX, DC, Eftpos

General Manager details
Ben & Courtenay Morley
bloomfield@tfaustralia.com
www.bloomfieldlodge.com.au

Peppers Ruffles Lodge Day Spa

Willow Vale (near Surfers Paradise)

A tantalising feature of Peppers Ruffles Lodge and Spa (read our review on page 183) is the sumptuous new day spa, which together with its superlative cuisine and accommodation makes this Gold Coast hinterland hideaway worthy of several days' stay.

This purpose-built spa facility has various treatment rooms, a relaxation space and a gorgeous pool with rainforest and coastal views. They provide the pinnacle of pampering for couples and a wedding party would revel in pre-nuptial bliss. Naturally, outside guests are also welcome.

For enquiries:
07 5546 7411
www.beautifulaccommodation.com/
ruffleslodgespa

Location
Peppers Ruffles Lodge and Spa
423 Ruffles Road, Willow Vale.
Map 8.

Spa menu
A full range of spa treatments

Products
Waterlily and Jasmin

Payment
Visa, MC, AMEX, DC, DD, Eftpos

Owner details
Jan and John Nicholls
jj@ruffleslodge.com.au
www.peppers.com.au/
ruffleslodge

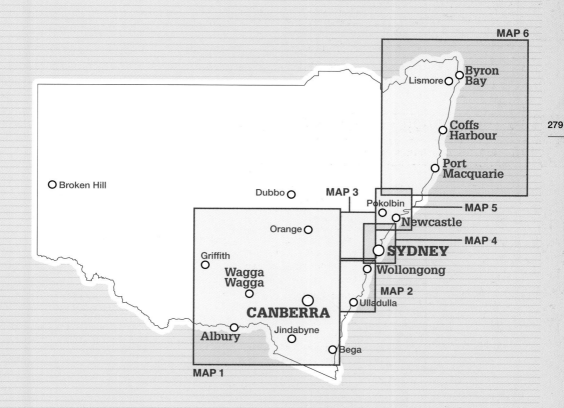

MAP 6

Byron
Bay

Lismore

Coffs
Harbour

Port
Macquarie

279

Broken Hill

Dubbo

MAP 3

Pokolbin

MAP 5

Newcastle

Orange

SYDNEY

MAP 4

Griffith

Wollongong

Wagga
Wagga

MAP 2

Ulladulla

CANBERRA

Jindabyne

Albury

Bega

MAP 1

All numbers in purple (10) refer to the page number of each property or day spa

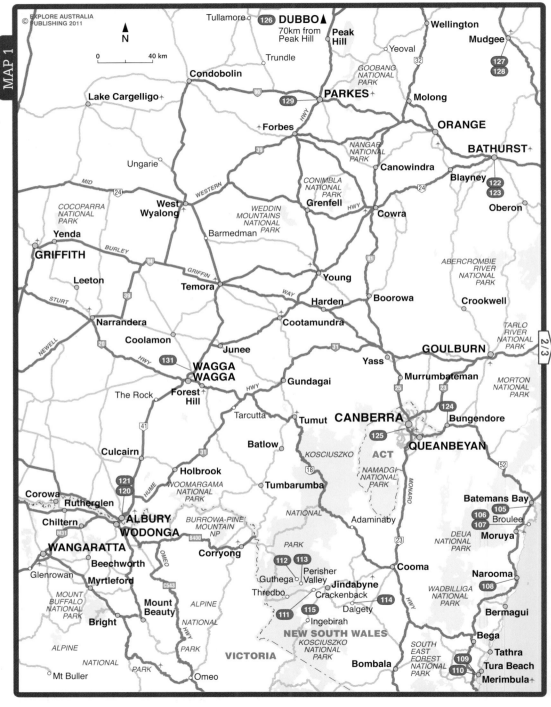

© EXPLORE AUSTRALIA
PUBLISHING 2011

MAP 1

N

0   40 km

280

Tullamore

126 DUBBO ▲
70km from
Peak Hill

Peak Hill

Wellington

Yeoval

Mudgee

127
128

Trundle

GOOBANG
NATIONAL
PARK

Condobolin

90

PARKES

129

Molong

ORANGE

32

Lake Cargelligo

Forbes

BATHURST

NANGAR
NATIONAL
PARK

Canowindra

Blayney

122
123

39

Ungarie

MID

24

West
Wyalong

WESTERN

CONIMBLA
NATIONAL
PARK

Grenfell

Cowra

Oberon

COCOPARRA
NATIONAL
PARK

WEDDIN
MOUNTAINS
NATIONAL
PARK

24

ABERCROMBIE
RIVER
NATIONAL
PARK

Yenda

Barmedman

GRIFFITH

BURLEY

GRIFFIN

81

Leeton

Young

Crookwell

Temora

WAY

Boorowa

2/3

STURT

Harden

Narrandera

Cootamundra

TARLO
RIVER
NATIONAL
PARK

Coolamon

Junee

31

GOULBURN

131

WAGGA
WAGGA

Yass

MORTON
NATIONAL
PARK

The Rock

Forest
Hill

HWY

Gundagai

25

Murrumbateman

23

NEWELL

20

HWY

Tarcutta

Tumut

CANBERRA

124

Bungendore

41

Batlow

125

QUEANBEYAN

52

Culcairn

31

Holbrook

KOSCIUSZKO

ACT

121
120

WOOMARGAMA
NATIONAL
PARK

Tumbarumba

NAMADGI
NATIONAL
PARK

Batemans Bay

106
105

Corowa

Rutherglen

NATIONAL

Adaminaby

107

Broulee

Chiltern

ALBURY
WODONGA

BURROWA-PINE
MOUNTAIN
NP

MONARO

DEUA
NATIONAL
PARK

Moruya

M31

WANGARATTA

PARK

B400

23

Cooma

Narooma

108

Beechworth

OMEO

Corryong

112 113

Perisher
Valley

Glenrowan

Myrtleford

C543

Guthega

Jindabyne

WADBILLIGA
NATIONAL
PARK

Bermagui

MOUNT
BUFFALO
NATIONAL
PARK

Mount
Beauty

ALPINE

Thredbo

Crackenback

114

Bega

Bright

111 115

Dalgety

HWY

Tathra

ALPINE

NATIONAL

Ingebirah

109

Tura Beach

NATIONAL

PARK

PARK

NEW SOUTH WALES

SOUTH
EAST
FOREST
NATIONAL
PARK

110

Merimbula

VICTORIA

KOSCIUSZKO
NATIONAL
PARK

Bombala

Mt Buller

Omeo

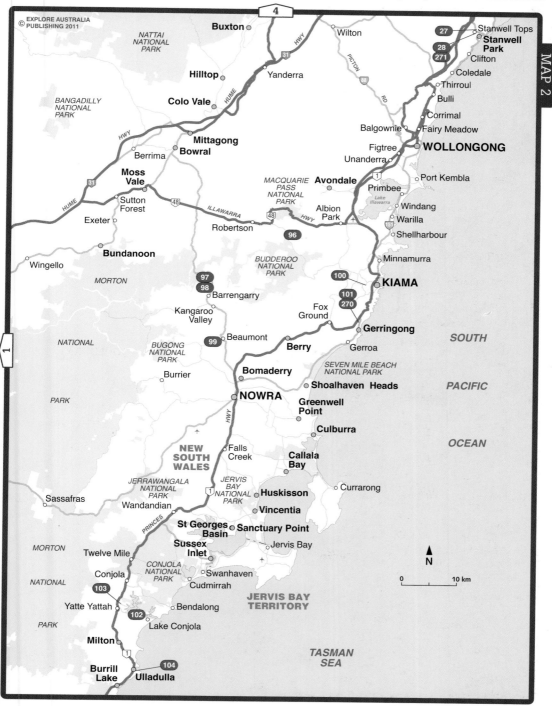

All numbers in purple (10) refer to the page number of each property or day spa

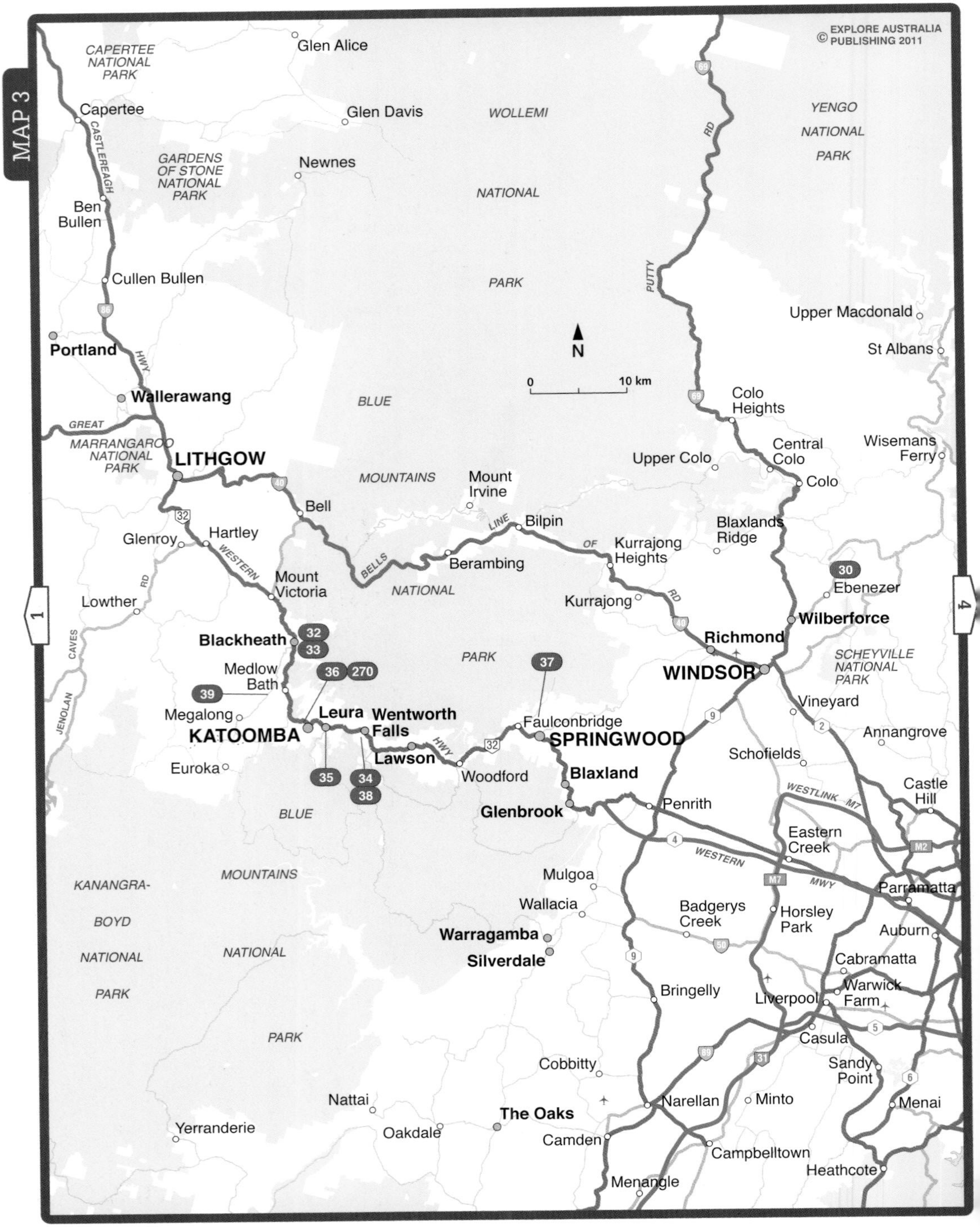

MAP 3

282

CAPERTEE NATIONAL PARK
Glen Alice
Capertee
Glen Davis
WOLLEMI
YENGO NATIONAL PARK
GARDENS OF STONE NATIONAL PARK
Newnes
NATIONAL
Ben Bullen
Cullen Bullen
PARK
Upper Macdonald
St Albans
Portland
Wallerawang
BLUE
Colo Heights
Wisemans Ferry
MARRANGAROO NATIONAL PARK
LITHGOW
MOUNTAINS
Mount Irvine
Upper Colo
Central Colo
Colo
GREAT
Bell
Bilpin
Blaxlands Ridge
32
Hartley
LINE
Berambing
Kurrajong Heights
30
Ebenezer
Glenroy
WESTERN
BELLS
OF
Kurrajong
Wilberforce
Lowther
Mount Victoria
NATIONAL
Kurrajong
Richmond
SCHEYVILLE NATIONAL PARK
Blackheath
32
33
PARK
37
WINDSOR
Medlow Bath
36
270
Vineyard
39
Leura
Wentworth Falls
Faulconbridge
Annangrove
Megalong
KATOOMBA
SPRINGWOOD
Schofields
Euroka
35
34
38
Lawson
Woodford
Blaxland
Castle Hill
Penrith
Eastern Creek
BLUE
Glenbrook
WESTLINK M7
MOUNTAINS
WESTERN
Parramatta
KANANGRA-BOYD
Mulgoa
Badgerys Creek
Horsley Park
Auburn
Wallacia
Cabramatta
NATIONAL
NATIONAL
Warragamba
Bringelly
Liverpool
Warwick Farm
PARK
PARK
Silverdale
Casula
Cobbitty
Sandy Point
Menai
Nattai
Narellan
Minto
Yerranderie
Oakdale
The Oaks
Camden
Campbelltown
Heathcote
Menangle

N
0   10 km

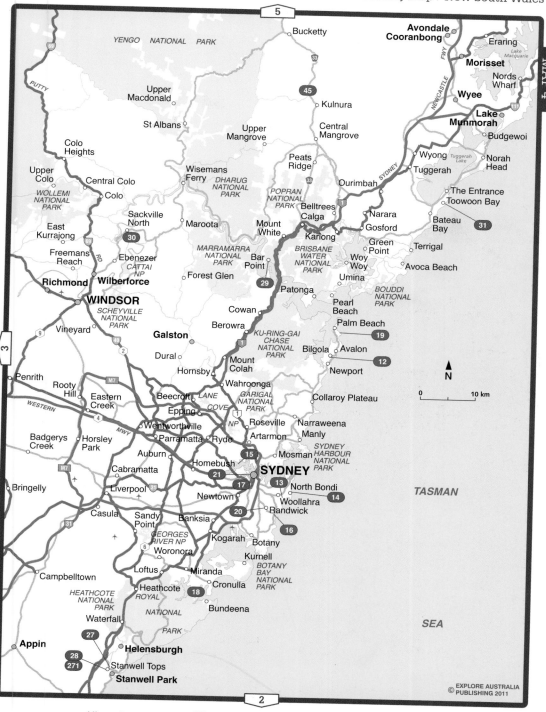

All numbers in purple (10) refer to the page number of each property or day spa

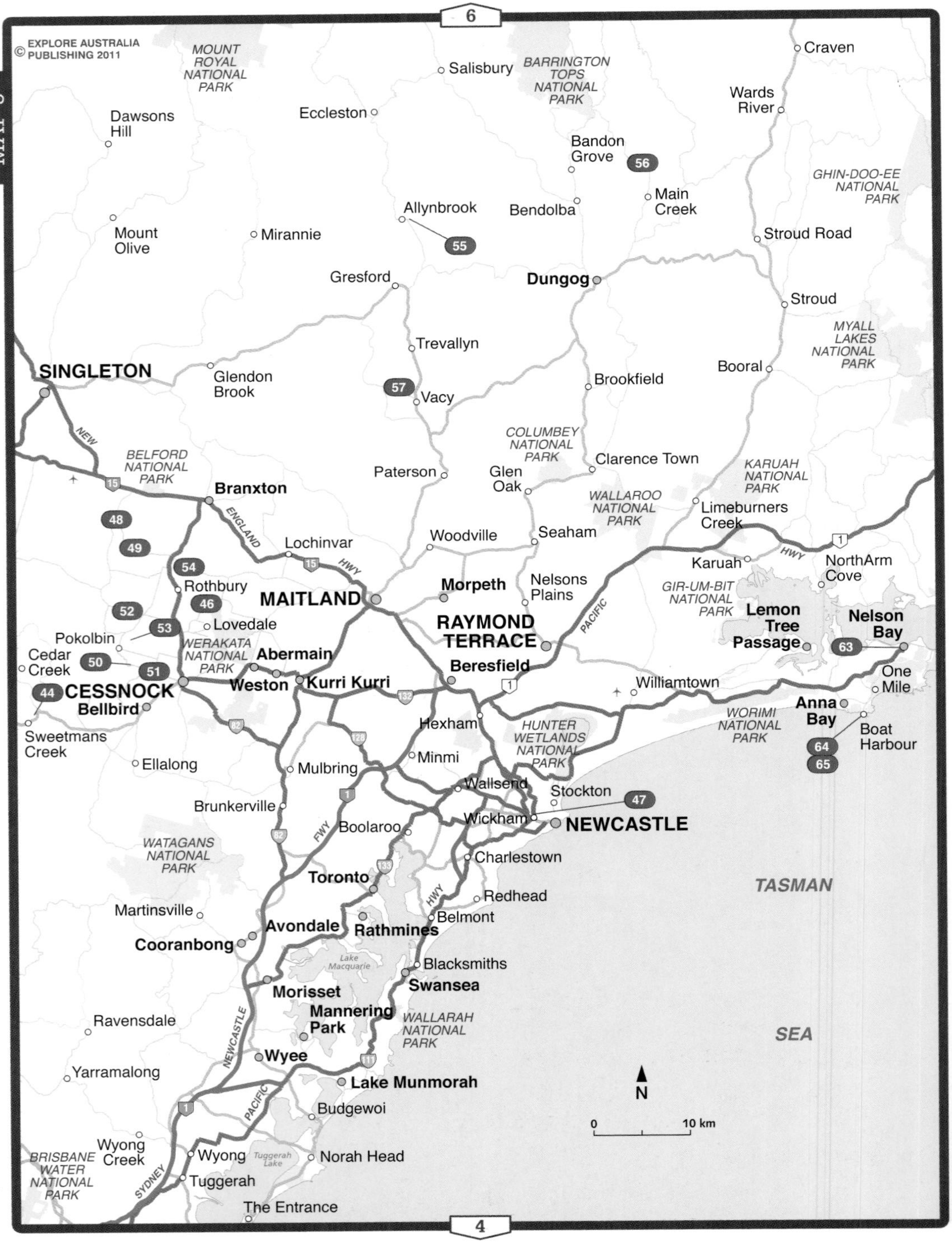

MAP 5

6

© EXPLORE AUSTRALIA
PUBLISHING 2011

MOUNT
ROYAL
NATIONAL
PARK

Salisbury

BARRINGTON
TOPS
NATIONAL
PARK

Craven

Wards
River

Eccleston

Dawsons
Hill

Bandon
Grove 56

GHIN-DOO-EE
NATIONAL
PARK

Mount
Olive

Mirannie

Allynbrook

Bendolba

Main
Creek

Stroud Road

55

Gresford

Dungog

Stroud

MYALL
LAKES
NATIONAL
PARK

SINGLETON

Glendon
Brook

Trevallyn

Brookfield

Booral

Vacy

57

COLUMBEY
NATIONAL
PARK

Clarence Town

KARUAH
NATIONAL
PARK

NEW

BELFORD
NATIONAL
PARK

Branxton

Paterson

Glen
Oak

Seaham

WALLAROO
NATIONAL
PARK

Limeburners
Creek

15

ENGLAND

Lochinvar

Woodville

Karuah

HWY

NorthArm
Cove

48

49

15

HWY

Morpeth

Nelsons
Plains

GIR-UM-BIT
NATIONAL
PARK

1

54

Rothbury

MAITLAND

RAYMOND
TERRACE

PACIFIC

Lemon
Tree
Passage

Nelson
Bay

52

46

Lovedale

53

Pokolbin

50

Cedar
Creek

51

WERAKATA
NATIONAL
PARK

Abermain

Beresfield

63

One
Mile

44

Weston

Kurri Kurri

33

CESSNOCK

Bellbird

Williamtown

WORIMI
NATIONAL
PARK

Anna
Bay

Boat
Harbour

Sweetmans
Creek

Hexham

HUNTER
WETLANDS
NATIONAL
PARK

64

65

Ellalong

Mulbring

Minmi

M1

Wallsend

Stockton

47

Brunkerville

82

Boolaroo

Wickham

NEWCASTLE

WATAGANS
NATIONAL
PARK

1

Charlestown

TASMAN

Martinsville

Toronto

33

Redhead

Avondale

Rathmines

Belmont

Cooranbong

Lake
Macquarie

Blacksmiths

SEA

Ravensdale

Morisset

Swansea

NEWCASTLE

Mannering
Park

WALLARAH
NATIONAL
PARK

Wyee

PACIFIC

Yarramalong

Lake Munmorah

N

0   10 km

1

Budgewoi

BRISBANE
WATER
NATIONAL
PARK

Wyong
Creek

Wyong

Tuggerah
Lake

Norah Head

SYDNEY

Tuggerah

The Entrance

4

All numbers in purple (10) refer to the page number of each property or day spa

284

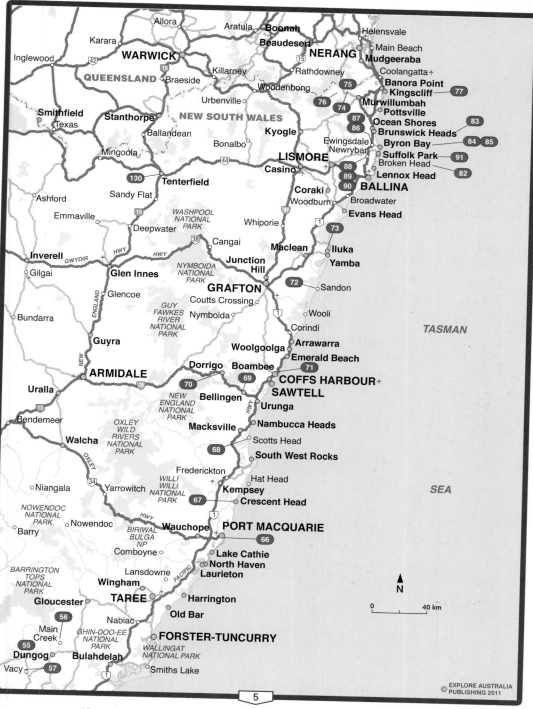

All numbers in purple (10) refer to the page number of each property or day spa

Locality maps for
Queensland

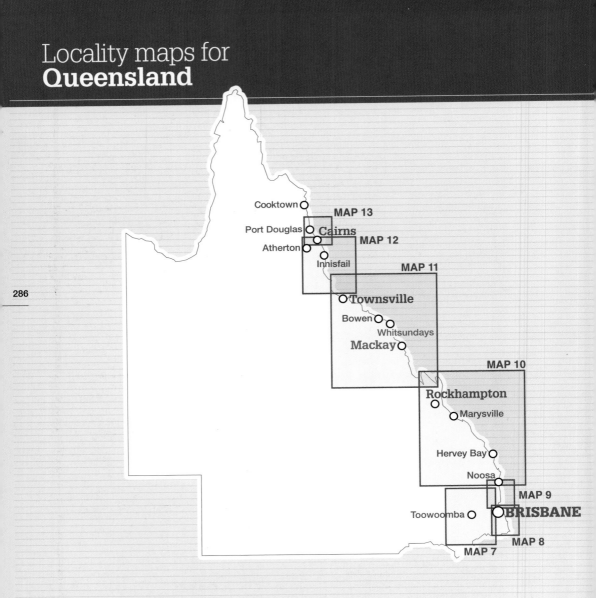

Cooktown

MAP 13

Port Douglas **Cairns**

MAP 12

Atherton

Innisfail

MAP 11

Townsville

Bowen
Whitsundays

Mackay

MAP 10

Rockhampton

Marysville

Hervey Bay

Noosa

MAP 9

Toowoomba **BRISBANE**

MAP 8

MAP 7

All numbers in purple (10) refer to the page number of each property or day spa

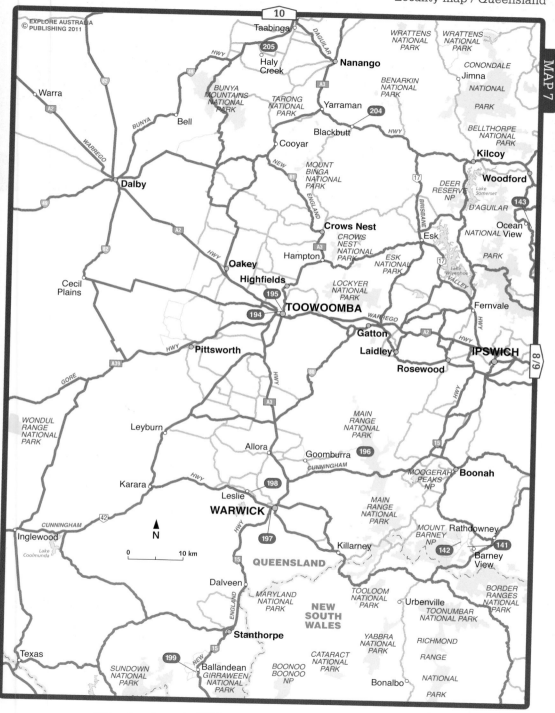

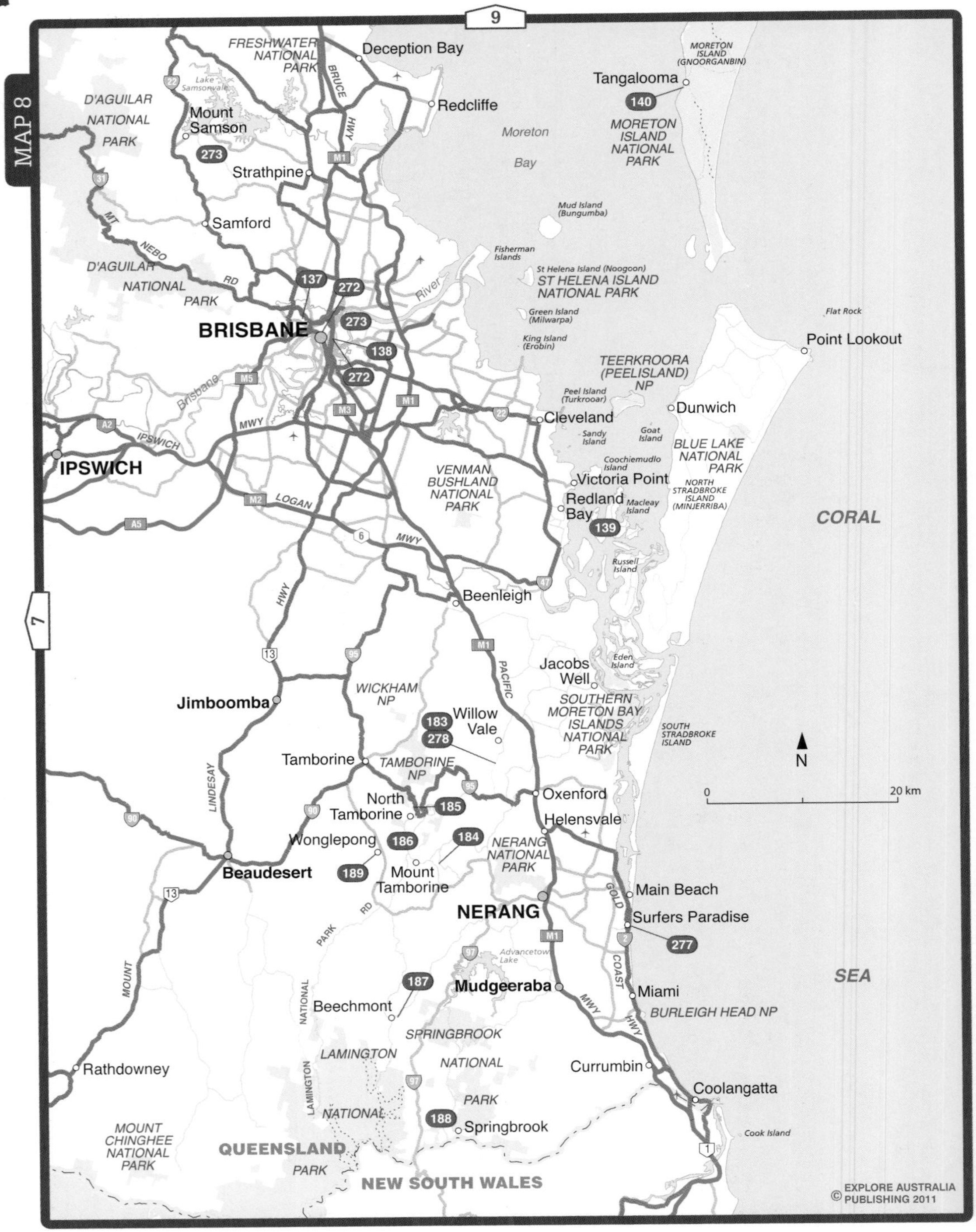
MAP 8
9
7
FRESHWATER NATIONAL PARK
Deception Bay
BRUCE HWY
MORETON ISLAND (GNOORGANBIN)
Tangalooma
140
Lake Samsonvale
D'AGUILAR NATIONAL PARK
Mount Samson
Redcliffe
Moreton Bay
MORETON ISLAND NATIONAL PARK
273
Strathpine
M1
MT NEBO RD
Samford
Mud Island (Bungumba)
Fisherman Islands
St Helena Island (Noogoon)
ST HELENA ISLAND NATIONAL PARK
D'AGUILAR NATIONAL PARK
137
272
River
Green Island (Milwarpa)
Flat Rock
273
BRISBANE
King Island (Erobin)
Point Lookout
138
272
TEERKROORA (PEELISLAND) NP
Brisbane
M5
Peel Island (Turkrooar)
M3
M1
22
Dunwich
Cleveland
A2
IPSWICH MWY
Sandy Island
Goat Island
BLUE LAKE NATIONAL PARK
IPSWICH
VENMAN BUSHLAND NATIONAL PARK
Coochiemudlo Island
Victoria Point
NORTH STRADBROKE ISLAND (MINJERRIBA)
M2
LOGAN MWY
Redland Bay
Macleay Island
CORAL SEA
A5
139
6
Russell Island
47
HWY
Beenleigh
M1
13
95
PACIFIC
Jacobs Well
Eden Island
WICKHAM NP
SOUTHERN MORETON BAY ISLANDS NATIONAL PARK
Jimboomba
183
278
Willow Vale
SOUTH STRADBROKE ISLAND
N
Tamborine
TAMBORINE NP
LINDESAY
95
Oxenford
0
20 km
North Tamborine
185
90
90
Helensvale
Wonglepong
186
184
NERANG NATIONAL PARK
189
Mount Tamborine
Beaudesert
13
GOLD
Main Beach
NERANG
Surfers Paradise
RD
PARK
M1
277
2
97
Advancetown Lake
COAST
MOUNT
NATIONAL
187
Mudgeeraba
MWY
Miami
HWY
BURLEIGH HEAD NP
Beechmont
SPRINGBROOK NATIONAL PARK
LAMINGTON
Rathdowney
Currumbin
LAMINGTON NATIONAL PARK
97
Coolangatta
188
Springbrook
MOUNT CHINGHEE NATIONAL PARK
QUEENSLAND
Cook Island
1
NEW SOUTH WALES
EXPLORE AUSTRALIA © PUBLISHING 2011

All numbers in purple (10) refer to the page number of each property or day spa

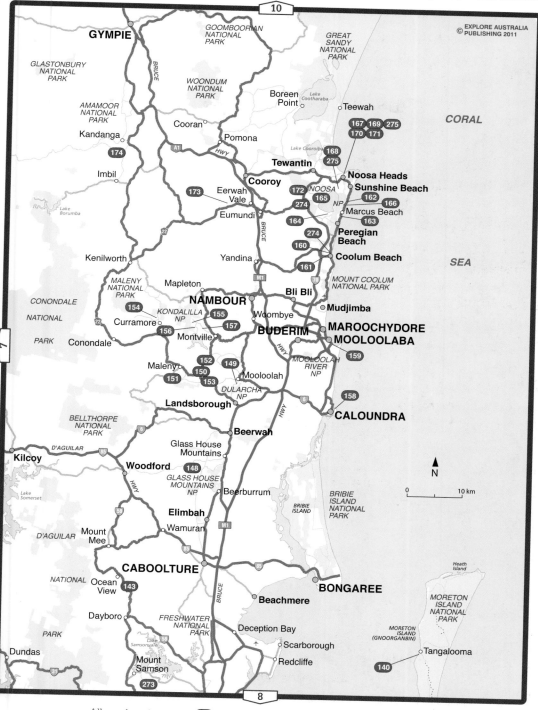

289

All numbers in purple (10) refer to the page number of each property or day spa

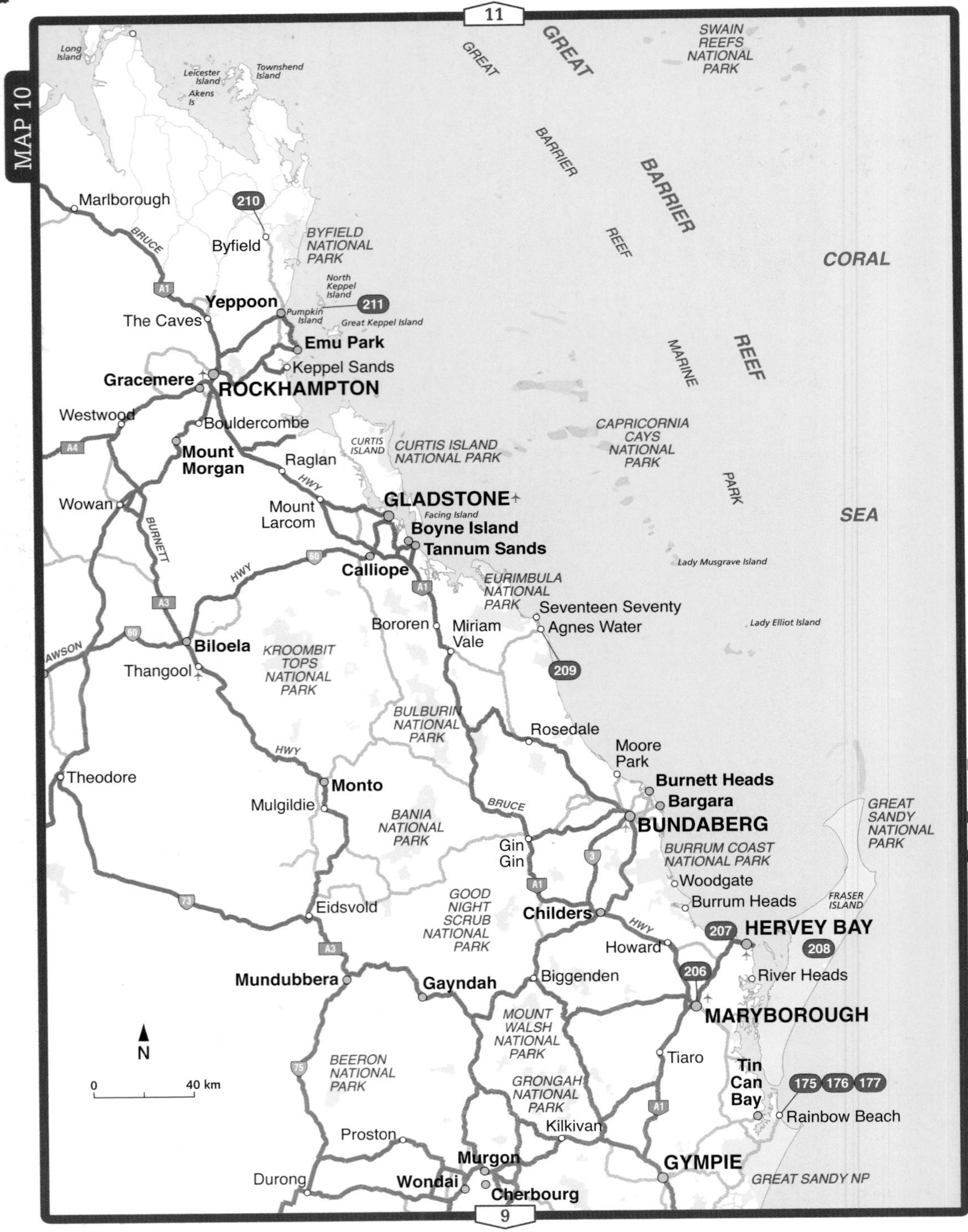

MAP 10

11

Long Island

Leicester Island

Akens Is

Townshend Island

GREAT

GREAT

BARRIER

SWAIN REEFS NATIONAL PARK

BARRIER

REEF

CORAL

Marlborough

BRUCE

210

Byfield

A1

BYFIELD NATIONAL PARK

North Keppel Island

Yeppoon

Pumpkin Island

211

Great Keppel Island

The Caves

Emu Park

Keppel Sands

Gracemere

ROCKHAMPTON

Westwood

Boulercombe

A4

Mount Morgan

Raglan

CURTIS ISLAND

CURTIS ISLAND NATIONAL PARK

Wowan

BURNETT

HWY

Mount Larcom

GLADSTONE

Facing Island

Boyne Island

Tannum Sands

HWY

60

Calliope

A1

MARINE

REEF

CAPRICORNIA CAYS NATIONAL PARK

PARK

SEA

Lady Musgrave Island

A3

DAWSON

60

Biloela

Thangool

KROOMBIT TOPS NATIONAL PARK

Bororen

Miriam Vale

EURIMBULA NATIONAL PARK

Seventeen Seventy

Agnes Water

Lady Elliot Island

290

HWY

BULBURIN NATIONAL PARK

209

Rosedale

Theodore

Monto

Mulgildie

BANIA NATIONAL PARK

BRUCE

Gin Gin

A1

Moore Park

Burnett Heads

Bargara

BUNDABERG

BURRUM COAST NATIONAL PARK

Woodgate

Burrum Heads

GREAT SANDY NATIONAL PARK

FRASER ISLAND

73

Eidsvold

A3

GOOD NIGHT SCRUB NATIONAL PARK

Childers

HWY

Howard

207

HERVEY BAY

208

206

River Heads

75

Mundubbera

Gayndah

Biggenden

MOUNT WALSH NATIONAL PARK

BEERON NATIONAL PARK

Tiaro

MARYBOROUGH

GRONGAH NATIONAL PARK

A1

Tin Can Bay

175 176 177

Proston

Kilkivan

Rainbow Beach

Durong

Wondai

Murgon

Cherbourg

GYMPIE

GREAT SANDY NP

▲ N

0   40 km

9

All numbers in purple (10 *) refer to the page number of each property or day spa*

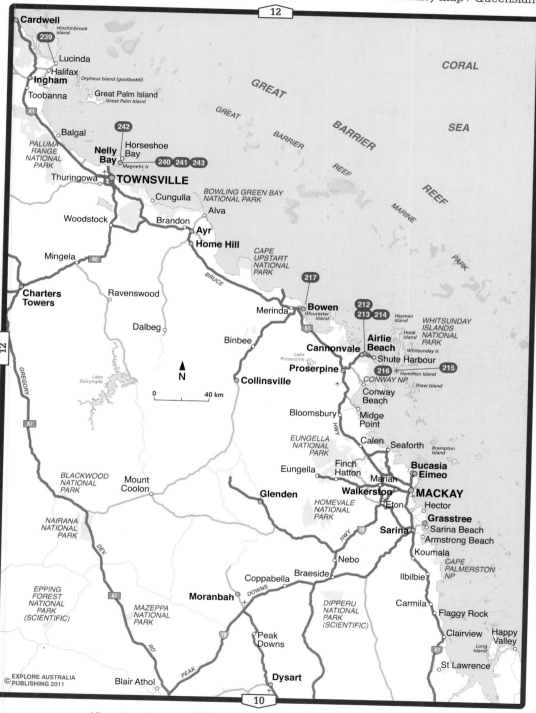

All numbers in purple (10) refer to the page number of each property or day spa

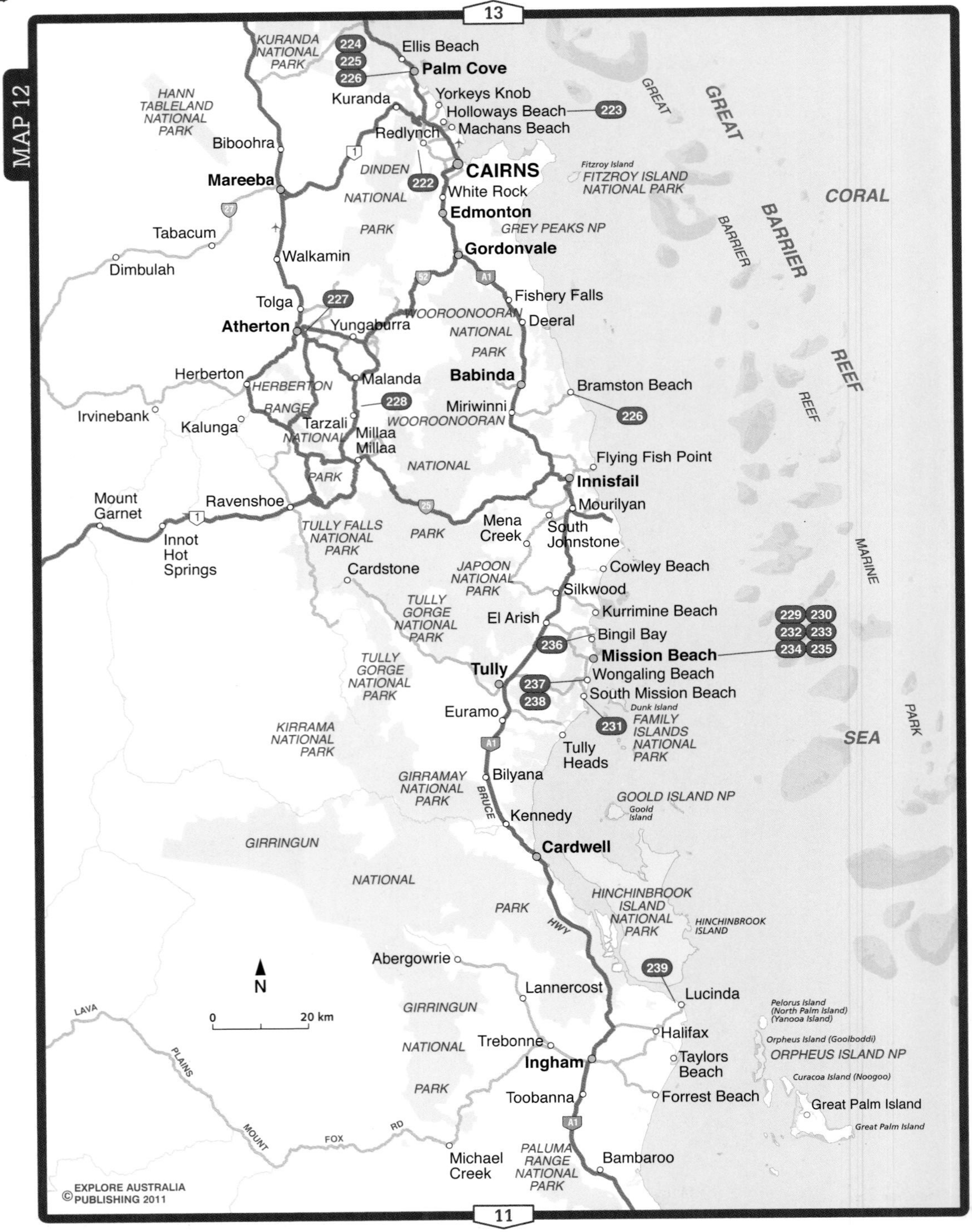

Locality map / Queensland

MAP 12

292

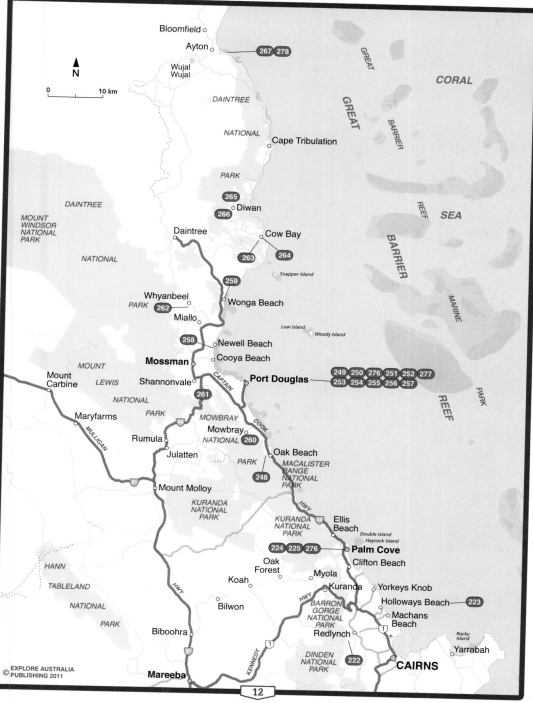

Bloomfield

Ayton
267 278

Wujal
Wujal

DAINTREE

NATIONAL

Cape Tribulation

GREAT

CORAL

GREAT

BARRIER

REEF

SEA

PARK

265
266
Diwan

DAINTREE

MOUNT
WINDSOR
NATIONAL
PARK

NATIONAL

Daintree

Cow Bay

263 264

BARRIER

Snapper Island

259

MARINE

Whyanbeel

PARK 262
Miallo

Wonga Beach

Low Island

Woody Island

258
Newell Beach
Cooya Beach

MOUNT

Mossman

Mount
Carbine

LEWIS

Shannonvale

CAPTAIN

Port Douglas

249 250 276 251 252 277
253 254 255 256 257

PARK

261

NATIONAL

PARK

MARYFARMS

MOWBRAY

COOK

REEF

PARK

MULLIGAN

44

Mowbray

Rumula

NATIONAL 260

Julatten

PARK

Oak Beach

MACALISTER
RANGE
NATIONAL
PARK

248

Mount Molloy

KURANDA
NATIONAL
PARK

HWY

Ellis
Beach

44

Double Island
Haycock Island

HANN

KURANDA
NATIONAL
PARK

224 225 276
Palm Cove

Oak
Forest

Clifton Beach

TABLELAND

Koah

Myola

Yorkeys Knob

NATIONAL

Bilwon

Kuranda

HWY

Holloways Beach

223

Machans
Beach

PARK

Biboohra

BARRON
GORGE
NATIONAL
PARK

Redlynch

Rocky
Island

HWY

81

KENNEDY

1

DINDEN
NATIONAL
PARK

1

Yarrabah

222

CAIRNS

Mareeba

N

0   10 km

All numbers in purple (10) refer to the page number of each property or day spa

Index

Property name
New South Wales

294

Queensland

Index

Suitable for children
New South Wales

Index

Suitable for groups
New South Wales

Queensland

299

Good food getaways
New South Wales

Queensland

Gardens
New South Wales

Historic properties
New South Wales

Queensland

Visit us online

www.beautifulaccommodation.com

Discover special packages and deals
See more images of each property
Check for rate updates
Book or enquire direct
No commission or booking fees

Credits

the invermay press

Published by The Invermay Press under licence from Hardie Grant Publishing Pty Ltd
Explore Australia Publishing Pty Ltd is a division of Hardie Grant Publishing Pty Ltd

hardie grant publishing

www.beautifulaccommodation.com.au

National Library of Australia Cataloguing-in-Publication entry
Author: St. John, Simon, 1967-
Title: Beautiful Accommodation New South Wales and Queensland/
Simon St John

ISBN 9781742702131

Cataloguing-in-Publication Data data is available from the National Library of Australia.
Dewey Number: 647.940994

Cover and text design by Hardie Grant Publishing
Principal photography, including cover image, by Ross Doonan
Supplementary photography by Tourism New South Wales, Tourism Tropical North Queensland, Tourism Queensland, Brisbane Marketing, Tourism Australia, winecountry.com.au, iStockphoto, Masterfile and Jon May
Maps by Explore Australia
Printed and bound in China by C&C Offset Printing

Front cover image: Noosa Holiday House, Sunshine Coast, QLD
Back cover (main image): Casa Belle Country Guest House, North Coast, NSW